Calling Elections

'Calling Elections,

The History of
Horse-Race Journalism

Thomas B. Littlewood

University of Notre Dame Press

Notre Dame, Indiana

Library of Congress Cataloging-in-Publication Data

Littlewood, Thomas B.
Calling elections : the history of horse-race journalism /
Thomas B. Littlewood.
p.   cm.
Includes bibliographical references and index.
ISBN 0–268–00833–7 (cloth : alk. paper)
1. Election forecasting—United States.   2. Journalism—Political
aspects—United States.   3. Press and Politics—United States.
I. Title.
JK2007.L57   1998
324.973′001′12—dc21   98–39984

∞The paper used in this publication meets the minimum requirements of
the American National Standard for Information Sciences—Permanence
of Paper for Printed Library Materials, ANSI Z39.48-1984.

Dedicated to the
memory of Jacob Scher
Newspaperman and Teacher

As some vast river of unfailing
   source—
Rapid, deep and exhaustless his
   numbers flowed.

Lord Byron

Much of political journalism is
an artful effort to disguise
prediction as reporting.

David Broder
1970

Contents

Preface

This book is the joint product of two disciplines that live in a constant state of alienation: the practice of daily journalism and the scholarly life of the academy. The working cultures of these two groups are so at odds as to defy all logical understanding. I spent almost twenty-five stimulating years as a newspaper reporter, many of those years covering national and state election campaigns and "calling elections." The transition to a highly satisfying though slower-paced second career of nineteen years as a professor of journalism was less painful than I had been led to expect.

I am grateful to many colleagues in both fields. Theodore Peterson, dean emeritus of the College of Communications at the University of Illinois in Urbana-Champaign, read an early draft, had many good suggestions, and was a source of encouragement until his death in 1997. A grant from the Freedom Forum foundation helped with the research expenses. Laurie Mikva, Christine Netznik, Zach Hart, Mary Lane, Evelyn Skinner, and Robin Price were involved at various times in the research and manuscript preparation. Another former colleague at Illinois, Carolyn Marvin, inadvertently provided some of my inspiration with her fine book, *When Old Technologies Were New.*

In less tangible ways, many others contributed to this work, beginning with the man to whose memory it is dedicated—Jacob Scher, a streetwise but uncommonly sensitive Chicago newspaperman who was my model as a journalism teacher. I should also mention several editors of the "old" *Chicago Sun-Times:* Milburn P. Akers, Larry Fanning, Dick Trezevant, Emmett Dedmon, and Ralph Otwell, all first-rate journalists; and among other associates at the University of Illinois, Steve Helle, Gene Gilmore, Bob Reid, James Carey, Fred Mohn, Kim Rotzoll.

Finally, this book could never have survived without the patient caring, manuscript oversight, and psychotherapeutic ministrations of my wife and partner, Barbara Littlewood.

Introduction

In today's world of telecommunications, the election of the president is news converted instantly and continuously into numbers. The process begins long before the parties have nominated their candidates. Once the campaign is actually underway, the status of the contest is arithmetically transcribed on a daily basis. Seated at random-digit dialing phone banks, high school student interviewers at the Gallup outpost in Lincoln, Nebraska, conduct their nightly national tracking polls for *USA Today* and the Cable News Network. Public opinion on a conveyer belt. No self-respecting news organization can afford to be without some sort of election season poll.

Polling intelligence colors the other news of the campaign. "Ephemeral spasms of mood" harden into numbers and thus into news, as one critic has complained.[1] The patterns that emerge in the opinion polls shape interpretations of reality—the perceptions of journalists, politicians, and (inescapably) the voters themselves. Some news organizations endeavor to breathe life into the sterile numbers by assembling subsets of voters known as "focus groups." When this happens, individuals whose only knowledge of the candidates can be the images propounded by journalists find themselves in the position of feeding back the same images which are then reported as fresh news by the same journalists.

New survey results from Gallup and others are available on the Internet. Communications conglomerates are in a rush to stake vague territorial claims in cyberspace. New systems are being developed that will deliver interactive polling and other information onto the news consumer's screen through a multisensual array of print, video, and audio media.

Reporters, editors, candidates, pollsters, and the keepers of data are in touch with one another by E-mail. The various "Usenet" electronic bulletin boards disseminate the latest state-by-state polling data. In 1996, PoliticsNow ("the political powerhouse on the Net") supplied daily polls and mock election matchups before the campaigning had even begun.

Campaigners, journalists, and camp followers were inundated with electronic measurements of the Body Politic—some raw, some parboiled. The

1

candidates all had their home pages on the World Wide Web. These days every conceivable partisan cause can be found spinning statistical data in the interminable cyberspace campaigns.

Burdened by their old-fashioned daily (and in some cases weekly) publication cycles, print journalists scramble for the attention of television and on-line audiences by "posting" reports of uncertain authenticity on their Web sites.

For any reporters who may still be confused, an on-line hotline service keeps them apprised of up-to-the-minute GroupThought, the conventional wisdom sanctioned by the celebrity journalists who achieve their elite status by virtue of their appearances on national television.

On election day, the television networks pool their resources in a massive nationwide cooperative exit-polling exercise carried out by a consortium called the Voter News Service.[2] Interviewers fan out across the country, carrying their clipboards and questionnaires into 1,500 carefully chosen precincts (out of 188,000) where representative voters are asked about their decisions as they leave the voting place. The findings are funneled into still more computers at an "input station" in Cincinnati, Ohio. From there they are relayed to statisticians in New York City and fed into the networks' mainframe computers. The state-by-state analysis anticipates outcomes while the voting is still in progress. On election night, intricate software makes it possible to blend the exit poll data with the incoming raw figures gathered in by the dependably authoritative Associated Press. The movement of data from election headquarters to media office can occur almost instantly. In some places, media computers access a county's official election results and print spreadsheet summaries as the figures come rolling in. Using their pagination systems, newspapers are able to swiftly publish entire pages of vote figures. Over special election night wires, the fifty state election centers of the AP speed tens of thousands of NewsAlert summaries over their DataStream circuits.

Minutes after the polls close in a state, the network anchor stars "call" the race, punching up projections on a touch-screen computer. The visuals dance dizzily across the "cyberset" screen, bar graphs and pie charts flashing their numerical previews of the day's results. Because they now share the same exit-poll data and the same raw returns, the networks compete chiefly through the gaudiness of their visual displays. NBC, in partnership with the software giant Microsoft, invited viewers on election night 1996 to discuss the figures on the Web with its expert correspondents who were available for consultation at their Web site "chat auditoriums."

As they have for many years, news organizations raced against one another—before, during and after the voting—to quantify the status of the contest, to gain an edge and be first with the news. News of the substantive dialogue between candidates and the electorate is overshadowed by the endless estimates of who is ahead and by how much. There is less attention now to the essential discourse of the campaign. All along the way, electoral politics is endowed with a scientific quality that practitioners know it does not possess.[3] The complexity of human attitudes is reduced to aggregate numbers on sheets of computer printout. As a consequence, political reporters—the campaign kibitzers—find themselves shouldering much of the blame for the failure of election campaigns to address complicated issues of public policy. As more readers and viewers shun the political system, many media decision-makers react by offering a more tantalizing, less issue-grounded brand of political journalism.

Though the technology obviously is far different now, the reporting of presidential elections as sporting contests has been evident in the United States for a long time. The origins of the horse-race tradition in American political journalism can be traced back at least to the 1820s. As soon as ordinary Americans were given an opportunity to vote in contested elections, the press was placed in the position of having to balance functions and responsibilities that were not altogether compatible.

On one hand, the Bill of Rights granted extraordinary privileges and protections to a private business—the "news business"—with what is generally assumed to have been an understanding that the free press would serve as an educational forum for the ventilation of policy disagreements and the enlightenment of the voters. Because news vendors sell their product in a competitive market, however, they are inclined to heed the buying habits of their consumers (their readers). Inevitably, a tension developed in the reporting of election news between what the editors as opinion leaders believed the people needed to know to be informed citizens and what their subscribers wanted to know about. Wanted sufficiently, that is, to pay the price of the product for sale.

What they wanted to know about has involved the press in another set of roles that the authors of the First Amendment could not have foreseen—as scorekeeper, bearer of the news of election returns, and increasingly as prognosticator. As newspapers competed to report the news ahead of the others, first against other newspapers, then against the much faster broadcast media, they were no longer content to wait for the voters to vote. They attempted to discern what was going to happen before it happened. The historian Daniel Boorstin believes this journalistic phenomenon, this drive to anticipate the news, can be traced to what he calls "the graphic revolution."[4] Once it became possible to give people an exact representation of reality (with photographs instead of word symbols), journalists thought they could remain useful by revealing what *tomorrow's* pictures would show. In David Broder's words: prediction disguised as reporting. "Anticipation," Broder said another time, "is part of a good journalist's equipment, closely linked to the desire to be first with the news."[5] While chief of the Washington bureau of the *New York Times,* James Reston and his staff were in dogged pursuit of "all the news that's fit to print," the famous slogan of that distinguished newspaper. And, added Reston in his memoirs, "we wanted it before anybody else and *preferably before it happened*" (my emphasis).[6]

In greater or lesser proportions, political journalism in America has always consisted of some of what we now call horse-race reporting and some "educational" information about the issues. Many editors went about their educational function out of partisan motives, leading them into scathing analyses of the defects in the character and integrity of the opposition candidates. Although the press is much less partisan now, news of what the candidates are saying about the policy issues must vie for space not only with the horse-race reporting but with the more titillating and sometimes scandalous "character" issues.

What some now call "gotcha journalism" was commonplace in the last century. Only the motives were different. Then they were predictably partisan; now the intense "feeding frenzy" is attributable mainly to intermedia competition as national news organizations compete for attention and exposure more than for actual audience ratings.

The aim of this book is to examine the origins of the horse-race political reporting tradition. In doing this, I will describe the interplay of various modes of political journalism: those involving partisan impressionism, the election campaign as folk entertainment, the journalist as civic watchdog, scandalmonger, educator and—alas—as scorekeeper.

The story will dwell on these specific aspects of journalistic practice:

— How journalists endeavored, before and after random sample polling, to forecast the outcome of an election before it happened.
— How news gatherers scurried, before and after the coming of the telegraph, to collect the inconveniently scattered news of election results.
— How newspapers, constrained by the slowness of their production processes, competed to make the news of the outcome known as quickly as possible. At first, this was done with electric lights and other crea-

tive technological means; now the news is posted on computer network "bulletin boards."

— And, finally, how television preempted the "hard news" reporting of election results, with the assistance of computer wizardry, causing print journalists to look for other roles to play.

The chapters that follow will concentrate on how and why the tradition of horse-race reporting prevailed over news of the campaign discourse. The reasons are related both to the psychology of news and the evolution of the unique American presidential election campaign. The dominance of the superficial over the substantive will be shown to have begun long before the Gallup Poll, Madison Avenue, or television sound bites. The focus throughout will be limited rather narrowly on how the journalist's perceived need to "call elections" as quickly as possible influenced the reporting of political news and with it the conduct of election campaigns.

One

The Colonel and the Key Precincts

Not lightly fall
Beyond recall
The written scrolls a breath can float;
The crowning fact,
The kingliest act
Of Freedom is the freeman's vote.

John B. Howe

The weeks of suspense are almost over. The last of the campaign oratory has sputtered to a close. The hastily erected polling apparatus is in place. On this, democracy's highest of holy days, the voters have performed their kingliest act. However holy, there has never been anything remotely pious about election day in America. Whiskey flows. Greenbacks change hands. Around the voting booths the milling crowds hoot and holler. Down the street, sounds of gunshots and firecrackers ring out. After the polls close, the people drift toward the only common source of trustworthy information available to one and all: the downtown newspaper offices.

It is the mid-1880s. Once the people have spoken, a familiar all-night ritual is about to begin on the editorial floor of the *Boston Globe*. At this early hour, as daylight fades into darkness, the crowning facts are still shrouded in obscurity. Workers at the *Globe* are not yet fully accustomed to the newfangled electric lamps dangling from the tangle of wires hanging from the old gas jets overhead. Tension builds to the clicking tempo of telegraph keys. Copy boys scurry about. Reports from the wire services, printed on thin, oily "flimsies," are delivered in leather cylinders shaped like dice boxes. Shot out of a pneumatic tube, the cartridges slam into a padded receptacle and fall at the feet of an office boy. Most of the reporters are still uncomfortable using the telephone as a news gathering instrument. It is awkward scribbling notes while talking into the bell-shaped contraption fastened to the wall. The first long-distance telephone line reached Boston from Providence in 1881. But the sound of voices still fades over distances.

Calling Elections

For the older hands especially, the face-to-face encounter with a source of news is more reassuring.

But this is a big news night. There is no time to be lost. "The highest state of fever," recalled one editor who had lived through many election nights, "attends the excitement and strain of the most intense work that falls to the lot of any men, except soldiers in war."[1]

The newsroom of the 1880s is fitted out like a schoolroom. Sheets of yellow blotting paper cover the rows of sturdy wooden desks. Paste pots, violet-ink stands, fresh pads of writing paper, new pens and penholders decorate each desktop. As dusk settles outside, a few men sit down "before the virgin sheets of paper," knowing that no later than 2 A.M. they must cover those sheets with the election returns of a nation of many faces and many voices. And this they must do weeks in advance of any official tabulations. "The craft has no more exacting, exasperating task," said another editor, "than to formulate on imperfect information at midnight or thereabouts remarks that must go to the press hours before conclusive news arrives, and that will be read in the light of statistics yet unknown or events impossible of prevision."[2]

Soon the air is clouded with smoke from briarwood pipes and stubby cigars. A brass spittoon on the floor defines each work station. As the evening wears on, weary men grow careless with their aim. Stale newspapers soak up the tobacco stains on the juicy slick floor. A water pail and a tin jar of ice water stand off in one corner of the room. The reporters wear white shirts, stiff celluloid collars, heavy dark suits, and high-laced shoes. Many of them feel more secure under their derby hats as they toil through the night.

Julian Ralph wrote a nostalgic memoir of that era, called *The Making of a Journalist.* The anxious newspapermen discern meaning in the numbers, he said, "as sparks might be counted while they fly from the shapeless iron on a blacksmith's anvil." How much simpler the task would be if the figures arrived in some predictable order. But, no, they "come in driblets and atoms and must be put together as the Florentines make their mosaics." Some don't come at all. The men in the newsroom then call on their years of experience to fill the empty spaces with a tentative, makeshift mosaic. Some of the figures are "plucked from the very air—as the magician seems to collect coins in a borrowed hat—begotten of reasoning, but put down beside the genuine returns with equal confidence and almost equal accuracy."[3]

Voting districts in the three parts of Massachusetts—Boston, the outside cities, and the rural towns—have all been covered by supposedly fail-safe reporting precautions. "To seize the returns from an entire state on the instant," said Ralph, "is as if a giant hand were put out to cover every hill and valley." Candidates and their managers have been beseeched to phone in whatever figures they have as soon as they are available. Special correspondents are deployed around the state to round up any straggling numbers.

Dispatches "rain in upon the workers," Ralph wrote, "like autumn leaves in a gale-swept forest." Close by the incoming tube, guarded by a semicircle of spindles, sits the journalist whose job is to sort the hundreds of slips of paper. Tonight's task is complicated because state and other federal offices are being filled on the same day as the presidency. Desk workers hunched over their tables of returns are filling in the blanks and looking for patterns expected or unexpected. They agonize. Why are the returns so damnably slow coming in? Why have we still not heard from Springfield? Those figures from the Third Ward in Worcester don't look right. Better double check. How was the turnout in the mill towns along the Connecticut River? What could have caused the bulge from the French Canadian wards in Fall River? The first returns always come in from the Brahmin districts of Beacon Hill and the Back Bay, "those sifted few" in Oliver Wendell Holmes' words, who live in less crowded households with fewer voters on the rolls. Not until much later will the figures drift in from the immigrant neighborhoods beyond the mud flats on the South Bay and in Roxbury and Charlestown and Dorchester.[4]

The raw vote totals are updated and distributed on slips of different colors—white, green, blue, yellow according to their destination: the copy desk, the composing room, the political editor, the bulletins for public display, the Colonel's sanctum. Analyzers will apply their "logarithms and formulas" to the mass of numbers, but eventually, as the deadline draws closer and many vital fragments of returns are still unreported, it will fall to one wise executive to risk the paper's reputation by engaging in some educated guessing.

At the *Boston Globe*, "the Colonel" is that man. His name is Charles H. Taylor. He is the editor and publisher, known all over Boston in the 1880s as "Colonel Taylor." It is an honorary military rank bestowed upon him by a grateful governor of Massachusetts in whose service he then toiled on the public payroll. Later, in 1891, another even more grateful governor would promote the Colonel to General, which title Taylor carried with him the last thirty years of his life.

On this night Colonel Taylor sits at the head of a table in an office just off the newsroom floor. This is where he receives the reports of his reporters and confers with them about his reading of the results. With him are a few of the bookkeepers from the business office—referred to by the gritty journalists in the newsroom as "the slide-rule boys." Their job is to run whatever mathematical calculations the boss may need. Newspapers everywhere were slow in taking advantage of the new mechanical devices available for processing data. The federal government used punchcards and "electrical counting machines" for the national census of 1890.[5] But decades would pass before the *Globe* could total the figures on election night with anything more advanced than the standard desktop keyboard calculators.

Adjacent rooms appropriately separated from the newsroom are occupied by the candidates and bigwigs of the Democratic Party of Massachusetts. A policeman stands outside at the entrance of the *Globe* building to keep out the hoi polloi, but the party leaders are there as special guests of the publisher. At intervals, Colonel Taylor rises from the table and joins his guests to impart the news of their electoral fate. These rooms are the nerve center of the vote tabulation process in Massachusetts. Occasionally Republican officials call on the phone from their hotel headquarters to glean from the Colonel whatever he chooses to confide about how they are doing.

As the evening progresses, the crowds in Washington Street outside grow larger. The people wait impatiently for the bulletins flashed by stereopticon slides that are projected from the *Globe*'s "magic lantern" onto the mammoth canvas sheet nailed to the side of the building. Crowds are also gathered in front of the other papers on Boston's Newspaper Row. When a sudden sound of cheering carries from down the street, it is disquieting for the harried workers at the *Globe* to know that the people are cheering something and there is no way for them to know what that something was. Can it be that they know something we don't?

Like so many editors in that era, Colonel Taylor was both politician and newspaper executive. The two pursuits mixed well together. *The Newspaper Maker,* a trade journal, once explained: "In the U.S., the secular newspaperman is always more or less of a politician. . . . Politics is business, and there is no better preparation for it than the all-around study of men and affairs which the newspaper calling necessitates."[6] William Allen White, the ever astute editor in faroff Emporia, Kansas, offered a further explanation in 1902: "Whether he likes politicians or not, the editor must get into politics; otherwise he becomes a journalist and writes of things which he knows nothing about."[7]

Born in the Charleston section of Boston in 1846, Charles Taylor got his

The Colonel and the Key Precincts

first job as a printer's devil when he was only fifteen. A year later, he enlisted in the Union army at the start of the Civil War. A Confederate bullet in the shoulder put an end to his military service. Back in his old job in the composing room of the *Boston Evening Traveller,* Taylor earned a reporting tryout by spending his lunch hours taking notes in the Charleston police court and delivering them to the city editor. While a reporter for the *Traveller,* he also wangled the Boston stringer's job for Horace Greeley's *New York Tribune,* then probably the most important Republican journal in the nation.[8]

Eager for a deeper understanding of political power, Taylor left the Boston newspaper for a position as private secretary to the governor, who was a Republican. Taylor continued his political training by being elected first to the state legislature and then as clerk of the state House of Representatives. While in these public offices, Taylor managed also to keep his position as Greeley's Boston stringer.

In the meantime, the *Globe* had been founded in 1872 in competition against ten other Boston dailies, only two of which were operating at a profit. The *Globe,* lacking an Associated Press wire-service franchise and on the brink of bankruptcy, hired the twenty-seven-year-old Taylor to be financial manager. The young man got the job because of his political rather than his business connections. He successfully revived the floundering newspaper and was promoted a couple of years later to publisher. As publisher, and despite his membership on the Republican State Committee, Taylor made a shrewd business decision. He turned the *Globe* into a Democratic Party newspaper. The party organization in Boston demonstrated its appreciation by pronouncing it "the duty of every Democrat in Massachusetts to aid personally in increasing the *Globe*'s circulation and influence." Before long, circulation went up. Taylor renounced his prior affiliation with the Republican Party and was forthwith named an officer of the Democratic Party of Massachusetts.

The *Globe* reported political news through the prism of the Democratic Party, albeit with faltering vision. Just before the election of 1888, the *Globe* placed the headline "Cleveland Elected" over a story relating to the prediction of another newspaper, the *New York World,* that the Democratic president would carry New York.[9] "President Grover Cleveland has done well, very well," proclaimed a *Globe* editorial, "and the omens all point to his election by a decisive electoral and popular majority."[10] (Unhappily for Colonel Taylor and the *Globe,* among others, Cleveland did less well in the unreported states and lost the election.)

Calling Elections

Come election night, however, newspaper editors put aside their partisanship and worked with the rest of the staff toward the same goal: to publish the results of the election and declare the winning candidates as quickly and accurately as possible—preferably more quickly and more accurately than their rivals.

Because of their early deadlines, morning newspaper editors often were required to indulge in some informed speculation before the results were known. By 1883, Colonel Taylor had used his knowledge of voting behavior in Massachusetts to perfect a method of projection which later came to be described as the key-precinct system. The precinct is the basic voting unit in each state. Voters cast their ballots at the precinct polling place, and the results are counted and reported precinct by precinct. Taylor's method called for the stationing of reporters at selected key precincts. The reporters would telephone the results to the *Globe* office as soon as the count had been finished. In New England, and in big cities generally, people of similar ethnic background and financial status tended to live in the same neighborhoods. Families might move, but ordinarily within their neighborhood. Not only did people of similar backgrounds live in the same precinct, but they were likely to vote like their neighbors with considerable partisan consistency from one election to the next. Under Taylor's tutelage, the *Globe* first identified clusters of like precincts in a community. Certain districts were identified as lower-class ("shanty") Irish, others as middle-class ("lace curtain") Irish. Others were labeled Italian, Portugese, Russian Jewish, Armenian, Syrian, Lithuanian, and Yankee upper-class, middle-class, or lower-class. Using mathematics, the "slide-rule boys" singled out precincts whose voting behaviors were consistently most typical of the others. Voting patterns in all the precincts were charted, based on previous elections. Computations that can be done instantly by a computer today were laboriously worked out then with pencil and paper. Thus, it was possible to assign a baseline vote to all the precincts and to identify those that could be safely used as representative models for similar precincts. Once the results were obtained from the key precincts, unless there were special factors at work (which the *Globe*'s political reporters were supposed to find out about in advance), the outcome of the election could be projected with only a few scattered precinct returns actually in hand. The analytical secret lay in sorting out the deviations from the expected pattern and, again by using mathematics, projecting how it would all turn out when all the votes were in. Although the Taylor method strikes us today as eminently logical and quite elementary, it was considered a daring innovation in the middle 1880s. Considerable courage was required for the Colonel and his editors to go to press with headlines announcing the election of a candidate who had been running second in the raw vote totals all evening long.

Although the *Globe* had mastered the techniques of "calling" state and local elections in Massachusetts, presidential elections required similar judgments from many states. In the 1880s, a centralized method of collecting the returns had not yet been perfected. The leading wire service, the Associated Press, was still only a series of regional networks leasing telegraph lines from the Western Union Company and attempting to pool the news of the election. The APs and Western Union were run by men who, like Colonel Taylor, had political interests to promote. Many of the collectors and transmitters of local results were telegraphers who were not above "editing" the figures to reflect their personal political preferences. The national reporting system left much to be desired. In 1888, the *Globe* had to look to the newspapers in the other big cities for news from their states and factor in their partisan biases before safely determining who had won there. It was not until Thursday, November 8, 1888, for example, that the *Globe* informed its readers: "IT IS SETTLED—Harrison is Elected President— New York Papers Unanimous."

As erratic and immature as that early data collection system was, when the copy deadline arrived, the ritual in the newsroom followed a familiar course. A young man in an inky leather apron dashed from one desk to another, inquiring "thirty for you?" (thirty being newspaper jargon for "the end.") When the last of the tables had been "footed" and sent upstairs to the composing room, the mighty presses would throb for hour after hour in the basement of the *Globe* building. Coffee, beer, sandwiches, and grapes were brought in to refresh the newsmen between editions. They gathered around the first copies of the paper, the ink on the pages still damp. Fresh copies of the opposition papers would also be rushed to the editors' desks for the test of comparison. By breakfast time, 400,000 copies of the 12-page edition would have been printed, bundled, and hustled into horse-drawn delivery wagons. Some were carried to the railroad station and tossed onto special trains destined for the farthest corners of New England. In a few fleeting hours, all the available election results had been collected in one building, filtered through Colonel Taylor's rich memory bank, and the inked words and numbers put on paper for the edification of the readers of the *Boston Globe*.

Other newspapers perfected their own key-precinct methods, anticipating on the basis of fragmentary returns how the vote totals would add up. To this day the development of the *Globe*'s key-precinct analysis techniques remains the single most important methodological advance in the history of electoral journalism. Journalists thereafter were working against one an-other to find new ways of reporting the outcome of an election without wait-ing for the votes to be counted—or even cast. The concept which under-lies key-precinct analysis—leaping from partial information to a broader conclusion—is central to the practice of horsc-race journalism, past and present.

Two

Old Hickory . . . and a Passion for Numbers

"Ours is a society of numbers."

Daniel J. Boorstin

The originators of the American constitutional system would not have envisioned the rush to interpret the meaning of vote figures from key precincts or anywhere else. The voting behavior of the common man did not become a matter of universal public curiosity until voting privileges were extended to most adult white males. That did not happen until the 1820s.

Before the revolution against the British crown, election campaigns in the American colonies usually were brief, perfunctory affairs. Editors opened the pages of their newspapers to announcements of candidacy and endorsement letters. One candidate in colonial Virginia conducted an advertising campaign so low-key that the ad neglected to mention his name. "To the Free and Independent Electors of the Borough of Norfolk," read his statement in the *Virginia Gazette*. "You are desired not to engage your votes or interest until the day of election, as a gentleman of undoubted ability intends to declare himself on that day, and hopes to succeed." The item was signed only, "A Freeman."[1]

Polls remained open for several days for the convenience of travelers. This enabled the clerks to keep a running tally, which information they gladly shared with anyone who cared. When the voting had finished, the result would be immediately announced to the interested onlookers. In some colonies, the wardens of election were required to post the results "at the church door or some other public place."[2]

Editors of colonial newspapers appear not to have been especially interested in the numerical details of the balloting. When the royal governor dissolved the lower house in Virginia and called new elections, as he frequently did, the *Gazette* would follow with notices such as: "Last Friday came on the election of a Burgess to represent the Borough of Norfolk in the present Assembly; when Capt. John Hutchings was declared duly elected;

and he has since qualified himself in the House."[3] No vote totals, no other details, no horse-race journalism.

Later on, after the revolution, some offices were vigorously contested. Even then, however, the political activists of the young republic appeared more interested in the scorekeeping details than were the editors. In 1792, when President Washington was reelected unanimously, Governor George Clinton of New York offered his name as an alternative to Vice President John Adams. Sensing that his patrons were curious about this development, the keeper of Fraunces Tavern in lower Manhattan queried his customers about their preference and posted a record of the results. Clinton was shown to have meager support, possibly because he had used family connections to dodge service in the revolutionary army. His boomlet went nowhere.

Because voters announced their voting decisions aloud, in full public display, it was possible to keep an accurate score with considerable precision. The impetus for the publication of this intelligence, however, generally came not from journalists but from supporters of candidates. The colonial printers who constituted "the press" were not reporters as we understand that term today. More comfortable publishing long ideological tracts, many of them had managed to use their political influence to get themselves appointed local postmaster. Wherever the print shop doubled as the post office, the proprietor was likely to be a significant political figure in the community.

Jonas Green was a typical example. Not long after founding the *Maryland Gazette*, editor Green was welcomed into The Tuesday Club, which consisted of the local inner circle—ministers, professionals, and elected public officials. Before he could straighten out his typecase, Green had become an alderman, vestryman, clerk of the [horse] races, secretary of the Masonic temple, and (for good measure) the postmaster.[4]

Our modern notion of news as fresh, sometimes elusive information that impartial professionals would dig out and deliver to a mass audience did not exist in the early days of our nationhood. The selection of the president was entrusted to a few well-respected electors. Hoping to avoid divisive political parties, the drafters of the Constitution knew nonetheless that strong-minded individuals would have differences of opinion and would solicit the support of allies. The role of the press in this system was to be, first, as a forum for the exchange of political ideas. Voting was restricted to men of property, so it seems clear that the press was also to be "free" independent trustees speaking, in effect, for the outsiders who were not invited into the political process.

Old Hickory . . . and a Passion for Numbers

Without reporters to gather news in distant places or wire services for its timely delivery, newspapers obtained most of their outside news by clipping and recycling stories from other newspapers. In recognition of that fact, Congress codified a practice begun in colonial America—the postage-free exchange of newspapers. Newspapers could exchange copies anywhere in the country, and the post office would carry them at no cost to the sender or the receiver.

Before the first president left office, the selection process began to change. Two members of Washington's cabinet—Thomas Jefferson and Alexander Hamilton—forged their separate alliances with other politicians. This led to the organization of continuing parties, which required a means of communication within the organization and with prospective voters. The presidential campaign of 1796, won by Adams, was waged in the pages of the Federalist Party newspapers. In all but two states, the presidential electors were selected then by the state legislators without any involvement by any voters at large. The casting of votes began in October, but it was not until a few days before Christmas that the electors had all marked their ballots in the various states and mailed them off to the capital. In that election the precedent was established that the parties would each have networks of loyal partisan newspapers and that the publications on the winning side would be rewarded with government printing contracts and other patronage enticements.

Members of Congress, having been drawn into one or the other of the parties, nominated their party's presidential candidate. Elections remained the business of a small group of interested citizens who read newspapers and exchanged ideas. The amount of raw (if colored) political information in the newspapers of that period would impress us today. Editors printed large quantities of political "news," much of it in letters and argumentative essays from like-minded contributors. Not much else was available. The job of the reporter did not yet exist. Enterprise journalism was unheard of.

A new dice game became popular with children in the 1820s. Players moved a marker across a board on which a map of the United States had been drawn. The states were identified by name and by their number of electoral votes. The object of the game was to accumulate enough states to be elected president. Youngsters who were learning their "ciphers" were also set to thinking about geography and how numbers and the knowledge of numbers could lead to political power. Then, as now, the apportionment of electoral votes was based on the number of a state's representatives in

Congress, updated every ten years to reflect state-by-state population changes. Political change was linked to the statistical act of counting heads. Arithmetic, geography, and civics were interrelated. Egalitarianism was a long way from being realized in this young nation, but those children became aware at an early age of the connection between statistical measurements and electoral achievment.[5]

A little later on, European visitors noticed how the American people seemed to have become infatuated with numbers. The English traveler Thomas Hamilton described the Americans he saw as "this guessing, reckoning, expecting, and calculating people."[6] The Frenchman Alexis de Tocqueville agreed that the minds of Americans "were accustomed to definite calculations."[7] This "passion for numbers" was something unique. It had not been detected before in the American colonial experience, and it was uncharacteristic of Europeans.

An American scholar who has studied the "numeracy" phenomenon, Patricia Cohen, notes that the American people chose specifically to count what was important to them. "Statistical knowledge was deeply gratifying because it was presumed to be objective, unimpeachable truth. It met an inner need for certainty. No other form of knowledge promised to be so clean and unambiguous." In her book, *A Calculating People,* she goes on to observe that "what people chose to count and measure reveals not only what was important to them but what they wanted to understand and, often, what they wanted to control."[8] In the nineteenth century, she emphasizes, "what was counted was what counted—people generally count only the things that matter." Numbers suggest objectivity and rationality, which are the opposites of feeling and intuitive judgment.

When the children's electoral college game was introduced, most of their fathers still took no part in the selection of the president. Some adult men were permitted to vote, albeit with difficulty, in local elections. But members of Congress nominated their party's candidate for president. State electors then chose one of the nominees to be chief executive. By the early 1820s the Federalist Party of Hamilton and Adams had about gone out of existence and the reigning Jeffersonian Republicans were breaking into factions, all with their own ambitious heroes and their own newspaper alliances.

As might have been expected, state and local politicians bristled at the exclusive control over presidential nominations by one set of elected representatives—the party members in Congress, who happened to be away from their home districts a good deal of the time. So when the last of Jefferson's Virginia dynasty, President James Monroe, declined to seek a third term in 1824, there was no screening mechanism in place to supplant the discredited congressional caucus. Candidates were put forward by various unofficial means, all intended to be expressions of popular support. Lacking effective long-distance communication, politicians tried as best they could to organize in behalf of would-be national candidates. Beginning at the township level, they picked delegates in a series of separate nominating conventions or caucuses. Thus the power over party nominations for president passed from members of Congress to widely separated state and local politicians.

More than two-thirds of the states chose their presidential electors by popular vote in 1824. Many of the newly enfranchised voters were supporting a military hero—General Andrew Jackson. Because Jackson was in no way the candidate of established power, it was necessary for him and his campaigners to activate new voters. The election campaign, as we know it today, did not yet exist. Candidates were not expected to make speeches or even to take positions on issues. There was little need to raise or spend money because there was very little visible electioneering by the candidates. Mainly they stayed at home and solicited the backing of opinion leaders by writing letters but without committing themselves on issues. Their surrogates in the various state legislatures did the speechmaking for them. And the editors of "their" newspapers spread partisan messages throughout the electorate. As more of the common people began voting, they read newspapers to become informed about where their economic self-interests lay. According to one account, European visitors were amazed to find a Pennsylvania farmer leafing through the cramped print of his weekly newspaper for news of the tariff debates in Congress. America was in the early stages of true representative democracy.

The campaign dialogue, such as it was, did not center on the candidate, however. Candidates tried to make as many friends as they could, relying on their reputations, while saying as little as they could get by with about the issues of the day. The "character" of the prospective candidates remained the paramount issue in the election of the president. Elect good people who would use their good judgment to make wise decisions as policy questions arose.[9] A later candidate, Zachary Taylor, said he had no opinions on public policy. If elected, he promised only to "serve the people." Even if there had been more nonaligned newspapers trying to report news of the issues objectively, the candidates and their advisers were doing all they could to avoid specific commitments on issues. As a result, the partisan press was filled with political information, but little of it tied candidates to explicit positions on policy differences. More than is generally realized, the candidates themselves and their managers have to be held responsible for a tradition of political discourse in the mid-nineteenth century that connected candidates and issues only in the vaguest terms.

Pennsylvania, Delaware, and North Carolina contained pockets of support for General Jackson in 1823. One of the most effective ways for the Jacksonians to bring the popularity of their candidate to public attention was with numbers. They held mass meetings and looked for opportunities to create the impression that a groundswell of enthusiasm was forming behind Jackson. Newcomers to presidential politics, many of them, they demonstrated their strength by arranging test votes and then publicizing the impressive results. In effect, they were using what would later be called straw polls to create a bandwagon effect by showing that "the silent majority" of previously uninvolved Americans wanted none other than Old Hickory.

The "proto-straw polls" of 1824 (a term coined by Tom W. Smith of the National Opinion Research Center at the University of Chicago) were different from anything that had been seen before.[10] Test votes were taken at ostensibly nonpolitical gatherings and the results were delivered to newspapers as quantitative evidence of the opinions of representative voters. All or nearly all of the polls were inspired by Jackson's supporters. Competition within different factions of what had been the same political party created confusion and curiosity in the general public. The best way to dispel the confusion and satisfy the curiosity was with numbers. Which of the candidates could appeal to voters across sectional lines? With three other candidates running, could any one of them win a majority of the electoral votes? What *were* other people thinking? How did *the numbers* look? The American people have always been strategic voters. How other people plan to vote *does* affect how individuals vote, which was then and is now one of the enduring reasons for their interest in opinion surveys reported as news.[11]

In North Carolina, where many of the military officers were active for Jackson, the militia musters were effective electioneering devices. A typical story in the *Carolina Observer* of Fayetteville reported in August:[12]

At a company muster held at Maj. Wm. Watfard's, Bertie County, on the 17th July, in the afternoon it was proposed to take the sentiments of the company on the Presidential question, when the vote stood as follows:

Jackson	102
Crawford	30
Adams	1
Clay	0

Old Hickory . . . and a Passion for Numbers

Most of the stories reporting news of the muster polls appeared in papers supporting Jackson. In 1823, the *Raleigh Register*, which was supporting William H. Crawford of Georgia for president, had been chosen by the legislature to be the state's official printer. The *Register* commented that the Jackson campaign's practice of "prematurely collecting the opinion of the people" had never been done before. A Crawford backer complained that the militia polls were rigged:

> In almost every captain's company the drums were beating and fifes whistling for the hero of New Orleans [Jackson]. The officers would treat their men, make them drunk and then raise the war whoop for General Jackson. Then the poor, staggering, drunken and deluded creatures would sally forth for the place appointed for them to vote. The result was always in favor of Jackson. I have conversed with some of them afterwards who told me they did not intend to vote that way at the proper election, they voted just to please their officers.[13]

From April until the voting in November, partisan newspapers leaped at every chance to cite fresh evidence of the popularity of the candidate of their choice. Reports were published of test votes taken wherever people came together. The *Carolina Observer*, which supported Jackson, gave special credence to "promiscuous assemblages of all parties when there is no public electioneering at the time, and the assembly are unexpectedly called upon to make their sentiments known."[14]

All manner of alleged quantitative intelligence found its way into print. Someone counted the toasts offered to particular candidates at a Fourth of July party in Pennsylvania. A sample vote was taken on the spur of the moment among the patrons of a tavern in western North Carolina. In other communities, poll books were left out at taverns, coffee houses, and other public places for customers to write in their preferences, the results to be reported to the press.

Most of the test counts were motivated by partisan considerations, true, but the editors welcomed them. Newspapers were responding to a public curiosity about what was fast becoming a form of popular entertainment— the election of the president.

It is important for our purposes to emphasize that the "proto-straw polls" were not initiated by newspapers. Editors were quick to recognize that their readers were interested in news of the relative strength of the candidates, but they did not awaken one morning and decide to send reporters out to interview voters. Once the practice had begun, some papers in North Carolina did endeavor to keep a running tally of the poll results. The

Calling Elections

Raleigh Star and North Carolina State Gazette—one of the leading Jacksonian voices in the state—had by early October in 1824 kept tabs on 155 separate meetings.[15]

As one might expect, newspapers supporting candidates who did not do well in the test voting tended to question the veracity of the polls. The pollsters made no attempt to screen out minors or other ineligible voters or to think through the simplest commonsense principles of probability sampling. In his study, Smith quotes the complaint of a paper which favored Crawford: "The most ridiculous misrepresentations are made of the sentiments of the People of Georgia. A few voters in a county out of as many thousands get together; and these meetings of the adherents of Gen. Clark, a violent personal enemy of Mr. Crawford, are paraded as evidence of his 'standing at home.'"[16]

The *Observer* printed a defense of its decision to report the test votes, an explanation that might be given today:

> The expression in black and white of numbers that are in accordance with facts rather than conjecture, is better evidence as to the popularity of men than whole columns of declamation. It is also better suited to the taste of the editor, who has a strong propensity to be what is significantly termed, one of the *matter of fact men.*[17]

Drawing on Smith's study of the election, we can reach three relevant conclusions:[18]

1. As long as competitive elections have existed, people have tried to anticipate their outcomes. High interest and uncertainty over the outcome inspired innovative ways of testing popular sentiment in 1824.

2. People began to understand that *national* leanings could only be assessed by somehow taking into account the sum of all the local information. They understood how the electoral college system worked then as well as they do now (and probably better).

3. Elections come down to numbers in the end. As Cohen reminds us, what counted was what was counted. Efforts were made, sometimes semi-independently, to measure voting intentions and report the results in the press before the election in an effort to influence the results of the election.

Traditionalists for the most part, editors were relieved when election day finally rolled around. "We are happy to have it in our power at last to make the results at the polls a substitute for calculations," confessed the *Observer* in Fayetteville.[19] When the electoral votes were finally counted, Jackson had a plurality of 90 to 84 for John Quincy Adams, 41 for Crawford, and 37 for

Old Hickory . . . and a Passion for Numbers

House Speaker Henry Clay. No candidate having received a majority of the electoral votes, however, the issue was placed before the House of Representatives. Speaker Clay threw his support to Adams, who won the prize and returned Clay's favor by appointing him secretary of state. This was exactly the kind of trade that the architects of the electoral college had hoped to prevent.

Newspapers scurried to be the first to report the news of Adams' victory. The *New York Evening Post* enlisted carrier pigeons to carry the news from Washington, but the birds went astray and the *Post* had to wait along with its competitors for the news to arrive by horseback.

Jackson ran again four years hence, and this time he could not be denied. Twice as many Americans voted in 1828 as in 1824. Money, organization, and stinging personal attacks were now part of the new stagecraft of politics. There were parades, rallies, barbecues, and souvenirs (Jackson's people gave out miniature hickory sticks). Voters learned to expect that the campaigners would "treat" them to hard liquor.

Voting in the several states stretched over several weeks. The *Carolina Observer* in Fayetteville pleaded with the postmasters to hasten the delivery of the exchanges: "We shall feel under obligations to the postmasters in the different Counties who will give us the earliest possible statement of the votes at the coming electoral election." An entire week elapsed after the voting in North Carolina, however, before the *Star and North Carolina State Gazette* reported: "The great contest has terminated, and although the result in all the States has not been received, sufficient intelligence has reached us to justify our announcing to our readers that the election of ANDREW JACKSON as President of the United States is reduced to a certainty, and that his majority is likely to exceed the sanguine expectations of his friends." The paper then listed the "Jackson states" in these categories: 1. Actual returns reached; 2. Certain but not heard from; 3. Doubtful but think it highly probable that General Jackson has received them (the electoral votes).[20] A week later, the paper was able to publish the county-by-county results from North Carolina along with items like this: "Kentucky—The Frankfort Argus of the 12th instant says that the present state of our information warrants the conclusion that Jackson's majority in Kentucky will not fall short of 8,000." (The Raleigh paper was giving its readers information on November 27 that had been clipped from a Kentucky paper of November 12.) On November 25, the *Register* conceded in Raleigh that Jackson had won.

It was a highly personalized campaign that excited many Americans who had never cared about politics before. "The election is the daily theme of the press, the subject of private conversation, the end of every thought and action," wrote de Tocqueville.[21]

The new president understood what newspapers had done to help whip up this excitement. And he knew how to command their loyalty through the use of patronage. For several years after 1828, citizen-initiated "proto-straw polls" almost disappeared from newspapers. Occasionally a partisan message would appear such as this: "At a large wedding given in Nash County on the 5th of the present month, where there were between 40 and 50 gentlemen, there was but one Van Burenite, and he would not express his sentiments. The Van Buren men are getting weaker and weaker in this section. We look for a complete revolution in 12 months."[22] Numbers were cited to suggest partisan strength at every opportunity, but the staged straw poll fell out of favor. Journalists made no effort on their own to initiate such surveys. There were two likely reasons for this. Most newspapers were clearly identified now by their partisan associations. Not even the most biased of readers were gullible enough to believe that reports of voter sentiment were unbiased. Instead editors devoted their energy and space to elaborate partisan pleadings. They published lengthy texts of speeches, statistical analyses, and briefs in the form of letters. The other reason was that improvements in the postal system made it possible for editors to print more timely news of the many state and local elections held elsewhere. Real voters casting real votes took precedence over misty estimates of voting predilections. Victories from afar became ammunition to bolster party morale at home. Editors loved to analyze figures from other elections as unfailing signs of favorable trends for their party. For now their partisan attachments overcame any desire to obtain unbiased information about the likely outcome of an election campaign.

Consider this item printed by the *Harrisburg Chronicle* in 1837, commenting on some comparative figures from New York:

> The *Albany Argus* has prepared a table comparing the Senatorial vote for this year with that of the Gubernatorial Vote of 1834. By this statement the Whigs have a majority in the state in 1837 of 15,213; but the *Argus,* to console itself for the overwhelming defeat which the Loco Focos [a Whig faction] have sustained this year, pretends to show a diminution in the Loco Foco vote since 1834, of 41,255, and of the Whig vote, 13,136, and deducting the Whig from the Loco Foco loss, and adding the Whig majority to the Whig loss, leaves what the *Argus* calls a majority (!) for the destructives of 13,985 votes. This elaborate mystification nine-tenths of the good people of this commonwealth can no more understand than they could the arithmetic of the *Argus'* Loco Foco brethren in this state.[23]

Old Hickory . . . and a Passion for Numbers

Partisan newspapers competed for patronage preference. Vying for the attention of patronage dispensers, some editors were led serendipitously into alien fields of enterprise journalism. Almost in spite of themselves, they began engaging in daring, aggressive, competitive journalism. James Watson Webb was a case in point. Webb founded the *New York Morning Courier* in 1827. It quickly became the largest and one of the best dailies in the nation. Webb wanted desperately to be a mover and shaker in the Jackson administration. He longed for an appointment to some high federal position. Several New York newspapers maintained pony express systems for carrying the news in 1830. That year, more to impress the president than his readers, Webb devised an elaborate relay plan to rush into print the news of Jackson's annual message to Congress. The text was carried from Washington to Baltimore on the back of a pony, from Baltimore to Philadelphia by steamboat, and on to New York by another fast pony. Twenty-two typesetters worked furiously to get out an extra edition. The *Courier* beat the arch-rival *Journal of Commerce* by twenty-seven and a half hours.[24]

Political news and election returns were among the few categories of news that newspapers of that period tried to deliver with dispatch and in detail. The rest of the paper was filled by clipping the exchanges and applying the pastepot. The *Carolina Observer* once gave its readers this front-page explanation: "No mail this morning north of Richmond—No news— our paper today presents a very barren aspect to the news-monger, being filled almost entirely with matter of a miscellaneous nature. We find nothing of the marvelous in the papers, not even a Kentucky murder. Congress is doing little besides debating the Tariff Bill, and from abroad the news is so late that we have hardly a right to expect anything additional for some time to come."[25]

Many new newspapers were launched in this period, founded typically by an ambitious local politician in partnership with an experienced printer. Not many of them were very enterprising. Consider an example: the Jackson administration's leading journal in the Michigan Territory was the *Democratic Free Press and Michigan Intelligencer.* The man who put up the money to establish that publication (which still exists today as the *Detroit Free Press)* was the first elected mayor of Detroit, one John R. Williams. Williams aspired to move up to the elected position of Michigan's territorial delegate in Congress. Two weeks after the election, the *Free Press* still could not give its readers the results:

> Sickness has prevented the editor from collecting the returns from several counties. All the counties have not yet been heard from. The anti-

Democratic candidate [the Whig] will no doubt be elected by a majority of
two or three hundred over either the Democratic or anti-Masonic candidates. Some remarks upon the late election and other subjects are omitted
this week to make room for the important public notice relative to the
supplies for the military posts, which was not received until yesterday.[26]

News of the election had been bumped by three columns of bid invita-
tions for supplies needed by the army—space for which the newspaper received payment from the government. Not until a week later did the *Free
Press* finally confirm that Williams had lost the election to his Whig opponent by a margin of almost 2-to-1.

The political journalism of the early 1830s was both easy and extremely
difficult. Reporting local voting was easy. Where the voting was by spoken
word, or with the placement of corn or beans next to a name, as sometimes
happened, it was a simple matter for all interested parties to keep score.
Some states allowed voters to make up their own hand-written ballots. After
the Whig Party became established as a counter to the Democratic Party
of Jackson and his successor, Martin Van Buren, the two strong parties
printed ballots listing only their candidates. Voters declared their party
preference by their choice of ballot. Secret voting did not become universal
in the United States until the early 1890s.

Statewide elections were another matter. Newspapers had neither the
means nor the inclination to organize a unified tabulating system. Typically.
the outcome of a state election would not be known until a week later, by
which time all but a couple of straggling counties had been heard from.

Information had to be physically carried from one place to another. The
bigger papers in New England, where the distances were shorter, organized
the first of the election-night horseback "overland expresses" in the 1820s.
By the 1830s railroads were running with steam-powered locomotives in
parts of Massachusetts, enabling the *Boston Atlas* to collect the election results from every town in the state by nine o'clock the morning after an
election. Some results arrived by train, others by horseback. Crowds of Bos-
tonians began gathering before daybreak in State Street to await the posting of the news bulletins in the windows of the *Atlas* office. As manager of
the first Massachusetts election reporting system, Major Richard Haughton,
who had been lured away from the *Journal of Commerce* in New York to edit
the *Atlas,* established a national reputation long before Colonel Taylor for
the swift "calling" of elections.

The movement of election news was much slower inland. Out in Illinois,
editors had to rely on mail exchanges with other newspapers and letters

Old Hickory . . . and a Passion for Numbers

from travelers, candidates, and volunteer correspondents. Cooperative ventures to exchange information in statewide elections invariably left the figures from some important counties missing. There was no central point for the collection and tabulation of results. Editors were reluctant to trust figures shared by papers loyal to the opposition party. Elections therefore were "running stories" for days and weeks after the votes had been cast. In 1836 it took more than two weeks for the *Alton Telegraph* to report the winners in three Illinois congressional districts, and even longer for the election of the president. A week and a half after the voting in Illinois, the *Telegraph* printed this story:

> The following returns are all that have been received by us, the mails from the north and east having been, from bad roads and other causes, unaccountably retarded. The statements below, it is proper to state, are given only from rumors . . . but we have taken pains to obtain the most correct information possible, and are of the opinion that the result will not differ materially from that given.[27]

The same edition of the *Telegraph* contained an unsigned letter from St. Louis: "A Boat this moment arrived from Louisville, bringing news that Ohio gave Harrison majority; Indiana 8,000; Kentucky 15,000. Nothing further. In haste, yours."

In its edition of November 30, the *Telegraph* still did not know which candidate had carried Illinois or been elected president. A week later, on December 7—one month to the day after the election in Illinois—the newspaper felt safe in reporting that Van Buren had been elected. Not until March of the following year were the complete nationwide electoral vote figures available to the *Telegraph* and its readers.

Three

Kicking All Politicians
to the Devil

Midway through a scorching August day in 1844, Philip Hone, a devoted Whig from New York City, joined the party faithful on a hillside in front of the courthouse in Albany. From there the fired-up Whigs paraded in close marching order through the city streets all the way to Patroon's farm, near the mansion house on the Troy Road. Hone stood in the sun for nearly five hours while the great Daniel Webster addressed the crowd. "Unfortunately," Hone wrote in his diary, "I was one of the tens of thousands who could not get near enough to enjoy this intellectual banquet. But I witnessed from a distance the commanding figure of the orator and occasionally caught the sound of his deep sonorous voice."[1] Hone said he read the speech in the newspaper the next day and was impressed.

Without electronic or other sound amplification, political speeches could actually be heard by few of those who were present. The others picked up a distant word now and then, basked in the fraternal ambience of the scene, and relied on party newspapers for the text—usually the edited text—of the speech.

The period beginning in the 1840s was one of strong, disciplined party organizations working hand in hand with their party newspapers. The partisan press filled their pages with the texts of partisan speeches. The reasons were both ideological and expedient. It was a time of unprecedented public interest in local, state, and federal politics (80 percent of the eligible voters voted in the 1840 presidential election). The party message had to be spread, the party workers had to be inspired. And Philip Hone had to be told what he had come to hear. Citizens who were interested in politics could indulge themselves in more uncooked political information (as distinguished from news and news analysis) than at any other time in American history.

By the 1840s almost all newspapers had enlisted, sometimes reluctantly, in one or the other of the partisan networks. Once welcomed into the party councils, their protestations aside, editors learned to enjoy the power. They became ever more arbitrary in their editorial judgments. "His party and the measures it advocated were wholly right," explained one such editor, "those of the opponent wholly wrong. The politicians were as intolerant and bigoted as were the members of different religious denominations. The idea that a man could be honest if his political opinions did not square with those of his opponent was not to be entertained."[2]

The party newspaper existed to serve the needs of the party. "Newspapers are the principal medium through which political lessons are learned," boasted an editor of the *Memphis Commercial-Appeal*.[3] During election campaigns, newspaper offices were used as reading rooms by party workers who congregated to scan the exchanges and keep up with the political gossip. Many reporters grew to detest the orders from politicians that they were obliged to carry out. "They put their feet on our tables and smoked our cigars," complained one reporter, and yet when the politicians had a good story to leak they usually gave the tip to an independent paper as an ingratiating gesture.[4]

Then, as always, successful indoctrination required the repetition of partisan themes. The paucity of accessible real news permitted newspapers to print the same political material over and over again. Later, when editors began publishing more real news, they resisted reprinting the same story. One of the principles of effective education being repetition, those who believe that responsible political journalism should fulfill an educational purpose are at odds with the journalist's understanding of the dynamics of news: the second time the story appears, it isn't news.

In the 1830s, however, newspapers had ample partisan inspiration, few reporters, and no practical way of receiving timely news from the outside world. Many editors in smaller communities were political pamphleteers, not journalists. The *Illinois Statesman* in Jacksonville routinely ran editorials thirteen columns long. Under the heading "Crimes and Casualties," the *Statesman* reminded its subscribers: "Our paper is small, and if our readers will for the present just have the goodness to imagine a certain due proportion of fires, tornadoes, murders, thefts, robberies, and bully fights from week to week, it will do just as well, for we can assure them that they actually take place."[5]

By the 1830s both the Democrats and the Whigs were holding national presidential nominating conventions. This made it necessary for state and local politicians to stay abreast of developments in other states. The consolidation of the nominating process also stimulated citizen interest in the mathematics of the competition. This occurred at the same time that railroads, canals, and better roads were improving the efficiency of mail deliveries.

Kicking All Politicians to the Devil

Faster transportation and the growth of cities created communitywide markets and the need for product advertising. Now advertisers would pay for access to a mass audience. Freedom from their dependence on a political subsidy awaited publishers who could put out inexpensive mass-circulation newspapers.

In 1835 James Gordon Bennett founded one of the most successful of the new "penny papers"—the *New York Herald*. Bennett had been among the first of the "Washington correspondents" for James Watson Webb's merged *Courier and Enquirer.* Bennett was very good at his job, which was to send back breezy, gossipy letters about the celebrities who were on stage in the nation's capital. The weighty substance of policy issues could easily be left to the official (politically sanctioned) Washington journals. Some of the correspondents were freelancers, forerunners actually of the syndicated columnists who did not come along until much later.

Bennett suspected that most of his readers didn't care about politics. He loathed most politicians. "In every species of news the *Herald* will be the earliest of the early," he pledged. "We care nothing for any election or any candidate from President down to a constable."[6] He served gleeful notice that his newspaper would "kick all politicians and parsons to the devil."[7]

In one of his first letters from Washington to the *Courier and Enquirer,* Bennett had written:

> Enough of politics for the present. It is often a dull, dry, and somewhat deceiving subject; yet it is full of fascination to minds of a certain cast. With it is mixed up human passion and feelings. It is the moral ocean of a nation. It ebbs and flows like its prototype, heaving some unfortunate individuals on the top of its billows, and overwhelming others in the gulf of forgetfulness—but from these tumblings and tossings arises the purity of the whole mass of national feelings.[8]

To compete in this new marketplace, the boss of the Whig Party in New York state—Thurlow Weed—hired a young journalist named Horace Greeley to edit a new penny paper that would be different: it would be inexpensive *and* partisan. Thus was born the *New York Tribune.*

Although Bennett cared little about dull political news, he did understand the interest that close elections had for the general reader. Greeley and the others were all running "expresses," relay systems combining various modes of transportation—pigeons, horses, steamboats, trains. When there was time to prepare for the movement of a big story, the penny papers would sometimes rent locomotives and race them against the opposition.

Besides being good fun for the journalists, the competition had the effect of sensationalizing some political news but diminishing the value of news about the substance of issues.

Partly for this reason, presidential campaigns became more entertaining in the 1840s. William Henry Harrison, a former army officer who had defeated the Indian chief Tecumseh at the Battle of Tippecanoe in the Indiana Territory, was the first candidate to "barnstorm" outside his home district. By cart, wagon, and ferry boat, Harrison traveled through Indiana and Ohio addressing groups of voters in person. Visual stunts contributed to the excitment.

Presidential voting occurred on different dates in the different states, spread over several weeks. Partisan papers hustled to report encouraging results from other states in advance of the election in their own states, as a propaganda ploy. The voting in 1840 started on October 30 in Pennsylvania and Ohio. Harrison carried Pennsylvania by only 343 out of 287,693 votes. Haughton had arranged for a railroad and horseback express to relay the news of the Pennsylvania election from Philadelphia to the *Boston Atlas* just before the voting occurred in the New England states and New York in the first week of November. Long before the electors in South Carolina were finally chosen by the legislature of that state on November 26, the nation knew that Harrison had been elected.

Bennett turned out to be less disenchanted with politics than he was with politicians. For all his snorting in print, he yearned to be a leader himself who would tell politicians what to do. He soon saw his independent, mass-circulation newspaper as an instrument of independent political power. His memoirs, written "By a Journalist" (Isaac C. Pray), contain this statement:

> [Wanting to be a party leader, not an errand boy] was a great sin in the eyes of politicians who, in that day, dictated to the Press. Editors were mere secretaries writing at the whim and will of political chieftains and their aids—the subalterns of King Caucus. There was not even a dream then of a new order of Journalism that would stand superior to, and independent of, the degrading influences of party spirit.[9]

Partisan journalism in America did not disappear with the establishment of the penny papers of New York City. Most newspapers were still predictably partisan. When the new owners of the *Hunterdon County Democrat* took over in New Jersey in 1867, they assured anxious readers that the change of ownership had been "approved and sanctioned" by the local Democratic committee. They promised to continue the paper's business policies, which included accepting cords of hickory wood in lieu of the two-dollar annual subscription.[10]

Nor did most newspapers cut back on their sometimes dull political news because of what the *Herald* and the other penny papers were doing in the big city. Looking at the country as a whole, journalism historian Donald Lewis Shaw found that the proportion of news devoted to government and politics (about one story out of every four) did not vary much between 1820 and 1860.[11]

Editors in other cities watched the New York press with interest. They sensed increasingly that readers everywhere were attracted to timely, readable news of the candidates as personalities—and the campaign as a horse race—instead of the long, tedious dissertations of the past. Alongside the many new sources of "human interest" news, political news had to be interesting not just to political junkies but to Everyman.

Electioneering practices also were adapting to changes in transportation and communication. By the mid-1880s, the campaign for president had moved from statehouse caucus rooms and the smoking parlors of businessmen's clubs to meeting halls and picnic groves. In the new electoral system, parties and candidates would need to attract the attention of voters who were less sophisticated, who were drawn to the political theater as spectacle.

Four

The Lightning and
the Fire

Alexander McClure, editor of the *Philadelphia Times,* reminisced often about an autumn afternoon of his boyhood in rural Pennsylvania. A group of men were gathered at his father's farm for a barn raising. The men were of mixed political persuasion; some were Whigs, others were Democrats. It was a Friday—two weeks and three days after the presidential election of 1840. Among the men, only his father was sufficiently eclectic to subscribe to *two* weekly newspapers, one Whig, one Democratic. That afternoon the weekly mail was due to arrive at the country post office. So, while the men worked on the barn young McClure was sent into town to greet the "post boy." He tore open the Whig paper first and saw a huge coon reproduced over the masthead. As the symbol of the Whig Party, the coon was meant to commemorate Whig candidate Harrison's victory in Pennsylvania by, it was reported, 1,000 votes. Hurrah for the Whigs. With less haste, the lad then proceeded to the Democrat paper. There he was greeted by a huge rooster at the top of the page. The rooster symbolized the Democratic Party, proclaiming the reported fact that the Democrat Van Buren had won Pennsylvania by 1,000 votes. Back at the farm, the conflicting news accounts were spread out on the lawn for the puzzled men to interpret as they would. "Both sides went home rejoicing in the triumph," McClure recalled in his autobiography. The editors had engaged in some wishful, if premature, extrapolation of incomplete results. An editor who lived through this period in Massachusetts said in his memoirs that election results were persistently falsified. It was not until two more weeks had elapsed that the definitive news finally reached the McClure household: Harrison had indeed won the state by 305 votes.[1]

Party weeklies entered the spirit of an election campaign with a special zest. "A presidential campaign lifts them as a heavy flood lifts stray chips of decayed wood by the river bank above the normal level," said a story in the *New York Herald,* referring to the weeklies in New York state.[2]

Reporting election results was no more exact a science for big-city dailies. The election of 1844, four years later, was one of the closest in

35

American history. Three days after the last of the voting, it was still uncertain who had carried New York. Whoever did win New York's electoral votes—either the Whig candidate Henry Clay or the Democrat James K. Polk—would be the next president. That much was certain. Enough voting results had been relayed from state to state, by train, boat, or pony express, to know that New York's electoral votes would be determinative. The figures were still not in from St. Lawrence County, far to the north. Whigs knew enough to be apprehensive. St. Lawrence was a Whig stronghold, true enough, but it had rained hard on election day and some of the farmers did not vote. Late that night Horace Greeley, the zealous Whig editor of the *New York Tribune,* sat anxiously in his office on Nassau Street. The last of the deadlines had passed, the presses were silent, and all the others had departed the news floor. The returns from St. Lawrence County were being carried south on the riverboat *Empire.* A crowd gathered at the pier waiting for the vessel to dock. Upon its arrival, a messenger brought Greeley the news: Clay had lost. Legend has it that Greeley broke down in tears. A switch of 5,000 votes anywhere in the state would have made Henry Clay president.

There would be other devastating disappointments ahead for Horace Greeley, but never again would he have to wait so long for the bad news. In May of that year a new communications device—the electromagnetic telegraph—had been used for the first time to send the news of Clay's nomination by the national convention of the Whig Party from Baltimore to Washington.

At first, the invention of the telegraph was considered important chiefly for railroad traffic control. It did not take long, however, for journalists to grasp the significance for them. "This is indeed the annihilation of space," announced the *New York Sun.* Instead of having to physically carry information from place to place, man could move coded signals electronically through a wire almost instantly. Election results from St. Lawrence County or anyplace else could be transmitted at the speed of light anywhere a wire could carry them.

Until then, journalists either observed for themselves what they needed to know, or were told about it (face to face) by others who knew what they needed to know. They could receive information through the mails, which usually entailed copying stories from other newspapers; or they could arrange to have the news brought to them from its place of origin (by "running expresses"). Even if the states all made their presidential election decisions the same way at the same time—which they did not—there had

The Lightning and the Fire

been no practical method for the information to be collected in a timely fashion in a central location.

The telegraph changed that. Not only did the technology now exist to transmit coded words and figures rapidly from place to place, but Congress wisely passed a law in 1845 requiring that the election of the president occur everywhere on the same day beginning in 1848: that day being the first Tuesday after the first Monday in November. The gathering of election figures would be more manageable in a nation which then consisted of thirty-three states. Simultaneously, the development of rotary presses powered by steam made it possible to print more newspapers faster. Newspapers could be carried longer distances by faster trains operating more safely, thanks to steam power and the telegraph.

Having the presidential election on a single day—and having the technical means now to transmit the results long distances quickly—contributed to horse-race journalism in another way. Although the voting for president occurred on the same day, countless state, local, and sometimes congressional elections were being held almost continuously all year long. Voting in Rhode Island and Connecticut in April—and in Indiana, Ohio, and Pennsylvania in October—was seen as an omen of how each state would go in November.

To help readers interpret the meaning of the voting installments, several New York papers published statistical reference books. The best of these was Greeley's *Whig Almanac and Political Register.* Thick with statistical trivia, here was a county-by-county compendium of past election records that sold for twelve and a half cents per copy beginning in 1838. The political junkies of the nineteenth century had their election reference books. The results of a municipal election in Buffalo could be compared with the one two years before—and with last week's congressional voting in central Indiana. Greeley himself loved to analyze and re-analyze election trends. He could not understand why everyone else did not share his fascination with the patterns formed by election pluralities. His former associate, Charles A. Dana, said Greeley "thought a newspaperman of little use who did not know the number of votes in every township in the State of New York and in every voting precinct, and who could not tell whether the returns from the Second District of Pound Ridge in Westchester County were correctly reported or not without sending to the place to find out how many votes had really been cast."

Newspapers needed the telegraph to bring them news from beyond their reach. But what would be the organizational mechanism for the collection and delivery of this news? Telegraphers could deliver the news, but could they also gather it? If they didn't, who would?

By mid-1846 the telegraph line from Washington was finished all the way to Boston, except for a few inconvenient gaps. The wire did not, for example, go under or over the mile-wide Hudson River. *Scientific American* proposed that the wires be supported with balloons, but that idea was abandoned.[3] Eventually the problem was solved by stringing two wires across the river between iron towers. Service had to be interrupted and the wires lowered into the river whenever a vessel with a tall mast approached.

New York City papers made use of the telegraph for various news-sharing arrangements at elections and other times. In 1847 six of them formed a cooperative organization they called the Associated Press. Several smaller regional wire services were founded outside of New York City to feed telegraphic news to the member papers from sources inaccessible to their own reporters.

Wherever telegraph lines were installed, the first general agent of the New York AP, Alexander Jones, tried to hire temporary correspondents to report the election results in 1848. Most of them were telegraphers—nonjournalists of varying ability to read. On through the remainder of the nineteenth century, many of the wire-service correspondents were telegraph operators with no training as reporters.[4]

Unhappily, the election service was expensive, unreliable, and hard to understand. It was difficult for the reader of the *Herald* to make sense out of items such as: "Fifth Despatch—Poughkeepsie, Nov. 7, 10 1/2 P. M.— Returns from six towns in Dutchess county show a majority of 1,256 for Taylor. Hudson City gives Taylor 467, Cass 423, and Van Buren 115."[5]

Now that all the states were voting on the same day, the telegraph made it possible for the news that a candidate had apparently carried this or that state to be transmitted rapidly. But the problems of piecing together incomplete results within a state perplexed the editors in a close election. There was no practical method of discerning which returns had not been received, and how the missing numbers might affect the result.

Other editors arranged independently to trade figures with newspapers in distant cities—telegraphically. The telegraph had stretched as far west as Illinois by this time, but no one was trusted with the responsibility of piecing together the results in that state. In its Friday edition, three days after the election, the *Alton Telegraph* reported in the last paragraph of a column and half of returns "By Magnetic Telegraph," this sentence with a St. Louis dateline: "It is conceded here and at the city of New York, by

The Lightning and the Fire

both party papers, that TAYLOR IS ELECTED." Even with the telegraph, the *Telegraph* in Illinois felt compelled to wait until the eastern party press reached a consensus. A week later, the paper reported additional details, "most of which," it said with less than ringing confidence, "are more or less correct."[6]

Until the mid-1880s, the job of AP telegrapher/reporters was limited to putting on the wire whatever items could be taken from their member newspapers. Generally they did not attempt to gather news on their own. After candidates began campaigning from place to place by railroad, journalists had to become more mobile as well. Many of the eastern papers printed verbatim texts of the Lincoln-Douglas debates in the Illinois senatorial campaign of 1858. Correspondents accompanied the candidates from debate to debate, insisted on adequate press facilities near the debate platforms where they could hear, and did an admirable job of portraying the color and excitement of the events. For the debate transcript, they relied on their new teammates: the "phonographic" stenographers who had mastered phonetic shorthand symbols. Reporting the Lincoln-Douglas debates ranks as an impressive example of how political journalism could, when it was so inclined, focus on public policy issues for other than partisan motives. Issues journalism at its best. Madison and Jefferson would have been proud.

When the voters went to the polls in that election, the *Chicago Daily Press and Tribune* was still having to urge "friends" around the state to "forward us election returns at the earliest moment." Though telegraph lines were in place in Illinois, newspapers lacked the necessary organization to collate the contests for the state legislature (which would determine the outcome of the U.S. Senate contest). On the day after the election, the *Tribune* reported:

> Returns from the election held in this State yesterday are presented to our readers as we have received them by telegraph—in a confused mass. In the main they wear an encouraging aspect, but they do not include a sufficient number of districts, nor are they decisive enough in their character to justify a conclusion as to the result in the State. We incline to the opinion that the Republicans have carried the Legislature. But it will take another day—perhaps longer—to determine the question. Let our friends await with patience and hope.[7]

Another column, labeled "Vote in the Interior," credited messages from editors of scattered downstate newspapers for some disjointed local figures. Two days after the election, with nine House districts still unheard from, the outcome remained in doubt. The following day, it was reported that Stephen A. Douglas had apparently won. A full week after the election, the *Tribune*, reporting results from all but three counties, declared Douglas the winner. "We have at last found out the vote of Springfield which the papers of that city have carefully suppressed up to this time," the Chicago paper complained.

Telegraphic news made the downtown newspaper the focal point of interest for the announcement of election results, rather than party headquarters. Most newspapers mounted bulletin boards in their office windows that could be consulted by passersby.

Once the *Herald* secured a solid circulation base in the New York market, Bennett gave more attention to his role as a molder of public opinion. Of the 1856 election, which the Democrat Buchanan won despite the *Herald's* opposition, Bennett's biographer says this:

> All through the night, the milling crowds surged about the newspaper offices, shouting, booing, cheering, whistling, as the reports of the election were announced. The staff at the *Herald* worked like madmen, from printer's devil to publisher. They were determined to keep their reputation of always being "first with the news." Not until 3 o'clock in the morning, when it was evident that Buchanan was elected to the Presidency, did James Gordon Bennett don his hat, coat and muffler and call it a day.[8]

Four years later, the *Herald* and its competitors had enough sketchy information in the early morning hours to declare Lincoln the next president in their Wednesday morning editions. The AP supplied dispatches from twelve of the thirty-three states indicating likely winners but without specific figures. All the AP could report from New Orleans was: "The election in this city passed off quietly. The result is not yet ascertained."[9]

Not until after the wire spanned the continent in 1861 did the telegraph become a reasonably efficient vehicle for the collection of national election results. The more perceptive editors understood all along that news reporting would never be the same again. Samuel Bowles of the *Springfield Republican* (Massachusetts) wrote in 1851:

> ... There is a great deal more news nowadays than there used to be. ... Publishers of country weeklies used to fish with considerable anxiety in a shallow sea for matter sufficient to fill their sheets, while dailies only dreamed of an existence in the larger cities. ... Now all is changed. The increase of facilities for transmission of news brought in a new era. The railroad car, the steamboat, and the magnetic telegraph have made neighborhood among widely dissevered states. These active and almost miracu-

lous agencies have brought the whole civilized world in contact. The editor sits in his sanctum, and his obedient messengers are the lightning and the fire.[10]

Of the many effects of telegraphic transmission of news, two are especially noteworthy for this study. The sea in which editors fished for news, using Bowles' metaphor, became much broader and deeper. There was more news available from more placcs. At first, because there were far more users than there were facilities, journalists filing stories could "hold the wire" for only ten minutes at a time. Reporters were encouraged to write briefly, to save money on tolls and to cram as much solid information into their ten minutes on the wire as they could. The language and the literary style of journalism changed. News was treated as a commodity. A "tighter, leaner" political journalism ensued with, as communications scholar James W. Carey has remarked, "the loss of the luxury of detail and analysis."[11] Political news had to compete for space in the paper. Editors were less likely to print long-winded, argumentative essays or the full texts of speeches. Substantive news of issues had to be made to fit into a smaller package.

New York's penny press editors thought more highly of political news as the number of readers who had a financial stake in the outcome of elections increased. Dana of the *New York Sun* estimated in 1880 that more than 50,000 New Yorkers were either on the public payroll or in jobs that were dependent on government purchases of goods and services. For these folks, voting numbers could mean paying the grocery bill. Dana calculated that daily circulation went up by 82,000 just before a presidential election. Good journalists "must feel the impulse [of politics], feel the heartbeat that thrills through the whole American people."

Two strong party organizations were now firmly established, led by professional politicians who agreed that the spoils of public office belonged to the winner. In Philadelphia, for example, the post office, the navy yard, and the mint were all "formidable reservoirs of ballots . . . reinforced by an army of internal revenue assessors, collectors, cashiers, clerks, and detectives."[12] The precinct captains, government payrollers, aspiring candidates, contractors, and vendors constituted the hard core of a vast audience for horse-race political reporting.

As reader interest in election races increased, newspapers were looking again for credible ways to measure the status of the contest. Some party papers resumed the publication of letters from curious partisans who claimed to have polled their fellow passengers on train trips. In the summer of 1856, for instance, one nosey traveler told the *New York Times* that he had sampled no fewer than 2,886 fellow passengers on a train ride through New England. He reported that seven-eighths of the "literary men, collegiate professors, teachers, etc." were Republicans, as were thirty-nine out of forty-two "ministers of the gospel." At about the same time, another staunch Republican organ, the *Chicago Tribune* revealed that a newspaper in New Haven, Connecticut, had seen a letter from a workman in Samuel Cole's pistol factory in Hartford indicating that 109 out of 146 workers in one department were planning to vote for the Republican candidate.[13] Editors were being told that their politically interested readers wanted to know about the numbers.

By this time editors had discovered another passageway to the reporting of election news with numbers. For much of the second half of the nineteenth century, straw polls conducted informally by readers were subordinate to the reporting of detailed information about the betting on the election. Whom did the professional gamblers think would win? What were the wagering odds? With these reports they were making the most of another old American passion—"The rapture of risk, the elation of gambling."[14]

Though hardly unique to Americans, gambling seems always to have been an addiction of special attraction to people who either practice or follow politics. Many of the leading politicians in colonial Virginia, for instance, were wealthy planters who bred horses for racing and high-stakes betting. At the beginning of the 1800s, according to one account, typical Americans "played cards, billiards, shuffleboard and dice [for money], bought chances or fractions of chances in lotteries and bet on contests between bulls, bears, cocks, badgers, horses, men and dogs."[15]

Neither moral reprimand nor the makers of laws ever succeeded in suppressing the urge to gamble. "Gambling at games is a substitute for relaxing in this heady country of ours," said one historian.[16]

The precarious nature of political life fascinated risk-takers. Among the most interested spectators standing in front of newspaper bulletin boards on election night were likely to be a certain number of men with unusually long beards. Almost always, their razors had been retired not out of personal or religious conviction but as the penalty for losing an election bet four years before.

Newspapers were involved in the betting on elections in at least three ways—by "booking bets" themselves; by sponsoring lotteries based on the vote figures; and by reporting in repetitive detail, as news, the bets that were being offered and placed either in gaming establishments or privately. Partisan papers backed up their public commitment to the candidates they were supporting editorially by booking bets. Two politically opposed news-

The Lightning and the Fire

papers in Little Rock, Arkansas—the *Arkansas State Gazette and Democrat* and the *Arkansas Whig*—wagered free subscriptions if their candidate lost in 1852. For several weeks preceding the state election in Ohio in 1880, the *Cleveland Plain Dealer,* a Democratic organ, taunted the opposition by printing at the top of the front page a standing offer to accept $5,000 bets against the Democratic presidential candidate, Gen. Winfield Hancock (who lost). In 1860 the editor of the *Chicago Press & Tribune* accepted bets of $100 at the newspaper office. "A chance to make enough to pay for a winter's clothing," the story said. "Accept my proposition or stop blowing!"[17]

Bennett's memoirs, written by Isaac Pray after the editor's death, proposed that "political betting [be made] a penal offence":

> Political betting, or betting upon elections, has been indulged in very extensively for many years; and a son of one of the Presidents of the United States has been shown to have extensive operations in this foolish and degrading practice, so common as to be vulgar, and so popular as to be dangerous. For many years it was not uncommon for journals publicly to propose and accept bets on the issues of a political campaign. In this way politicians sometimes sold principles and every consideration of justice and propriety, to save their money, or to add to it, or in the hope to strengthen the prospects of their cause.

Another New York newspaper, the *Journal of Commerce,* proposed in 1834 that betting on elections be outlawed:

> We do not introduce this subject because we think anything we can say will do much good. There is too much interest in gambling of all sorts to be checked by anything but stern principle. . . . Betting upon elections is putting the high franchise of freemen at the stake of the gambler. It is a political sacrilege. Besides this, it throws into our contests with one another, at the polls, a spirit of violence, when without this addition, the mass of passion would be quite sufficiently great. Every man who bets on an election encourages, perhaps begins, in himself and in his antagonist, a practice which often has led, and may again lead, to ruin.[18]

Newspapers in Boston and Cincinnati, two cities with large immigrant populations, were unmoved by such appeals to moral principle. They seized an opportunity to capitalize on the interest in the election and increase circulation. Toward the end of the century, papers in both cities attempted to boost sales by sponsoring and advertising lotteries based on the election figures. The *Boston Globe* promised $5 a week for life to the person who came closest to predicting the total vote in 1892. In Cincinnati, the *Enquirer* announced in 1904 that its "profit-sharing bureau" had set aside $100,000

for a contest that it said would stimulate interest in the election. Only subscribers were eligible to participate.

The churches were less tolerant of games of chance in Germanic Cincinnati, however, than they were in Irish Boston, and a committee of a hundred
of the city's clergy and business and professional leaders protested to the
federal government. "The schemes stimulate the spirit of gambling, encour-
age breaches of trust, create profligacy and mendicancy, and . . . they are
as detrimental to public morality as any lottery ever devised," asserted the
protesters.[19]

Urban newspapers also reported betting on elections as news, the last of
the three ways journalists were involved in election campaign gambling.
Until random-sample polling evolved much later out of the straw poll, editors continued to report betting odds and the volume of wagering as measures of the probable outcome of the race. Betting news was reported in a
tone which indicated that the gamblers probably had some inside dope that
the general public did not have.

Betting on elections, and on other events—notably horse races—was
transacted during this period through the pooling of wagers in public betting parlors. During election seasons, newspapers kept their readers informed about the betting conditions.

Here are fragments from typical stories in the *New York Herald* one week
before the election of 1876. The headlines read: "Betting—Pool Selling
and Private Wagers on the Presidential Election—Speculation North and
South—No Decided Indication—Tilden Slightly the Favorite." With the approach of Election Day, "betting on the result becomes more excited," the
story said. "The pool rooms are nightly crowded with an eager throng."[20]

On the Thursday after the election, the outcome was still in doubt, and
part of the *Herald's* coverage was entitled "in the pool rooms":

> "We have sold Tild'n for twenty thousand majority in New York state,
> for twelve hun' dollars; what am I bid for under twenty thousand?"
> "A hat," sung out somebody in the crowd.
> "Five dollars," shouted some more feasible individual.
> "Gim'me ten dollars," vociferated the auctioneer. But no one would and
> sale made at 5.

Reportorial talent and newspaper space that might have been given over
to the debate over issues was devoted to stories like this from the *New York
Times* in 1908:

> Colorado Springs—James Burns, the Colorado Springs mining man, last
> night offered to bet $2,000,000 that Bryan would carry Colorado. Burns

was seated in an uptown cafe with John Cary, the wealthy Denver manufacturer, when they were introduced by the proprietor of the place to a
wine merchant from Hoboken.

"I came from Hoboken," said the stranger. "Your name is Burns, isn't it?
I'll bet you that Taft carries your own State."

"All right," said Burns.

"How much money can you scare up?" said the wine merchant. "I'll just
take all you've got."

"Well, I have about two million to bet that Bryan will carry Colorado,"
replied Burns easily.

The bet was not covered, and the discussion of politics was discontinued.[21]

The American people—women as well as men—were interested in election
pluralities, betting odds, and the mathematics of the electoral college. Pitts
Shoe Store placed an ad in the *Columbus Dispatch* in 1896 inviting women to
guess the state-by-state electoral vote received by each candidate. "A pair of
our superb $3 specialty shoes for women" were awarded to all who guessed
the correct figures.

James Bryce, the British ambassador to Washington in the 1880s and an
astute student of American life, saw something in the American psyche that
explained this excitable attraction for electoral competition:

> . . . Americans like excitement. They like it for its own sake and go wher-
> ever they can find it. They surrender themselves to the enjoyment of this
> pleasure the more willingly because it is comparatively rare, and relieves
> the level tenor of their ordinary life. Add to this the further delight which
> they find in any form of competition. The passion which in England ex-
> presses itself in the popular eagerness over a boat race or a horse race
> extends more widely in America to every kind of rivalry and struggle. The
> presidential election, in which two men are pitted one against the other
> over a four months course for the great prize of politics, stirs them like any
> other trial of strength and speed; sets them betting on the issue, disposes
> them to make efforts for a cause in which their deeper feelings may be
> little engaged.[22]

Five

The Unholy Alliance of the AP
and Western Union

Members of the Electrical Club of New York City met in the front parlor of their Manhattan clubhouse on election night in 1880 to watch a race between the telegraph and the telephone. Which would transmit the returns first? Would it be the coded signals over a wire? Or the other wires that could carry the sound of the human voice as far as 250 to 300 miles? The *Boston Globe* had just installed its first office telephone, but the instruments were not in general use to gather news. The election night race was said to have been "pretty even." The captains of the electrical industry had reason to be doubly pleased, both being powered by electricity.[1]

New technology—the railroad, the telegraph, and then the telephone—made it possible for newspapers to collect election returns and get the news out much faster than before. Morning papers made every effort to report the winner the morning after election day. Sometimes extraordinary measures were justified. To gather returns from two congressional districts in the mountainous region of Georgia, the *Atlanta Constitution* once hired relays of horseback riders, installed temporary telegraph wires, engaged teams of operators, and chartered locomotives.[2]

In big-city newspaper markets, the competition and therefore the urgency were more intense. Just before the election of 1856, the *New York Herald* acknowledged in a story on the front page that "the public will be looking for the result the next morning." For this news to be available, the editors tried to explain, "it will be necessary for the inspectors of election throughout the United States to aid the telegraphic operators and for the telegraphic operators to aid the editors in every town, village and city, and for the editors and reporters to aid each other."[3]

New York City papers used a primitive version of the stereopticon projector to enlarge their election bulletins across the entire side of a building for the first time in the presidential election of 1860. Transparencies were projected by the *Herald* onto a large outdoor canvas. At first a gas light illuminated the words and figures through the lenses and prisms of what

47

came to be called the "Magic Lantern." Before Edison's invention of the electric light bulb, cylinders of lime or calcium provided the light.

The next morning the *Herald* described the wondrous experience for its readers: "Like a new moon, the brilliant calcium light shed its rays upon the transparency, which at intervals proclaimed the state of the momentous horizon and the loud bursts of enthusiasm at once manifested the mighty interest which the concourse of citizens took in the event."[4] In 1872, the *Herald* described the scene in equally grandiose terms: "A great, glaring, calcium light shot down its lurid, silvery rays upon a surging sea of upturned faces."

The irregular pace of election results from distant locations invited partisan manipulation. Perhaps the most notorious of the journalistic double agents was William Henry Smith, for many years the head of the Western Associated Press. Editors in "the West"—principally Chicago, Cincinnati, St. Louis, and Louisville—had broken away from the New York AP in 1865. Previously an editor in Cincinnati, Smith also represented the political interests of his friend, Governor Rutherford B. Hayes of Ohio.[5] The AP leader used his contacts with newspaper editors and his control over the selective release of election returns to help Hayes win the Republican presidential nomination in 1876. Smith was accused of holding back some figures, inflating others, and pressuring editors who were AP member-customers. The subsequent general election campaign against Governor Samuel J. Tilden of New York remained in doubt long after the election while the two sides fought over the electoral votes from three southern states.

"The Dance of a Phantom Majority"—"Is Tilden's Election a Snark or a Boojum?"—"Who'll Come out of the Woods?"—"Lightning Flashes out of the Clouds of Doubt," shouted the exciteable headlines in the *New York Herald*.[6]

As the controversy dragged on into the winter, Smith suppressed AP news favorable to Tilden. When Tilden's backers met to protest that the election was being stolen, Smith wrote to an AP reporter in Ohio: "I suggest that we can best subserve the interests of the country and of the press by making no reference to them [the Democratic meetings] in our reports. . . . Our general rules exclude political matters anyhow and there was never a better time to bring them into action."[7]

Eventually Hayes was declared the winner. William Henry Smith was rewarded with one of the most lucrative patronage posts—as customhouse collector for the Port of Chicago—while continuing as full-time general manager of the AP.

Partisan newspapers printed pre-election news that supported their biases. Some were reporting the results of what were depicted as spot polls. Instead of relying on letters from like-minded readers, reporters now were being assigned to question voters themselves on excursion trains, steamboats, and other public conveyances. The *Chicago Tribune*, for example, uncovered a preponderance of sentiment affirming the overwhelming popularity of Republican candidates.

Other stories described the voting views of certain prestigious occupational classes, such as clergy, college professors, judges, and philanthropists. "The main effort of a candidate's orators and newspapers is to convince the people that their side is the winning one," noticed the British Lord Bryce.[8]

Occasional stories were devoted to what the candidates were saying about the issues, but a typical one in the *New York Herald* in 1876, headed "Campaign Issues," applied the proper spin with this unambiguous second-deck headline: "Democratic Pledges of Reform a Sham and a Snare."[9]

AP's election reporting system underwent congressional scrutiny after the infamous stock-trader Jay Gould obtained control of Western Union Telegraph Company in the 1880s. AP and its newspaper customers leased their wires from WU free of charge on election night. In exchange, the telegraph company was allowed to sell AP's returns independently to private homes, clubs, and other clients.

As the gatherers and purveyors of piecemeal election news, WU and AP made many collaborative decisions about what to report, when and how to report it, and when to call the election. A Senate committee opened an investigation into whether Western Union "restrict[ed] the free and independent use of the telegraph by the press." Senator Charles A. Sumner had already made up his mind. "The Western Union has a twin connection with another incorporated thief and highway robber called the Associated Press," said the senator. "They are banded together in a strong bond of mutual plunder and rapacity against the people."[10]

The publisher of the *New York World*, Joseph Pulitzer, was one of those who suspected Smith and Gould of tampering with the transmission of results of one of the hardest fought of presidential elections: Republican James G. Blaine's loss to Governor Grover Cleveland of New York in 1884.

Newspapers on both sides slanted the news outrageously. The *Chicago Tribune*, which was supporting Blaine, posed as an appropriate issue the relative proportions of the candidates' "brain pans" and necks. Cleveland had a head that was small at the top and what today would be called a football neck. "His Beefy Neck—Beef Instead of Brains" declared the *Tribune's* headline.[11]

In Springfield, the *Illinois State Journal* took its cue from the *Tribune* and introduced news of Cleveland's speeches with a standing headline: "What the Fat Boy Says."[12]

The *New York Herald,* which was backing Cleveland, saw events a little differently. These headlines appeared above the lead story of October 24:[13]

The Campaign of Filth

Blaine Managers Deluging the Country
With Obscene Literature

Stories of Boccaccio Revamped

Disgust of Decent Republicans at the
Infamous Attacks

The AP and Western Union were supporting Jay Gould's candidate: Blaine. Gould was first accused of manipulating Western Union's transmission of returns in the Ohio state preliminary elections. The AP apparently overreported the Republican vote in Ohio by misplacing the returns from some Democratic districts and timing the release of results from selected blocs of counties to benefit the Republicans.

Emotions peaked on election day. "Large Sums Wagered—Jay Gould Backs Blaine Heavily," reported the *Chicago Herald.* Theaters in Chicago used leased wires to announce the results from the stage. By now Western Union wires connected Chicago with New York and Washington. The *Chicago Tribune* boasted that its "special despatches" would "far surpass the reports of the Associated Press." The Washington Boulevard Ice Rink advertised: "Election Returns—Without standing on the corner and taking a death cold—See beautiful and graceful skating—And with great comfort see the election returns every 15 minutes."

To learn the results of the election as soon as possible, most Americans had to leave their homes and venture out into the night in search of the information. And in cities big and small most of them headed not for the theater or the skating rink but to the newspaper office. By the tens of thousands, they massed in the streets and sidewalks of New York's Newspaper Row in lower Manhattan. Thomas Edison's invention of the electric light bulb in 1879 made it possible to shed more light on the bulletins in newspaper windows. Out in Springfield, Illinois, the *Illinois State Journal* borrowed a locomotive headlight to shine on its bulletin boards.

On that night the *Herald* estimated that more than 500,000 people poured into Manhattan across the recently completed Brooklyn Bridge or by steamer from Staten Island, Jersey City, and Hoboken.

Pulitzer and other Democratic editors alleged that Gould and the AP were falsifying the results in some New York counties. It became clear by midnight that if Cleveland carried New York he would have won. The *New York Herald* and the *New York World* proclaimed Cleveland elected, but the two *Tribunes* in New York and Chicago insisted that Blaine was ahead in New York State. The *Chicago Tribune* printed scattered items like "Cleveland will probably carry Peoria County by 300 to 400" and "Escanaba, Mich.— Delta County is Republican by 350 majority," but still it was unable to bring together statewide figures in a coherent fashion.[14] The AP awarded New York to Blaine, though thirty districts were still outstanding.

At eight o'clock on Wednesday morning, 5,000 people were standing in front of the *Herald's* white marble building on Broadway. All that day and night, men and women milled about in the streets, drifting in waves from the *Tribune* building, which continued to post AP totals showing Blaine increasing his lead, to the other papers which had Cleveland on top.

Newsboys were hawking contradictory editions.

"'Ere you are. Er's your hextra. Cleveland carries the state by 3,000!"

And minutes later—

"Ere you are. Er's your hextra—Blaine carries the state and's elected!"

Other lads moved through the crowd offering "tickets to Blaine's funeral—2 cents apiece."

The *New York Times*, a "mugwump journal" supporting the Democrat in 1884, claimed later in the week that Gould was personally supervising the filing of AP news reports "and keeping back returns favorable to Cleveland." Returns were being sent out in lumps of unidentified election districts, the story said, which were reported "in amounts and at times to suit the schemes" of the Blaine camp. Western Union messages from Democrats were bungled and the figures revised by the operators, according to the *Times*. The AP was accused by the *Herald* of "indulging in the same trick [as in Ohio during the state election] by wishing to make a state which was clearly for Cleveland appear to be in doubt," thereby delaying the outcome.

The *Chicago Tribune* reported in its Friday editions that the Democrats were "trying to steal" New York State. "Cheating!" screamed the headline. "Democrats Trying to Carry New York by Fraud."

On the sidewalks of Manhattan, meanwhile, the scene grew more tense as supporters of the two candidates taunted one another. Janitors secured the iron doors of the *Tribune*. Squads of police dispersed the pro-Cleveland demonstrators. Thousands of protesters then tramped into Madison Square and on to the Western Union building.

"Who buys up Presidents?" shouted a man who had shinnied up a light pole.

"Jay Gould!" chanted the mob.

"Who are we after?"

"Jay Gould!"

"Hang Jay Gould! Blood, blood, Jay Gould's blood! We'll hang Jay Gould to a sour apple tree."

Finally, late on Friday, Gould sent a telegram to Cleveland from the financier's 150-foot yacht in the Hudson River. He congratulated the president-elect, thus signaling an end to the crisis. Only then did the AP finally put New York in the Cleveland column. "Cleveland Has Won—Jay Gould Gives Up New York State," announced the *Chicago Herald*. The crisis was over—everyhere, that is, but on the pages of the *Chicago Tribune*. "Which? The Presidency Still Trembling in the Balance," the paper stubbornly headlined on Saturday. "Information showed that Mr. Blaine is honestly elected," said Monday's edition. On Saturday, November 15—11 days after the election—the headline in the *Tribune* declared: "Done Up! Almost the Last Chance of Blaine's Election Now Passed—Cleveland Still 872 Ahead—The Demon Bull of Luck Still Pursues Him." The next day—on November 16—Editor Joseph Medill conceded that Grover Cleveland had carried New York by 1,100 votes. The game was over.[15]

Six

The Journalism of Magic Lanterns and Heavenly Hieroglyphics

Counting ballots was still a slow process, but an element of regularity was introduced into the centralized tabulation of national returns in 1883 when the nation honored a request by the railroads that it convert to four "standard time" zones. Until then there were many wildly different voting hours within a single state.

Standard time did not, of course, prevent the polls from closing (and the counting of the votes beginning) in the eastern states before the termination of voting in the western states. Indeed this became a more significant problem later on in the twentieth century with the transcontinental communication of exit-poll-induced broadcasting of the outcomes in some of the eastern states.

New technology continued to speed up the process of calculating results and fitting them into the mosaic. Reporting news by printing words on paper could not hope to keep up, regardless. The words had to be set in type, the forms prepared for the printing press, and the copies carried to the readers. In the late nineteenth century, some big-city newspapers chartered special trains to hasten the delivery of their product to outlying towns. The newspaper in Memphis sent "election specials" steaming through Arkansas and Mississippi. But the outcome of the election was a story that readers wanted told as quickly as it was known. Wealthy individuals, as well as clubs, theaters, restaurants, saloons, and hotels, could subscribe to the telegraph or telephone election services. In Fayetteville, North Carolina, the managers of the local armory charged twenty-five cents admission to defray the telegraphic costs. The *Observer* warned the citizens of Fayetteville that "nothing stronger than lemonade will be allowed in the armory."[1]

For many Americans, election night was a social experience—a communal celebration of citizenship. An effort was made even to satisfy the curiosity of citizens who happened to be confined. In Chicago the Cook County Jail and several hospitals were among Western Union's list of customers.

As soon as the polls closed, most interested Americans would converge on the counting centers in the downtown newspaper office. Major advertisers, political leaders, and other influential personages sometimes were admitted into the building, but the ordinary folks had to stand outside on the sidewalks and in the streets.

Here, particularly in the big cities, many of the spectators had been primed by a beverage stronger than lemonade, and the group dynamics were considerably more volatile. Hundreds of thousands gathered around the New York City newspaper offices on election night in 1896, "a howling mass of humanity blocking the streets and sidewalks," according to one account. "Every man, woman and child in the vast crowd carried a tin horn, a rattle or a megaphone, frequently all three."[2]

At first, newspapers answered the demand the only way they could, by displaying hand-painted numbers on large sheets of paper pasted onto bulletin boards in their office windows. Only those who were close enough could see the bulletins, obviously, and the crowds grew restless when fresh figures were slow in coming. Editors felt obliged, therefore, to entertain as well as inform their visitors. The *Minneapolis Journal* sponsored a vaudeville program. In New York, as the bulletin boards got bigger, the news bulletins were interspersed with moving pictures, portraits of the candidates, and "bright little skits" about the election.[3] William Randolph Hearst's *New York Journal* built a bandstand in front of its offices. Brass bands played patriotic music, and "chalk artists" were hired to distract the spectators during the intermissions.

In cities like Chicago, where the street crowds were not partial to lemonade and where fisticuffs were likely to interupt the chalk artists, newspapers sometimes hired an auditorium for the announcements of the returns. The *Tribune* played host one election night to 25,000 in the Coliseum at Wabash and Fifteenth Streets. To accommodate those with imperfect vision, P. T. Barnum's lead circus barker, "Foghorn Lou" Graham, who was billed as the "man with the mighty mouth," gave a vocal rendition of the results.[4]

On the night before the momentous election of 1896, the new owner of the *New York Times,* Adolph Ochs, strolled from lower Manhattan to Herald Square, according to Meyer Berger's history of that newspaper. Ochs noticed Hearst's bandstand in front of the offices of the *Journal.* A large map of the United States featured colored lights in each state that would be switched on whenever the winner of that state had been declared. The *World* had installed an 80-foot screen that stretched from the second floor all the way to the thirteenth on the Franklin Street side of its gold-domed tower.

"Election Day in New York is recognized as a holiday," Ochs wrote to his wife Effie in Chattanooga. "Everything is shut down, business generally suspended. It is as quiet about the office as on Sunday, but I think it is only the lull before the storm. I suppose we will have a howling mob of about a million about the office about dark. We are prepared to make a great display of the returns. At Madison Square I have the choice place of the city. The newspapers are vying with each other in their efforts to display the returns."[5]

Bennett's *Herald,* meanwhile, was well into the next generation of stereopticon projection. To fill the intermissions between the election figures, the *Herald* had arranged the motion-picture display of dancers and contortionists "in life-like activity visible blocks away." The crowd was said to have gasped when another of the early movie projectors, the "vitascope," showed a picture of the Grand Canyon at sunset. The election night enterprise, "directed by Professor Northrup of the Polytechnic Institute of Brooklyn," had, the *Herald* boasted later, "all the novelty of a theatrical production. A vast army, magnificent in its numerical strength and its mad enthusiasm, fought for places in Herald Square to enjoy the most rapid and striking presentation of election returns ever given by a newspaper."[6]

Ochs of the *Times* was not yet prosperous enough to compete with such displays, says Meyer Berger in his book:

> He had five modest bulletin boards set in as many windows on the second floor at 41 Park Row, three facing on Printing House Square, two on City Hall Park. At the southern end of Madison Square he had a twenty-foot screen under the electric slogan "All the News That's Fit to Print." He had worked out something new in stereopticon slides—a gelatine sheet that took print without blurring, as other slides did. "I suggested that to one of the stereopticon operators when we discussed our display," he told [his wife] Effie bitterly, "and he spread the idea all over town. All the newspapers copied it."
>
> On election night Ochs stood at his window in the *Times,* awed by the sea of upturned faces in City Hall Park, where 50,000 persons were jammed watching the returns. His display, he had to concede, was surpassed by the *World's,* but it exceeded any his scholarly predecessor had achieved. Around 10 o'clock helmeted policemen helped him through the crowds when he left the office to see how his Madison Square screen had drawn. The turnout in Madison Square was larger than downtown's and Ochs' heart beat fast when the crowd roared, "Hoorah for the *New York Times!*"[7]

His heart beat still faster the next morning when he saw that his newspaper had been able to claim that "The *New York Times* stereopticon flashed the first message of the New York City election four minutes ahead of its contemporaries."

While the *Times* under Ochs was beginning to become the serious newspaper of substance that it is today, it did not shy away from the stereopticon sweepstakes either. Four years later, in the election of 1900, an even larger canvas than the *World's* was hung by the *Times* between two poles next to the Bartholdi Hotel on Twenty-third Street. More than 75,000 people joined a crowd that stretched almost as far as the Sixth Avenue elevated station.

In Chicago the *Tribune* and the *Daily News* carried on their own competition. The *Tribune* borrowed a vitascope from one of the local theaters and hired a glee club to sing the Illinois state song while the state's natural attractions were being featured on the screen hanging across Dearborn Street.

On the Thursday before the election, the *Daily News* promoted its service with headlines that declared:

Hundreds of Funny Pictures to be
Displayed During "Waits" for Election Returns

Everybody Invited to See
The Truth in Figures

Elsewhere, the *Atlanta Constitution* told its readers in 1896 that it would be feeding fresh slides into alternating stereopticons, changing them every thirty seconds all through the night. The newspaper said that many local merchants had pleaded for the purchase of advertising time on the screen during the intermissions, "but they have been flatly refused—there will be no advertising fakes run in by the *Constitution*."[8] In Ohio, a professor from Ohio State University engineered the *Columbus Dispatch's* "writing on smoked glass!" magic lantern with such spectacular success that the newspaper conducted public tours of the operating room on the second floor.

More efficient calculating machines shortened the time needed to compute the results. Other innovations were directed at getting the news of the results of the election to more people more quickly. The masses of people who joined the jostling crowds outside the downtown newspaper offices were evidence of the great public interest in the "horse race." Editors in the big cities began thinking about how to circulate the news over a broader area—beyond the sight of images on a screen; beyond the range of Foghorn Lou's mighty mouth.

The first of their bright new ideas, thought up by the *Chicago Tribune*, utilized color-coded "aerial bombs"—fireworks that could be seen in the distance—to identify the leading candidates. In 1896 the *Tribune* announced just before the election that its "mortars" on the rooftop garden of the Great Northern Hotel, one of the tallest buildings in the Windy City, would fire skyrockets into the air every hour on the hour. Exploding at heights of a thousand feet, the bombs could be seen all over Cook County. A blue-colored "bomb" meant that the Republican candidate, William McKinley, was leading. A red burst would signify that the Democrat William Jennings Bryan was in front. One flash signaled the results in Cook County only; two bombs in succession would refer to Illinois; three would signal national success. All Chicagoans had to do was walk outside at the top of the hour and look toward the Loop downtown for what the *Tribune* was certain would be "a shower of blue stars."

Just before the next presidential election, in 1900, the newspaper announced its plans to repeat the election night bombardment. But the ever imperious editors of the *Tribune* failed to reckon with the mischief-making instincts of a new newspaper in town—Hearst's *Evening American*. All of the Chicago dailies had supported McKinley four years before, which was reason enough for Hearst to start his paper as a Chicago voice for the Democrats. The *American* followed up the *Tribune*'s announcement by a story stating that it (the *American*) would launch *its* aerial bombs on election night—a red bomb if McKinley were ahead; a blue bomb if Bryan were on top. The *Tribune* responded immediately with this solemn proclamation on the front page:

TO THE PUBLIC

The *Tribune* regrets to announce that it has been forced to abandon its plan for signaling election returns on Tuesday night by means of colored bombs. This is rendered necessary by the usurpation and reversal of its signal code by a Democratic newspaper. . . . Only confusion and misinformation would result. So, in order that the public may not be misled, the *Tribune* regretfully abandons its project. The lateness of the announcement by the other paper prevents the *Tribune* from securing bombs of different colors, they all having to be made to order.

The next day the *Tribune* added to the confusion with the headline warning that "Democrats Plan False Reports."[9]

But this was also a time when many urban newspapers were erecting tall buildings as monuments to their journalistic grandeur. While thus commanding the heights, it soon occurred to editors that they could signal the election results with the help of lofty electric lights that could be seen far away.

Pulitzer had erected the world's tallest skyscraper in lower Manhattan in 1890. On election night the great gilded dome was rigged with strings of lights that were illuminated according to a preannounced color scheme to designate the winning candidates. The *New York Tribune,* which already occupied the city's second tallest skyscraper, capped by a magnificent Florentine clock tower, decided in 1896 to reach even higher. "For the benefit of people at a distance from City Hall Square," the *Tribune* revealed its "absolutely novel and original scheme." The strings of colored lights would be hoisted five hundred feet above the building by large kites. Red, white, green, and orange lights would be "flung to the eye" each three minutes. An elaborate code that readers were instructed to clip out and carry in their pockets was spelled out in the paper. There were general signals and state signals. Each state was given a number and a combination of different light colors, the meaning of which would be a severe test of the cognitive agility of the spectators. Although the *Tribune* did not say so, readers who wanted to make any sense out of the heavenly hieroglyphics were well-advised to stick to lemonade until after the election had been decided. "The answer to [Bryan's] silver craze may be read, as it were, in the stars," the newspaper cleverly observed.

Unhappily for the *Tribune,* the wind died down at nightfall and the armada of nine kites had to be taken in. For want of an evening breeze, the editors were foiled in their grand plan to flash the news from a loftier vantage point than their competitors. The lights were lifted instead upon halyards strung on the roof of the building.[10]

While the managers of the *Tribune* were playing with their kites on that night in 1896, they had also installed a searchlight on the rooftop, which the paper said "flashed its powerful eye over the city." Although the *Tribune* was using its mighty light only to attract attention to the color-coded lights that signaled the results of the election, other urban newspapers already understood how powerful lights on tall buildings could beam the news of an election over a much bigger area than either skyrockets or strings of colored lights. Furthermore, the coding system could be made much simpler to understand.

It must be remembered that this was long before news by radio. To find out who had won the election, one had to go to where the information was available, which might mean the pages of a newspaper or, if that was not quick enough, it might mean traveling to the newspaper bulletins displayed downtown or scanning the night sky for a precoded visual signal. Searchlights apparently were used for this purpose for the first time on the night of November 3, 1891. The results of the New York gubernatorial race between Jacob S. Fassett and Roswell P. Flower were signaled by the *Herald* from the light on the top of Madison Square Garden. When Fassett seemed to be winning, "a brilliant pencil of light pierced the western gloom" (the light shone to the west). If Flowers was leading, "the eastern heavens were illumined." "The light shone east so much," joked the *Electrical Review*, "that roosters crowed, thinking day had dawned." The *Boston Post* also "issued a sky edition" on the same night with the results of state elections in Massachusetts, New York, and Ohio. When the Democratic governor was re-elected in Massachusetts, the *Post* "stabbed the zenith with a perpendicular ray of light for ten minutes. Large Democratic yells could be noticed floating up from the earth in the beam of light like motes."[11]

For the presidential election a year later, the *World* outfitted its dome with vertical bands of high-candlepower incandescent lamps of different colors, which were flashed on to "give the hungry thousands news of the great political battle." The *Herald* again used the lantern on the tower of Madison Square Garden. When the beam of light swung to the south, it meant that Grover Cleveland had carried New York. If New York had been won by Benjamin Harrison, "Harlem would have been illuminated, and if Harrison had been reasonably sure of carrying the country, the darkness of New Jersey would have been pierced by the penetrating pencil of light."[12]

Newspapers in other cities with access to tall buildings also used searchlights to report election results, including the *Chicago Herald* and the *San Francisco Chronicle*. Its lofty sand hills made San Francisco an ideal site for searchlight journalism. The *Chronicle* posted a powerful searchlight on the top of its new ten-story building, the first steel skyscraper on the West Coast. First used in 1892, the white, red, blue, and green beams could be seen fifteen miles away, the strength of the light multiplied ninefold by special prisms and reflectors, which enabled the newspaper amazingly, it said, to "print the news in the heavens." On election day, the *Chronicle* was excited:

> A shaft of light, cutting its way through the night, illuminating the Berkeley hills, losing itself against Tamalpais' rocky crest, touching the summit of the San Mateo hills, flashing in the windows of mansion and cottage on every eminence about the bay, told last night how the *Chronicle* will make known election returns to the thousands who stay at home as quickly as it does to those other thousands who will throng the streets about its bulletin boards. [When the system was tried yesterday] the rays bore their way through the gloom and glowed like shafts of painted lightning.[13]

The next morning the *Chronicle* claimed that it had scooped the New York papers. "Red flashes swinging like fingers of flame through the black of the night told the people of San Francisco of the election of McKinley at 7:15 o'clock last night. [10:15 New York time.] The *Chronicle* had beaten the world. . . . On hilltop and in valley, from Marin hills to Alameda marshes, the *Chronicle* flashed the news earlier than a national result was ever before made known."[14]

Seven

Pack Journalism and the Modern Campaign

The Australian paper ballot, adopted universally in the 1890s, weakened party control over voting and marked the beginning of the end of an era of intense political interest and participation. Between the Civil War and the 1890s, more people were active in political parties, more people voted, more people were knowledgeable about at least one side of the partisan debate than at any other time in American history.

This does not mean that the discourse at the grass roots was altogether noble. Much of the "issues politics" of that period echoed the clash of highly emotional sectarian religious values. Irish immigration stirred anti-Catholic fears. The Democratic Party fell into decline as Irish Catholics wrested control over party organizations in many of the big cities. Elections turned on such monumental concerns as whether beer-loving German-Americans would stand still for the closing of saloons on Sundays.

Though less subservient to party officials, many newspaper editors were active players in national politics. They wrote about these matters in a simplistic, biased fashion. Some newspapers published columns of information about, for instance, the tariff issue. But these were news stories devoted to the case for *or* against the tariff. Few were factually balanced. It is mistaken to hark back to an imagined golden age in the history of American journalism when newspapers reported in depth: Here is the argument in favor of the tariff; here is the argument opposed; here is the background information you need to help you make up your mind on this matter; here are the forces who would be helped by this and who are lobbying in its behalf; here are the forces who would be hurt by it; here is how this proposal would affect you and how it would affect others who are not like you.

It should also be noted that candidates were doing all they could to *avoid* sensitive issues. In the case of the tariff, Lord Bryce noted that the Democrats, being a coalition of different regional interests, tried to blur the issue.[1]

The more independent, and in most cases more sensational, urban newspapers of the 1890s spoke of a politics that one historian has characterized as "less simple and less accessible."[2] Truly secret voting, tighter voter registration laws, and better organization by interest groups all contributed to a diminution of party allegiance, more ticket-splitting, a drop in voter turnout, more cries for reform, and generally a journalistic devaluation of election campaign news.

These trends were beginning to form in one of the most memorable of all presidential campaigns: the election of 1896. Anti-Catholicism, severe economic depression, and wrenching differences over monetary policy set the stage for that campaign. The central issue was the supply of money and the value of the dollar. Behind the complicated talk of bimetallism, seigniorage, fiat currency, and the silver standard, the election was about whether the supply of money should remain as it was (and continue to be "sound," as the people who were well-off liked to phrase it); or whether the amount of money in circulation should be increased, which would lessen its value, bring lower interest rates and have the effect of reducing personal debt while driving wages and farm prices up.

The American people were thoroughly aroused by the debate. Without benefit of public relations counsel, a lone citizen would lug a soap box to the courthouse square and deliver a noon-hour oration.

Not many newspaper owners were members of the have-not class. Adolph Ochs, for one, told his wife that he "doubted very much whether there were many men in the United States whose future was so heavily dependent upon (McKinley's victory) as mine."[3] He led a *Times* contingent that carried American flags down Broadway in a march of Businessmen for McKinley. The *New York Times* was far from neutral in that election. With the notable exception of William Randolph Hearst, whose family owned extensive silver mining interests that would stand to gain from the free coinage of silver, most American newspaper owners were, like Ochs, strongly opposed to the reform nominee of the Democratic Party, William Jennings Bryan.

Bryan's support was concentrated in the western and southern states. Farmers and small businessmen resented their higher railroad freight rates, compared to those in the urban Northeast and Midwest. Bankers, corporate America, Main Street U.S.A. were backing the Republican nominee, Governor William McKinley of Ohio.

The campaign of 1896 was a compelling news story. It was obvious what would determine the outcome of the election. Farmers and ranchers in the south and west were drawn to Bryan's fiery brand of populism. But would they be joined by "the toiling masses" of low-wage manual workers and farmers in the north and east? Anyone who was interested in politics knew the election would turn on that question. More than ever before, the potential for massive party switching made individual voting intentions newsworthy. Some voters were in a mood to switch parties. But how many? Would the shifts balance out? How better to find out than to ask them?

Journalists had to tailor their coverage to two quite different kinds of campaigns. McKinley stayed on his "front porch" in Canton while his manager, Mark Hanna, made the rounds of Wall Street financiers raising money and implanting a simple campaign theme ("McKinley and the Full Dinner Pail") in the minds of publishers and other opinion leaders. Trainloads of Republican voters were shuttled in and out of Canton to pledge their support.

In his dusty black alpaca coat, Bryan embarked, meanwhile, on a tour of the nation. He traveled 18,000 miles and delivered up to twenty speeches a day from the rear platform of the last car of his railroad train. Still there were no microphones or loudspeakers—no electronic amplification of the sound of the human voice—but Bryan's voice could be heard a block away.

Whistle-stop campaigning brought with it new pressures for uniformity in political journalism. Railroad travel increased the mobility of political reporters, but because it was considered inappropriate for a woman to travel unaccompanied on a train, women were discouraged from entering the political press corps. Of more lasting significance, whistle-stop campaigning gave rise to the peculiar culture of pack journalism. Shaped by the psychology of the group, the traveling press corps took on an institutional character. The needs of the press had to be tended to by the campaign organization. Because reporters had to file their news stories at a prescribed time every day, the candidate was compelled to say something new and different each day. Together on the train for day after day, journalists and campaigners learned to exchange confidences and to adapt to one another's needs. They began to share a common interest in the mission of the campaign—and in their common creature comforts. The gruelling day-to-day pace of Bryan's campaign began to wear on the reporters. By the first week of October, according to the trade journal *The Fourth Estate*, the Bryan press corps was "utterly fagged out."[4] In one small town the train stopped for the night and the Bryan party rolled into a local hotel after the last speech of the day. The reporters were trying to get some sleep, but the voters who had heard Bryan's speech were so captivated, apparently, that they lingered under the hotel room windows chattering about the money question. "The boys" in the press corps, desperate for rest, had encountered an actor who was also staying at the hotel and who looked vaguely like Bryan. They rousted the actor out of bed and persuaded him to step out onto the hotel balcony, repeat the campaign theme yet again, and beg the crowd to disperse. The people cheered one last time and walked off.

In every presidential election year, the campaign circus takes on a life of its own. A strange group camaraderie envelopes the press corps. The reporter Edward Riggs said the two essential qualities of a good political reporter were "a strong stomach and liver, both in good working order."[5] A veteran campaign trouper of the modern era, David Broder, has noted that "something about campaigns breeds strange behavior. Reporters are away from home and office, enduring long passages of boring routine broken by moments of high-pressure action and drama."[6] In such close proximity the journalists compete for the stylistic approbation of their brethren on the road as much as their bosses back home. Displays of wit are admired. Any reporter who has ever covered a presidential campaign tour will understand the satirical code of rules that the Bryan correspondents adopted later in October:

> Any person undertaking to give his views on the financial issue shall be compelled to listen to the speeches of William J. Bryan. Any person showing symptoms of talking tariff shall be compelled to read the speeches of William McKinley. . . . 21 hours is fixed as a working day for the members of this party. To insure the enforcement of this regulation the Associated Correspondents agree that no record shall be made of any speech, reception, bonfire, salute or any other occurence between the hours of 1:30 a.m. and 4:30 a.m. The 53rd Sunday of the year shall be observed as a general holiday. On that day all telegraph wires shall be cut. All members of this party shall be entitled to three triangular meals a day, subject to appetites of local reception committeemen. Sandwiches from railway eating houses shall be used as fodder for the cannon from which salutes are fired. Campaign cigars shall be smoked only on the open prairies.[7]

It was soon discovered that traveling with the candidate's entourage is never a good place from which to gauge the success of a campaign, and furthermore that reporters are likely to exaggerate "their" candidate's popularity. Melville Stone, general manager of the AP, said this happened to the AP correspondents who traveled with Bryan in 1896. "[They] told me of the millions who gathered to welcome the itinerant, the wild enthusiasm displayed, and the certainty of his ultimate victory," Stone wrote later. "I replied that they failed to take into account the human curiosity involved and that nine out of ten in the great crowds greeting Bryan would have been equally excited by a visit of a circus."[8]

Pack Journalism and the Modern Campaign

Knowing that Chicago and the other northern cities would be crucial battlegrounds, Hanna oversaw the expenditure of $3.5 million, then an enormous sum, for voter surveys. Party workers conducted three separate citywide canvasses in Chicago alone. The surveys were intended to identify persuadable voters, who would then receive special literature prepared by the McKinley campaign's "literary bureau." Targeted messages were used systematically for the first time in a presidential campaign. Special appeals were directed, for one example, at bicycle riders.

Two competing Chicago morning newspapers—the *Tribune* and the *Record*—also set out to do what no newspaper had done before. They assigned their own personnel to try to find out—without partisan finagling—which candidate the voters preferred, and to report the findings as news. This was to be done not just on excursion steamers and trains, but by a sampling of the entire electorate. The *Record* had been started by Victor Lawson, the publisher of the afternoon *Chicago Daily News*. Stamped postcards were mailed by the *Record* to all 328,000 registered voters in Chicago, requesting that the sample ballot on the card be returned with the name of the preferred presidential candidate marked. Almost two out of three voters responded. The *Record* retained a team of mathematicians (astronomers actually) who were paid to venture a guess that the responses were probably sufficiently representative to conclude that McKinley would carry the city with 57.95 percent of the vote. The Republican candidate's share on election day turned out to be 57.91 percent—a remarkable coincidence.

Sophisticated techniques for the use of mathematics in statistical analysis had been developed decades before—in observational astronomy rather than the social sciences. Error theory was applied to the telescopic observation of the movement of stars and planets long before other scientists got interested in sampling theory.

Outside of Chicago, the *Record* was not as lucky with its postcard ballots. From various convenient sources, the paper assembled lists of approximately 12 percent of the voters in downstate Illinois and in eleven other midwestern states. The sample therefore was much smaller, it was not randomly chosen, the response was much less, and the results were not nearly as accurate. McKinley's vote was vastly overestimated. The astronomical consultants advised adjusting the figures based on 1892 district election returns, but even with the adjustment the projections were still tilted in McKinley's favor.[9]

The circulation of Lawson's paper surged while the poll results were being reported. Lawson also gained national notoriety by offering the poll findings free of charge to editors who were friends of his at the *New York Herald* and the *St. Louis Republic.* He estimated that the postcard ballot project cost the *Record* $60,000.[10]

Less ambitious were the *Tribune's* plans. The newspaper assigned reporters to solicit secret ballots from approximately 14,000 factory and railroad yard workers who were approached on the job. The newspaper reported that 80 percent of the respondents expected to vote for McKinley. The actual vote of manual laborers for the Republican nominee was far less than that.

Under the circumstances, what with the *Record,* the *Tribune,* and all the other Chicago dailies supporting McKinley editorially, Bryan Democrats suspected that the straw polls were less than objective. Particularly in the other midwestern states, it was alleged that the postcards had been mailed primarily (and deliberately) to Republicans. The Democratic National Committee denounced the *Record* poll: "The whole scheme is one of fraud and debauchery, and may be taken as a first step in a conspiracy to do away with popular elections under the law, and place the molding of public opinion in the hands of millionaires and corporations."

Other editors endeavored by various means to forecast who would win the election. It is less than astonishing that their guesswork tended to confirm the editorial policies of their newspapers. On the Sunday before the election, the *New York Times* published a headline—"M'Kinley Sure to Win—Bryan May Not Receive One Hundred Electoral Votes." To substantiate this information, the *Times* cited the reporting of the Washington correspondent of the *Kansas City Star,* Albert Miller, who had traveled through twenty-four states. "He has an opinion," said the *Times.* "He believes that there is to be a landslide, and that it will be for McKinley." Other stories in the same issue were headlined: "Free Silver is Doomed—Sound Money Will Have a Majority in Congress"—and "Battle Over in Illinois—McKinley Will Carry the State—Silver Men are Disorganized."[11]

In California, the *San Francisco Chronicle* reached the same conclusion before any votes had been cast: "Forecast of the Result—The Election of McKinley Certain—Sure of a Big Majority."

Although Joseph Pulitzer was backing McKinley, the editor of his paper in St. Louis—Charles H. Jones at the *Post-Dispatch*—was for Bryan. Prior to the voting, the *Post-Dispatch* reported: "Bryan Has Won—the Issue and the Management of the Campaign—the Gold Party is Defeated—Review of a Remarkable Campaign of Blunders." Another story said Bryan would win "by a triumphantly great majority."

Down in North Carolina, the Fayetteville *Observer* was so committed to

Bryan's cause that it published the full text of the platform of the state Democratic Party *every day* on the editorial page all during the campaign. On the eve of the election, the *Observer* told its readers in a news story on the front page:

> William J. Bryan will be elected President Tuesday. We feel confident of this. A review of the latest news received at this office leaves no room to doubt Bryan's triumphant election. . . . The returns this year will probably be very slow. The pivotal states are larger than is usual, and as Bryan will largely depend upon the gains in the rural districts, it may be a day or two before the result is known.[12]

Although its kites were grounded that night, the *New York Tribune* decided before 9 P.M., along with most of the other metropolitan papers, that McKinley had won. By stereopticon, colored lights, bulletin board, and searchlight, the news went forth. At opposite ends of the continent, the *New York Times* and the *San Francisco Chronicle* both claimed to have been first, but who noticed?

The *New York Herald* exulted in typical fashion on its stereopticon screen:

> Now the night is over,
> Day is drawing night,
> McKinley in the White House,
> Bryan Knocked Sky High.

In 1896 the election returns were still being tabulated by "the Press Bureau" of Western Union. Not all the wire service clients were as trusting of the AP-WU partnership as they might have been, especially in the South. The day after the election, the Fayetteville paper said the "wild telegraphic reports from the North" were suspect.

> Most of the machinery for the ascertainment of news is controlled by the enemies of democracy, and all of the machinery for its dissemination. This time the inducement to falsify the returns is a hundredfold greater than usual, because plutocracy recognizes that the death struggle between it and democracy has begun.[13]

There were two reasons for this, according to the *Observer.* First, the early returns came primarily from the cities, which were "controlled by the gold-bugs." The second was that those at the helm of the AP "manipulate the returns and intend by claiming everthing in sight to establish a moral status of popular belief that puts the burden of proof on the democracy."

Jones at the *Post-Dispatch* reported initially that Bryan had won, but then backed off, warning that the election would be stolen.

Has 1876 Come Again?

Is Fraud Being Practiced
With the Returns?

Same Peculiar Tactics

Bryan Crowding McKinley to the Wall
and Essential Votes Being Held Back

On Friday the Fayetteville paper conceded that "the anarchists" had won.
Not until Sunday did the St. Louis paper acknowledge that Bryan had lost
by 567,692 popular votes. A switch of 37,000 votes in six states—less than
one-third of 1 percent—would have won in the electoral college for the
"Great Commoner."

Not all towns were reachable by telegraph or telephone in 1896. It wasn't
until the next day that horsemen rode into Buffalo, Missouri, in the Ozarks,
bringing the news from the telegraph station on the railroad, twenty miles
away.

Bryan ran again in 1900. This time Democratic leaders in Chicago advised their party faithful to shun the *Record*'s postcard poll. This had the
intended effect, temporary though it was, of disabling the poll by distorting
the sample. The residue of anger left by the 1896 campaign affected the
circulation of many northern urban newspapers and prompted some of
them to promise more objectivity in their news columns.

Most newspapers, in fact, had devoted considerable space to the money
issue. Many years later someone compared the coverage of the campaigns
of 1896 and 1952 in the San Francisco newspapers. Although there were
four times as many column inches devoted to news generally in 1952 than
in 1896, the study found that the San Francisco papers had printed twice
as much political information during the 1896 campaign.[14] It must be reem-
phasized, however, that the reporting of the issues in 1896 consisted mainly
of argumentative prose. A voter would have been hard put to arrive at a reasoned judgment about the bimetallism issue based on the reportage from
a single newspaper. A clerk in a farm implement store in Missouri, for example, did not find clear, objective, probative information in the Kansas
City papers about why it cost more to ship freight by rail in the plains states.
The model of what good political journalism might have been was no more
mysterious then than it is now. What is the background of this subject? How
do railroad economics really work? What are both candidates saying about
this? What do I need to know to understand this issue that the candidates

are *not* saying? Who benefits under the policy advocated by McKinley? Who stands to benefit under Bryan's program? How and why? What pressure groups are enrolled in this fight? Is there a contextual setting for this subject, in the overall economics of capitalism, that I need to understand? Will you explain it to me, please, so that I can understand it? What is the factual information that will help me evaluate the partisan arguments? For all of the many inches of "political information," the press did not do that kind of reporting in 1896.

Nevertheless, the clerk in that store probably did understand much or most of what the money supply issue was about. The most cogent information and arguments were being delivered not by newspapers, though, but by partisan tracts. More clearly than any newspaper, William H. Harvey enunciated the case for free silver in his book, *Coin's Financial School*. "Unless you have been West recently," observed one writer, "you can have no idea of the influence which is being exerted by this somewhat puerile little book. Debate and controversy upon silver are endless and Coin . . . is everywhere accepted as gospel. . . . Dozens of men in this community can quote chapters and chapters in the book."[15]

Voters everywhere clamored for information about the money issue. The Republican Literary Bureau prepared over two hundred different pamphlets in twenty-one languages. More Americans made it their business to be informed about public issues then than now. And there were "opinion leaders" around then to help them understand. The owner of the store. The leaders of the local Grange. The friends he met on the courthouse square. Even his customers.

The point is that information was available to inform the voters about complex substantive issues—but they were one-sided presentations prepared by the parties, the candidates, interest groups, and sometimes newspapers. Historian Michael McGerr says that the period of "spectacular" campaigns had given way to a new age of "educational" appeals to persuadable voters.[16] He associates the "educational" campaign style with the distribution of pamphlets and other printed materials. Samuel Tilden's "Society for the Diffusion of Political Knowledge" was the first to mass-produce circular letters and printed copies of speeches and position statements in the 1870s. Newspapers did print stories about the issues in 1896, but most of the reports were partisan propaganda or impossibly abstract, or both.

Why was that so then? (And why is it so today?) The answer is partly in the working culture of political journalism. It was not necessary for journalists to be confined to a railroad car on Bryan's train (or on an airplane or bus as they are today) to be gripped by the strictures of pack journalism.

The next chapter will explain how more political reporters are sports-directed (and now personality-directed) than they are policy-directed. Non-specialists on policy issues, they find it hard to bore into the substantive details of an issue. They prefer to believe (and it may usually be true) that the personality and character of the candidates *are* the major issues in the election of the president. They contend (and this may also usually be true) that academics and others who complain about the deficiencies of issues reporting are really complaining that the news is not being reported so as to *cause* voters to vote as the academics would like them to vote. Hustling around the nation on Bryan's train, reporters were, as Stone recognized, in the worst possible position to make sense of the campaign. Their manifold uncertainties about the meaning of what was going on caused them to seek solace in the conventional wisdom of the pack. Journalists judge the news by certain predictable standards: novelty, irony, differences between what is and what is expected, the firing of words that "give off sparks," developments that can be made suspenseful, and "hard news" like the numbers in a poll. These are all highly valued in political journalism. Uncertain of their judgments, political reporters search for consensus in the brotherhood of the pack. The timelessness of that phenomenon was expressed many years later by Theodore H. White's observation in *The Making of the President—1960*. "The talk of the corps of correspondents who follow the candidates is not simply gossip," White wrote. "Gossip is only its surface form. It is consensus—it is the tired, emotional measuring of judgments among men whom the weeks on the road have made into a brotherhood that only they understand. And the judgment of the brotherhood influences and colors, beyond any individual resistance to prejudice or individual devotion to fact, all of what they write. For by now they have come to trust only each other."[17]

At the turn of the century, newspapers were moving rapidly towards pre-election forecasting as an element of horse-race political journalism. Some relied on interviews with unspecified party sources. Some of the predictions were grounded in the expertise of reporters and of editors. And, once the passions of the two McKinley-Bryan races had worn off, newspapers engaged increasingly in various forms of what were still straw polls (as distinguished from probability sampling polls). Reporters for the *Boston Globe* spoke to voters in Hull, Massachusetts, in 1900 inquiring about how they had voted in 1896 and how they intended to vote this time. This represented an effort to derive meaning from the survey. Instead of presenting the data objectively, however, the editors of the Democratic paper applied their own spin, stressing disproportionately the percentage gains by the Democrats compared to those in 1896.

Most of the campaign reporting in 1900 was both partisan and horse-race oriented. The *Globe* gave only glancing recognition to the predictions by many others of a Republican landslide, while continuing to give prominent play to claims by Democratic officials of a Bryan victory. According to one article, it was "prophesied by those who know" that 75 percent of the New York German vote would go to Bryan (October 17). According to another article in the *Globe,* former President Cleveland predicted a landslide for Bryan (October 30); and a headline from November 1 read—"Ohio Sure—That's the Way Bryan's Friends Feel." The *Chicago Journal* announced on the Saturday before the election—"McKinley's Election Now a Certainty." The morning after the election, the *Journal* indulged in some "mild gratification":

> Four weeks ago the *Journal* took the position that President McKinley's reelection was so fixed a certainty that it was idle to discuss Mr. Bryan's success, even as a possibility. . . . [We] experience a mild gratification in the reflection that it succeeded, some little time before the actual battle, in imbuing its doubting contemporaries with some share of its own confidence.[18]

Eight

Politics as a Sporting Proposition

Baseball mirrors the American character with astonishing fidelity; . . .
in its boundless obsession with averages, records, and other statistical
desiderata. . . . In short, baseball is us.

—Jay Tolson, editor,
The Wilson Quarterly[1]

In virtually all human societies anthropologists find ritualized game-playing and the spirit of gambling. In the United States this *agonic* or competitive impulse is expressed in what has been called its "struggle-play-gamble Big Game culture."[2] The perception of electoral activity as a "big game" and its linkage to the rabid American interest in spectator sporting events are factors in the shaping of political news.

A previous chapter touched on the parallels between gambling on horse races and gambling on elections. In both instances, newspapers tried to satisfy their readers' hunger for numerical measures of the status of the competition by reporting "news" of the betting.

What is especially interesting about the history of horse racing for our purposes is how rapidly it became systematized with trustworthy standards for the collection of reliable statistical information. We are told that stop watches were available in the colonies as early as the middle of the eighteenth century. This made it possible to compare the winning times, record the details in print, and establish probability odds for future races. Betters could consult turf publications for voluminous information about racing.

Visitors from abroad thought it odd how the American people were so aroused by the presidential election as the quadrennial Big Game. One of the reasons for this, of course, is the elimination-tournament aspect of the selection process. There are preliminary "heats" and then the final contest for the championship. This cannot help but cast the activity in the tournament mold so captivating to spectators.

It is of more than incidental significance that Americans have insisted that their most popular sports be subjected to extensive statistical scrutiny. Not just horse racing, but others as well—including, most importantly, the "national pastime" of baseball.

Over the years, politicians and the journalists who wrote about them learned to compete for public attention with baseball and other sports.

The man who is venerated in the National Baseball Museum in Cooperstown, New York, as "the father of baseball" was a newspaper reporter. His name was Henry Chadwick, an itinerant sports writer who was, like so many of his contemporaries, also a sports promoter. He helped organize the teams and leagues that he wrote about in his newspaper accounts. In 1858, the year that he joined the staff of the *New York Clipper* as its first baseball editor, Chadwick was appointed chairman of the rules committee for the first professional baseball league—the National Association of Baseball Players. He wrote the original baseball rule book and reigned for many years (while continuing to report baseball news) as the supreme arbiter of the many disputes that arose over the interpretation of his rules.[3]

Before long, Chadwick introduced the baseball scorecard and box score, in essentially the same forms that exist today. An insatiable record keeper, he was baseball's first stats freak.

The game had its own special language. In 1874 Chadwick published a lexicon of baseball jargon to help British journalists make sense of a tour of American teams in England. On through the 1890s, he edited or contributed to such journals as *Beadle's Dime Baseball Player, DeWitt's Baseball Guide, Our Boys Baseball Guide, Haney's Book of References,* and *Spalding's Official Baseball Guide.* All were loaded with statistical information about the game and its players. Chadwick originated the most basic of baseball's statistical concepts, that of the cumulative batting average as a measure of individual achievment.

Newspaper editors, meanwhile, were fanning the waves of baseball excitement. The *Cincinnati Commercial* assigned a full-time beat reporter to the first professional team, the Cincinnati Red Stockings, founded in 1869. The first ball players were a rowdy, hard-drinking band, oblivious to their public image, which made it easier for the club owners to take control of the game. This they did in 1876 by establishing the National League of Professional Baseball Clubs. Soon after that, the baseball writers met to organize the Reporters National Association. The stated purpose of their association was to promote the welfare of the national game by standardizing the scoring of games and by the collection of playing statistics. An "official scorers' league" was created to work for greater uniformity in the definition of hits and errors. The group even adopted a model for game stories, called the Orr-Edwards Code.

Scholars and philosophers have written of the evocative character of organized sports—and especially baseball—in American life.[4] By creating a "playful world" above politics, a world rich in drama and symbolism, baseball provided a pastoral retreat from the crowding and evils of city life, above the corruption of the urban political landscape.

The modern writer Robert Lipsyte draws a comparison between politics perceived to be something dirty and baseball as something beautiful. The public mind became convinced that "politicians were connivers; that ball players had the hearts of children; that the smoke-filled caucus room was the hellish furnace of democracy and that a sunny ball park was its shrine and reward."[5] James Reston, one of the foremost of modern-era political journalists at the *New York Times*, saw the worlds of politics and sports as being apart: "The world of sports has everything the world of politics lacks and longs for. They have more pageantry and even more dignity than most occasions in American life, more teamwork, more unity and more certainty at the end than most things."[6]

Sports conversation binds a diverse community together in a quasi-patriotic way that political activity does not. The "lyrical" nature of organized play was altered forever, historians have noted, when the outcome of the contest took on civic significance. Community pride is invested in the local ball club.

After the two professional leagues joined in the "major leagues" in 1903, a fan literally could not hope to follow the game without a scorecard, which cost a nickel. There were no numbers on the players' uniforms, no public address system. An announcer would take the field and shout out the starting lineups three times in succession, once standing at home plate, again at first base, and at third base. Thus the spectator was encouraged to "keep a scorecard" and doodle with statistics.[7]

It is this last characteristic, the obsession with statistical trivia, that connects baseball most directly to our subject: how journalists report political news. Under newspaperman Chadwick's early direction and then later on, one can see how "organized baseball" reinforced the horse-race tradition in political journalism. The game that became America's national pastime was uniquely suited to multiple and minute statistical "desiderata." Achievment is best explained in numbers.

Baseball's durable popularity meant that election contests would have to compete with "real" spectator sports for the attention of voter/fans.

Politicians—and the journalists who covered them—shared an interest in making the electoral process more exciting by presenting it as another kind of athletic contest.

In this century this effect has been especially noticeable in the linguistic infusion of sports language into politics. Many of the leading political journalists have been men who began their careers in the "toy department" of the newspaper—the sports department. Although I am not aware of any academic or other censuses of reformed sports writers who were converted to the political beat, there is considerable anecdotal evidence that journalists drawn to politics are disproportionately either sports department alumni or lovers of baseball. Prior to his distinguished career on the *New York Times,* "Scotty" Reston covered sports news for newspapers in Ohio and for the Associated Press. In his autobiograpical recounting of fifty years in journalism, Reston used a sports metaphor to explain how "as an old sports writer, I had always kept a box score of runs, hits and errors at the end of the [public affairs] game."[8] Tom Wicker, Reston's successor as Washington bureau chief of the *Times,* was sports editor of the *Robesonian* in Lumberton, Robeson County, North Carolina, in his younger days.

Examples abound in the biographies of political reporters past and present. Raymond P. (Pete) Brandt, for many years Washington bureau chief of the *St. Louis Post-Dispatch,* can be considered typical. Brandt worked his way through the University of Missouri by covering sports for a string of papers. George Will and David Broder are only a couple of the many contemporary baseball lovers who write political columns today.

The movement between the toy department and the political beat helped to establish shared attitudes about competition and journalistic standards. Among all journalists, it is hardly coincidental that sports writers and political reporters were most affected by the zestful, audacious writing style of Mark Twain.

More important in the long run is how the newsroom traffic between sports and politics contributed to the considerable rhetorical overlap of sports jargon and the vocabulary of political journalism. Politics and sports are metaphors for one another. Richard Lipsky points out in his studies that sports provides the emotional feedback and fulfillment so lacking in an impersonal and abstract political system. The learning process begins at an early age. Youngsters who collect baseball cards gain status with their peers by being able to cite the statistical data on the backs of the cards. Athletes demonstrate courage and grace under pressure, equal opportunity, team play, community pride, ethical standards—elements that many Americans are searching for. Politicians responded by appropriating the

Politics as a Sporting Proposition

language and some of the methods of the sports arena. The remoteness and impersonality of political action was overcome through the symbolism of entertainment and the arena. National sports consciousness finds expression, Lipsky reminds us, in a language that reaches people in a concrete, tangible, and emotional way.

Lipsky explains convincingly how the sports symbolism of politics helps to tip the balance away from issues journalism and toward what we here call horse-race reporting:

> Sports is a universe of controlled conflict. By using sports symbolism in political discourse the politician or commentator tends to transpose sport's ideologically unproblematic nature onto politics. This has the effect of underscoring the organizational (instrumental) imperatives at the expense of articulating substantive goals. It promotes an interest in who is "winning" or "losing" without looking at the reasons why one *should* win and the other should lose. . . . The power of sports language, as an agent of sports symbolism, forms a network of national and social communication that provides large masses of Americans with communal warmth and personal identity.[9]

Beginning late in the nineteenth century then, spectator politics had to compete as entertainment (and as news) with the new national sports mania. It was around this time that newspapers established sports departments and separate sports pages—pages filled with scores of games. Urban newspaper circulation boomed along with attendance at sports events. Believing sports to be in the same class with crime and sex as tantalizing circulation builders, editors promoted baseball, prizefighting, six-day bicycle races, and the new Big Game on Saturday afternoon—college football. By then, journalism historian Gerald Baldasty points out, urban newspapers were devoting a fifth or more of their space to news of leisure-time activities—sports but also theater, reading, hobbies, and music.[10] Politicians and horse-race journalists would have to learn to attract the attention of spectator/voters by employing the language, and evoking the images, of the sports page.

This "ethos of spectatorship" had another less obvious ramification. Reuel Denney studied the use of language and what he described as the "industrialization" of college football as commercial entertainment. In his book *The Astonished Muse,* first published in 1957, Denney contended that newspaper sensationalism, mass spectator sports, and the audiovisual media (movies, comic strips, comic books, television) were responsible for "the deverbalization of the forum."[11] Campaigns are less verbal and more visual because of the mass media and the Big Game, in his trenchant view.

Nine

Political Speech at Space Rates

The Oratorical Gasbags Homeward Fly.
—Headline in *New York Herald*
after the 1872 election

At the dawn of the new century, torchlights with marching brigades of faithful campaign workers were a flickering relic of the past. The mass marketing industry brought more productive methods to national elections.

Newspapers in the meantime were growing more profitable, more independent, more powerful. Trolley cars made it possible for consumers from all over the city to shop at the new downtown department stores. Citywide markets created a need for product advertising. Newspapers were more independent while politicians were getting better at controlling the images of their products-for-sale—a coincidence that led to the further diminution of substantive news of issues.

Editors had long since convinced themselves that their readers were as bored by the oratorical "hot air" from candidates as they were. They had also come to believe that their editorial page opinions were guiding voting behavior. Speech-making is "the picturesque foam" of a campaign, said the newspaper trade journal *The Fourth Estate*, but "the grand ground swell [is] the waves of editorial conviction that roar with the music of the pressroom booming and breaking on the shores of common sense, wearing away the unevenness of prejudice and building up the coastline that is strong and straight."[1]

Some publishers ran for public office themselves. Hearst started a newspaper in Chicago to be a voice for the Bryan Democrats, only to awaken to the sudden revelation that he would make an even better presidential candidate himself.

The inbred cynicism of journalists about politics had sharpened into an adversarial relationship, based not on ideology but in opposition to politicians as a class. Indeed, a reporter who did not view with disdain the self-serving pronouncements of the "oratorical gasbags" who inhabited the world of politics was regarded as professionally irresponsible. In the 1890s the *Commercial-Appeal* grumbled in Memphis, Tennessee, that the long presidential campaigns were "public nuisances . . . especially to the newspapers." The reason the editors gave for this editorial page pronouncement was surprisingly frank: the return in revenue and in new subscribers was not worth the effort. "Politics is the most thankless and profitless of discussions," the paper said, without mention of the First Amendment. Another time the same editors commented that political oratory and "the old race of practiced stump speakers are nearly extinct" because of "the universality of newspaper circulation."[2]

By then this notion that self-interested political discussion by candidates was beneath the dignity of the free press had become widespread in the newspaper business. The *Baltimore Sun* told its readers at about the same time that "we shall give no place to religious controversy nor to *political discussion of a purely partisan nature*" (my emphasis).[3]

There was more to it, of course, than the startling proposition that "political discussion of a purely partisan nature" was unworthy of publication as news. The corollary is that editors and publishers had decided that there *was* an appropriate place for partisan discussion in the newspaper: as *paid advertising*. The industry found a good deal of logic in the thought that newspapers should do all they could to divert partisan debate from the (free) news columns and into the (paid) advertising columns. The newspaper trade journals of that period were filled with expressions of newspaper managers' resentment that they were not profiting financially from the appeals of candidates for votes. Newspaper executives came to believe that candidates and parties ought to pay advertising rates for the publication of their partisan messages. Some editors in smaller communities where commercial advertising opportunities were more limited went a step further. They asked to be paid for their editorial page support.

A typical expression of this point of view appeared in an editorial in one of the trade journals, *Newspaperdom:*

> The average publisher toils and spins, works and perspires, for the political party to which he [belongs]. . . . Column after column and page after page are contributed gratuitously to the war of words that go to make up a campaign. And what does he get for it all? On occasion he is tossed a 2 x 4 bone, but the fat pieces go to professional politicians who do not contribute a tithe of the money and the energy given so freely by the publisher. . . . The man who confers a benefit upon the public is surely entitled to a just recompense, to our way of thinking.[4]

Political Speech at Space Rates

The rationale of newspaper managers is revealing. It was rooted in the conviction that most election campaigns were boring per se; most people did not care about issues or about politics. *Editor & Publisher* said in midsummer of 1908 that the election news was "duller than ditch water." The magazine the *Nation* agreed: "Dullness has already marked the presidential election for its own."[5]

During the last three months of a campaign, "a party paper needs to be somewhat absorbed with party matters," conceded Owen Scott of the Decatur (Illinois) *Herald* in 1903, but as a general matter "people do not read labored editorials on affairs of state" and "little interest is taken in tariff, or trusts, or imperialism, or free silver or the gold standard, or other so-called issues." Subscribers would rather read "a string of personals, an account of a local horse race, a Sunday school entertainment, a slangy account of a baseball game, or other local doings than all the editorials you can print." News should be our preoccupation, counseled Scott, "if we would make money and wear good clothes and be respected." He acknowledged that the publisher of a party paper usually paid an assessment to the party, the same as an officeholder. But Scott emphasized that everything else should be paid for as advertising.[6]

After the election of 1900, *The Journalist* was relieved that the speech-making was over:

> Election now is over, let us heave a long-drawn sigh;
> Calamity has passed away, the spellbinder has gone
>   by,
> If he'll work his brain and muscle
> As he used to do his chin
> A share of true prosperity may even come to him.

"Presidential campaigns are trying times for the newspaperman, especially in the [rural] areas," declared the same issue of *The Journalist*. "There his time is taken up with attending political meetings, writing arguments by the yard, and neglecting real news events for the mouthings of excited politicians. Election night finds him worn out with the struggle, brain fogged and disgusted with politics. Privately he is extremely glad that it is over and doesn't care a rap who won."[7]

Many learned Americans are under the mistaken impression that the news media's present-day obsession with personal scandal is a recent phenomenon. Writing more than one hundred years ago—in 1888—the Englishman Lord Bryce put his finger on a significant difference between elections in the United States and in Europe.[8] American elections turn much less on the views of the parties and more on "the character and conduct" of the candidates, he said. When the sound of personal scandal can be heard in a campaign, "the canons of decorum which American custom at other times observes are cast aside by speakers and journalists." Because "unmitigated publicity is a condition of eminence in America," news stories about the peccadillos of men take precedence over policy differences, more so, he said, than would be expected "in a country where equality is so fully established and the citizens are so keenly interested in public questions."

Based on his observations of the 1880 and 1884 campaigns, Lord Bryce identified three categories of criticism: (1) The candidate's war record (then meaning the Civil War); (2) Impeaching the nominee's personal integrity; (3) Charges made against the private life of the candidate, particularly in his relations with women. Few experienced public officials could avoid "occasionally finding themselves in situations capable of being misrepresented . . . [and] it takes no great invention to add details which give a bad look to the facts. You have the spectacle of half the honest men supporting for the headship of the nation a person whom the other half declare to be a knave."

This, he said, tends to "draw attention away from political discussions and thereby lessen what may be called the educational value of the campaign." Lord Bryce went on to tie this problem to press responsibility. In every campaign there are subjects worthy of debate. But they are subjects "so difficult to sift thoroughly before a popular audience that the orator has been able to evade them or to deal in sounding commonplaces." Unless journalists insist on a meaningful election-year discourse, the election of the president will continue to turn on personalities. This would suggest, at the very least, that newspapers devote their newsprint and their human resources to the "sifting" job that the candidates prefer to evade.

Most American reporters were convinced in the past (as they are today) that most voters make their decisions on the images of the candidates rather than on policy issues. Peter Finley Dunne's Mr. Dooley said the issues in 1904 were very clear: There weren't any.[9] At the turn of the century, the distaste of journalists for dull partisan discourse, plus their attraction to personalized conflicts of character and reputation, made it possible for many editors to agree that political speech was, or should be, a commodity to be sold like any other. "Why should not politicians be encouraged to pay space rates for what they want printed in the newspapers?" asked *Newspaperdom*. "Why should ordinarily sane newspapers be expected to load up the news columns for weeks and months before elections with arguments, correspondence and flings at the other party? A good deal of our politics is mere scramble for office. Much so-called patriotism is simply shouting for a good-sized slice of the spoils."

As an extension of this argument, it was sometimes asserted that instead of the newspaper management paying an assessment to the local political party, the transaction should be reversed: parties and candidates that benefit from a newspaper's editorial policy should pay the newspaper. In 1895, for example, *Newspaperdom* quoted approvingly this article in *The Nebraska Editor:*

Booming Politicians at Space Rates Only

The day will probably come when the newspaper will be no longer a free horse in politics; as a free horse it has been ridden nearly to death, and it will have to emancipate itself.

When John Jinks runs for an office he has to put up for all the aid he receives except from his party's newspaper; every ward-heeler and worn-out speaker who helps his cause is paid for it; but the editor, who does more than all the heelers in the wards, and all the speakers in the district, frequently goes without even thanks.

The office-seeker is generally selfish above everything, and it is not necessarily patriotism to support him because his politics dovetails with yours. He will not support you, should you even ask for a few crumbs that fall from his table; he may say that he will, but he generally lies.

The most prosperous newspaper in Kansas charges candidates as much for booming them as it charges merchants for advertising, and its support is considered well worth having, although everybody knows that the support is bought and paid for.[10]

For whatever reasons, candidates and parties responded by buying more newspaper advertising in the early 1900s. Both parties hired publicity experts. Associations of commercial and other special interests, fusion committees, and "good government" leagues also bought space in newspapers and magazines. Instead of sending reporters to interview distinguished people about their voting intentions (which Lord Bryce had noticed in the 1880s), newspapers now solicited paid advertisements from the same celebrities. Henry Ford, for example, bought space in 500 newspapers for an ad, captioned "Humanity and Your Vote," endorsing President Woodrow Wilson for reelection. John Wanamaker, George Harvey, Amos Pinchot, and other prominent Americans purchased endorsement ads. Political advertising had burst upon the scene so suddenly that in 1917 Congress considered trying to regulate it.

As political advertising increased, the proportion of political news allocated to talk about policy questions decreased still further. Newspapers had to compete for the campaign advertising dollar with filmed spots in movie theaters, billboards and display ads on streetcar panels.

Another factor helps us make sense of the journalistic (and public generally) intolerance of "oratorical gasbags." Jean Baker reminds us that much of the humor of the nineteenth century derived from politics. American humorists "dressed up elections in their worst clothes . . . and invariably sharpened the incongruity by writing in an incomprehensible, phonetically spelled version of the way Americans talked," she says.[11] Minstrel shows, songs, and cartoons ridiculed candidates and voters alike, treating elections as farce. The American people have always been ambivalent about the ideal of what government was meant to be and the often corrupt system that actually exists. Baker suggests that Americans ridiculed politics so as to blur the difference between the ideal and what they knew was really going on.

Ten

The Literary Digest and the Pundits

Straws in the Wind

The way people intend to vote is news of the first importance.

Claude E. Robinson,
Columbia University
sociologist, 1932

The preelection straw poll became a fixture in the larger-circulation urban newspapers during the first two decades of the twentieth century. In 1908, when Bryan ran for a third time as the presidential nominee of the Democratic Party, the press was tired of him. News demands novelty above all else, and by that time the indefatigable Mr. Bryan could no longer be made novel. No U.S. election, before or since, occurred with more prognostication and less reporting of what the candidates were saying about the issues than that one.

Newspapers formed interregional combinations to share the costs and the results of their preelection forecasting. The *New York Herald, Chicago Record-Herald, Cincinnati Enquirer,* and *St. Louis Republic* made one such combine. Far more so than before, reporters went out and asked conveniently available voters about their intentions. Factory workers, streetcar crews, sewer gangs, store clerks, theatergoers, travelers on trains, farmers visiting the county seat on Saturday afternoon were solicited.

Canvassers for the *Record-Herald* in Chicago collected more than 100,000 secret ballots in seven midwestern states. The purpose of this "investigation into political conditions," the editors informed their subscribers, was "to get at the real political drift." The newspaper took pains to explain that it was not predicting the outcome of the election, only showing "which way the political wind is blowing at the time."[1]

Nevertheless, the theme of the campaign story in all four papers, from beginning to end, was the hopelessness of the Democratic cause, spelled out repeatedly in hard numbers. On each of the six Sundays preceding the election, the *New York Herald* published a state-by-state projection of how the electoral votes would fall. In the middle of October, the *Herald* documented its electoral vote projection with three pages of reports of sundry straw polls of undetermined legitimacy in scattered states.[2] One told of polls taken on the same night in theaters in New York, Cincinnati, St. Louis, and Baltimore. Sample ballots were given to patrons as they entered vaudeville, burlesque, and other theatrical houses and were collected by attendants during the intermissions. The data from New York showed that Taft was doing well in "the melodrama houses and other first-class houses" whereas Bryan had more of a following in the seedier burlesque establishments.

On the last Sunday before the election, the *New York Herald* forecast 306 electoral votes for the Republican, William Howard Taft, and 177 for Bryan. Entire pages given over to similar forecast stories—"Nebraska Safe for Bryan by 8,000"—"Give Montana to Taft by 2,000." The *Herald* also printed elaborate tables listing indicated pluralities in New York state broken down by boroughs and counties.

The editors of the *Herald* were proud of their massive display of horse-race journalism. "*Herald* Forecast Praised as Fair and Impartial," asserted a headline in the next day's paper.[3]

The Chicago member of this combine, the *Record-Herald,* reported on the final weekend: "It is almost certain that on Tuesday next William Howard Taft is to be elected President."[4]

The fact that the *New York Times* did not conduct straw polls did not stop it from predicting the outcome of the election, the same as the other New York papers. A story at the top of the front page reported on October 25, "Vote for Taft Probably 286." The *Times* said the estimate had been based partly on results received direct from Republican and Democratic chairmen. In the same issue the *Times* printed a story reporting the *Chicago Tribune's* electoral vote forecast made, the *Times* explained, "after a careful study of the conditions in the various states and considered in the light of the predictions of the leaders of both parties made in private reports."

Projecting electoral votes was more risky in the next election, in 1912, because there were three horses in the race. Former President Theodore Roosevelt ran as a third-party candidate against President Taft and the Democratic nominee, Woodrow Wilson.

By then the oratorical discourse of the presidential campaign had been made more sterile by the wire services' insistence that candidates furnish "canned" speech texts in advance. It was cheaper for the AP and the other wire services to mail a week's supply of speech stories that could be set in type before the speeches were due to be delivered. Wilson, a former professor, found this practice onerous. "I cannot make speeches to a stenographer," he complained.[5] As a consequence, little of the vitality in the campaign oratory could be detected in the news stories.

Changes in the nominating process that gave more power to primary election voters—advocated by Roosevelt's Progressive movement—also created more reader interest in measures of the strength of the candidates.

The *New York Herald* accompanied its final poll on the last Sunday before the election with this editorial page comment:

> The Great Forecaster insists on turning prophet and says that Wilson will be elected. . . . If the result should be different, then the Chief Forecaster is not only a prophet without honor in his own country, but friendless, hated, pursued, a lost soul, a pitiable spectacle in the outer darkness. In this important crisis he stands absolutely confident and insists that it is a democratic avalanche which is coming.[6]

In big type across the top of the front page, the headline declared:

> Wilson the Next President
> And Congress Democratic,
> Herald's Canvass Indicates

Nervously the newspaper reduced its poll figures to 360 electoral votes for Wilson, 27 for Taft, 7 for Roosevelt, leaving 137 doubtful.

The *Boston Globe*, meanwhile, spiced its New England poll with the prediction of "Dr. Derolli" that the election would be so close as to be decided in the House of Representatives. Dr. Derolli was an astrologer who had gained fame by predicting that President McKinley would die a violent death, which transformed the doctor into a future and forever authority on everything uncertain.

Besides consulting the same Dr. Derolli, the *San Francisco Chronicle* conducted straw polls at Market Street theaters, of women on Tennessee Street, and of employees of the California Barrel and Glass Works.[7]

Although Wilson received less than 42 percent of the popular vote, he won 435 electoral votes to 88 for Roosevelt and only eight for Taft. With a field of three contenders, the published instructions on how to read the flashing lights in the skies over the big cities were more intricate than usual. The *Chicago Tribune* for instance, told its readers that a circular sweep from west to east would mean one thing, a circular sweep from east to west would mean something else, and a zigzag sweep would signify the third possibility. Some papers were still making do with stereopticon shows, enlivened in the case of the *Chicago Record-Herald* by "cartoonographs" and moving pictures.

Calling Elections

The week-by-week publication of forecast numbers by newspapers was now accepted by politicians. After the initial resistance by Democrats in 1896 and 1900, partisans made no further effort to disrupt the newspaper straw polls other than to exploit them. Candidates and parties viewed as the underdog in a campaign generally believed they were not helped by published polls. Psychologists know that some voters prefer to be on the winning side, although the "bandwagon" influence of polls has never been definitively measured. More obvious is the dampening effect on the morale of campaign workers when the polls keep telling them that the cause is hopeless. And overconfidence is a danger when a candidate is declared a sure winner long before the election.

Although politicians had reasons therefore not to welcome the publication of straw polls, there was usually only one way they could sway the results to their advantage. That was by arranging to have as many of their supporters as they could muster in the path of the pollster.

Preelection newspaper straw polls became more common for at least a couple of reasons:

First is the obvious fact that people wanted to know how the competition was going. The way people intend to vote is, as Professor Robinson understood, news of the first importance. Newspaper editors have always understood the old adage which says, if you want an audience, start a fight. Before the fight starts, people want to know who is favored to win. Once the fight starts, they want to know who is winning. As soon as it is over, they want to know who did win.

Newspapers that had relied on their "special scouts and correspondents" to divine the electoral vote prospects in the various states were now in a position to systematically gather information at the source—which is in the minds of the voters.

There was a third reason recognized by Robinson and others why newspapers loved straw polls: the advertising and promotional benefit for the newspaper itself. Reporters who carried ballot boxes emblazoned with the name of the sponsoring paper into some crowded place, like a theater or store or train station, were spreading the name of their employer. For a worker in the railroad yards to be asked whether he wanted to participate in the *Daily Bugle's* simulated election was to impress the worker with the identity of a publication he might not even have known existed. As Jean Converse points out in her history of survey research in the U.S., ample evidence suggests that editors were more interested in circulation growth than they were in serious measurement of attitudes.[8] The scientific sampling and question design techniques of commercial market research were already known. Advertisers were able to question predictably representative samples of their consumers about their product preferences. But, as *Fortune* magazine later described the typical preelection straw polls, they consisted of inquiries "chucked at the hinder parts of the population like bird shot at a rising duck." Journalists were not concerned, said *Fortune,* about "the possibility of treating public opinion as the steel people treated the ore trains at Hibbing—sampling every tenth car."[9]

Even more amazing was the frequency with which the straw polls came close to the actual vote. Polling in thirty-seven states in 1912, the *New York Herald* group achieved a median average plurality error per state of 7 percent. However, Robinson's study of the electoral vote predictions in 65 metropolitan dailies between 1904 and 1928 found that they guessed right almost as often without polls as with polls. Newspaper predictions were right about three-fourths of the time in close states.[10]

Although Robinson was convinced that most of the polls were conducted as objectively as the editors knew how, he found that they were not above manipulating the figures. This was done to make it appear that the race was close and the lead was changing hands from one day to the next. This, the editors hoped, would stimulate interest in the race—and the poll— causing readers to want to buy the next day's paper. The true leader would be allowed to "bound out ahead in the home stretch." Robinson thought it inconceivable that newspapers would risk the loss of reader confidence by deliberately distorting the final count. "If there is one sure way for a newspaper to commit suicide," one editor told him, "it is to conduct a fake straw vote."[11]

Sending reporters out to solicit sample ballots themselves was one straw poll technique. Another cheaper method was to print blank coupons in the newspaper and invite readers to cut them out and mail them back filled in. Because of the choice involved in spending money for a stamp, the response was less likely to be an accurate cross section of the electorate. It was especially tempting for organized groups to buy extra copies of the paper and stuff the ballot box. A third method, favored by national magazines, was to send postcard ballots in the mail to lists of voters and ask the recipients to vote and send them back postage-paid.

All of these methods suffered from the same defect: there was no way of knowing whether the straws were being cast into the wind by a representative cross section of all the voters. Rural residents, Republicans, and educated voters tended to be overrepresented in straw poll samples, according to Robinson. Opportunities for error were manifest in national surveys that sought to project the winners of the electoral votes in each state separately. The sample had to be representative of each state's electorate separately in order to be a fair sample.

One of the first newspapers to conduct straw polls using proportional quotas was the *Columbus Dispatch* in Ohio. An effort was made by the *Dispatch* to obtain straws from roughly proportional numbers of manual laborers and white-collar workers, urban and rural residents, and the different major ethnic groups. Beginning in 1906, canvassing crews were dispatched by the newspaper to specific locations where targeted groups of citizens were likely to be assembled for business and pleasure. By identifying different residential voting blocs and then soliciting a proportional representation of straw votes, the editors had transferred the key-precinct method of election night tabulation to the measurement of preelection voting intentions. The *Dispatch* was careful to continue polling through the Saturday night before the election so as to detect any last-minute shifts.

Not until many years later did such diligence in the operation of newspaper polls become the norm. In most newspaper offices, editors labored under the mistaken belief that they could best guard against error by increasing the sample. Pollsters did not realize that the error would be compounded by making a flawed sample larger.

Not all thoughtful men and women—indeed, not all journalists—were pleased by the measurement of what was portrayed as public opinion. The People were being asked by the press to react to "news" images simplistically conveyed by the press, which "opinions" would then be reported as news and the cycle would begin anew. "Public opinion now became synthetic, believable, passive, vivid, concrete, simplified, and ambiguous as never before," said the historian Daniel Boorstin much later. "If you wanted to know what the public thought, you could simply pick up a newspaper. Changes were recorded daily or twice daily. [Opinions] were forced into being by earnest newspapermen trying to make news. They were played against one another."[12]

"The great question so far as public opinion is concerned is not what it wants, but what it ought to want," said an earlier scholar, Lindsay Rogers. "The pollsters cannot make this discovery. . . . [When] there is clearness on what public opinion ought to want, it usually wants it. Even if the yeses and noes had real meaning, two important questions would remain: How heartfelt are the yeses and noes? How many people really care one way or the other? . . . The more men are moved emotionally, the greater their reluctance to disclose their real opinions to strange interviewers. . . . Decisions that are reached have to be accepted, and without a broad basis of consent, democracy does not work."[13]

As more newspapers offered their own straw polls across the country, issues reporting continued to change. The AP's Melville Stone won President Wilson over to the efficacy of canned texts in the 1916 campaign. Stone was less successful with the Republican candidate. A former Supreme Court justice, Charles Evans Hughes did not take orders from newsmen. Stone warned Hughes that "touch-and-go talking" from the rear platform of a railroad car would be futile. A hurried news report would be handed off at the next town to a telegraph operator "who would probably be an incompetent." "The report would necessarily be greatly abbreviated in order to secure transmission," Stone said he tried to explain to the candidate. "On its receipt by a newspaper in the rush hour it would again be cut down so that when Hughes read the story as it appeared in print he would probably be unable to recognize it as his own speech."[14] In the pages of newspapers, the discourse of the campaign appeared lifeless, without texture or context.

The most distinctive innovation in the political journalism of the 1916 campaign occurred not in the pages of any newspaper but in a magazine. Funk & Wagnalls booksellers owned a popular national weekly magazine— *Literary Digest*. The editors of *Literary Digest* came up with a brilliant election-year scheme: they deputized their subscribers to be political reporters.

Readers were invited to "act as special correspondents and tell us how feeling is running . . . in the circle of a man's or a woman's daily occupation and residence." The volunteer correspondents were instructed to report specifically on what the Roosevelt third-party voters of four years before were likely to do this time. Here the editors were onto the importance of identifying shifting streams of voting groups. "If we can catch the voters in the glare of the searchlight as they are shifting from one political camp to another and count them," the *Digest* explained to its readers, "we can tell which camp will be found to have the heaviest battalions [on election day]."[15]

A surprising number of subscribers took their assignments seriously. If nosey neighbors went around snooping into "the politics" of other people on the block today, someone would be sure to call the cops. But the spirit of community was still alive and well in 1916. More than 3,000 reports were received. The conductor of a cross-country train mailed in a lengthy summation of his interviews with passengers. Traveling salesmen took the political pulse of their customers. Dentists and druggists became reporters. Housewives canvassed their precincts and sent in comparisons with the figures of four years before. An article based on the survey, headlined

"Political Reports from 3,000 Communities," made what turned out to be the telling prediction that Wilson would benefit more than Hughes from the votes of Progressives who supported Roosevelt in 1912.[16]

Almost as an afterthought, *Literary Digest* also endeavored to test public opinion on its own. As early as 1895, the staff had been collecting names and addresses of potential subscribers for solicitation. So, in addition to the random canvass by its readers, postcards were mailed to several hundred thousand names on its list, in five selected pivotal states. The postcards consisted of a sample ballot and a subscription blank: the sample ballot to vote in the straw poll, the subscription blank to read about the results—an ingenious mass solicitation of new subscribers through the mails. The *Digest* received some 30,000 responses from New York, New Jersey, Ohio, Illinois, and Indiana. Hughes was estimated from the returns to have a considerably bigger edge in all five states than he actually recorded on election day. The projected pluralities were off by an average of 20 percent—5 percent in Illinois, 19 percent in New Jersey, 20 percent in Ohio, 22 percent in Indiana, 28 percent in New York. The cause of the error would be painfully obvious today: Upper-income voters were disproportionately represented on a list of people who might have enough money to subscribe to a weekly magazine.

Aware of that problem, the *Digest* made a further effort in the same campaign to combine analysis and polling by surveying 457 labor union leaders. The unionists were asked to speak the sentiments of their membership as a whole. As expected, the survey published on October 7 showed a big advantage for Wilson.

Four years later, in 1920, the *Digest* mailed 11 million postcard ballots to a nationwide list of residential telephone users. This time the plurality error in six key states that were selected for analysis averaged 21 percent. Later in the 1920s, the magazine added to its mailing lists names taken from automobile registrations—totaling as many as 18 million mailings one year. Again the managers simply ignored what they knew to be the fact that car owners and telephone subscribers were hardly a meaningful cross section of the U.S. population, certainly not in the 1920s.

The reporting of straw polls could not help but affect how journalists perceived the other news of the campaign. Some papers now had political experts on their staffs. One of them, James Morgan of the *Boston Globe,* wrote a daily column called "The Progress of the Campaign," which included commentary on various polls. The *Globe,* as a partner in the *Herald*'s straw poll combine, reported on the Sunday before the election that Wilson would have more popular votes, but Hughes would win the election with

The Literary Digest and the Pundits

295 electoral votes to the incumbent's 236. An editorial entitled "How to Analyze a Straw Vote or Early Election Returns" explained that the analysis had been based on straw poll results in individual states.

In New York, the *Herald* was quite uneasy about its own poll. For although the paper was strongly supporting Hughes editorially, the final combined straw poll figures showed an apparent trend toward Wilson. Almost apologetically, the editors projected 307 electoral votes for Wilson and 224 for Hughes. One entire section of four pages on the last Sunday before the election was devoted to various aspects of the poll. Columns upon columns of tables were subjected to intricate analysis. Three days before, a story on the front page reported "President Wilson Leads Herald Poll in Minnesota by a Good Margin"—461 to 408. The *Herald* was pleased that nationwide interest in the straw poll had boosted circulation. But the editors took pains to state in a final editorial:

> Without partisanship and without bias, the *Herald* has used its best endeavors to make the poll just what it purports to be—a fair indication of the political sentiment of the country as this is gauged by expressions of individual preference. The element in this situation concerning which no man can feel certain is the great silent vote. . . . The *Herald* undertakes no analysis of that phase of the situation, for the reason that it knows nothing of the intentions of voters who have not declared themselves.

It was a new experience for a newspaper to be predicting the *defeat* of the candidate it was supporting editorially. The subeditors were protecting their hindquarters. They were also betraying their ignorance of the theory of sampling because a true random sample would presumably have been representative of those who were not asked for their views.

Out in Ohio, the *Columbus Dispatch* was now polling the entire state. Its poll, which projected a Wilson victory in Ohio, caused consternation among prominent Republicans. The purpose of the poll, the newspaper hastened to explain, was to "detect, and not direct, the mind of the great determining state, Ohio. . . . to make plain the drift of public sentiment in regard to the national question. At great expense and in spite of much contumely, [we have] honestly and faithfully performed this function."

The *New York Tribune* predicted that Hughes would win. The *New York Times* was not sure. "Dispatches From All States Indicate a Close Election," said the *Times*. "Result May Depend on Ohio and Illinois." In this story, "based on dispatches from correspondents of THE NEW YORK TIMES," 207 votes were considered safe for Wilson, 158 for Hughes, and 11 other states, including New York, were classified with their 166 votes as doubtful. The situation, the newspaper admitted, was "too baffling to enable trained political observers accurately to forecast the result."[17]

If the *Times* was baffled, Stone knew the AP would have its hands full on election night. It would be a close election, one in which editors would award electoral votes on incomplete key-precinct projections at their peril. Two of the nation's leading newspapers that had access to the same straw poll information had interpreted the electoral vote significance differently—the *Globe* and the *Herald*.

The AP had finally succeeded in preventing Western Union from pirating its figures and marketing them in competition with the news service. One of the executives in the AP New York office, Wilmer Stuart, spent months traveling around the country organizing the first centralized election night tallying system. In some places the AP relied on member newspapers for returns; in others (like the solid Democratic South) arrangements were made to obtain returns from the dominant party organization. Stone and Stuart decided to report raw vote totals only, rather than attempting a district-by-district comparison with the figures of four years before. For each state, the AP would keep a running count of the number of districts tabulated, the total number of districts in the state, and the votes received by the candidates.

Despite Stuart's yeoman planning, some glitches developed in the communication system. Some counties in northern California and in the southwest were not yet reachable by either railroad or the telegraph. Results were carried to San Francisco by stagecoach from some parts of the Sierras. Men on horses and mules tried to make it through mountain passes choked with snow. Nor were the telegraph lines always strung to the specifications of news distribution. Sections of the eastern slope of the Cascade Mountain range in California routed their election reports to Reno, Nevada, instead of the coastal cities, because the lines of communication ran that way. The leading newspapers in the eastern cities would be tempted to take chances and make assumptions based on definitive figures from the big eastern states that came in first.

Both parties invested heavily in advertising for their candidates. A group of Chicago advertising men formed a "truth in politics" committee with the intention of giving the Republican Party a permanent organization of trained publicity experts. Hughes' advisers made a tactical decision to concentrate their newspaper advertising in the crucial states east of the Mississippi River.

By this time, in 1916, electric lights were being used to signal the results of elections over vast expanses, not only in cities with skyscrapers. At its laboratories in Schenectady, New York, General Electric Company had developed powerful new pressed-filament tungsten lamps that could be mounted in oversized searchlights. A light five feet in diameter which GE said could be seen under the right weather conditions 100 miles away was made available to the *Albany Daily Press & Knickerbocker.* Wanting also to signal the news of the gubernatorial race, the New York papers used ever more complicated codes. From the Metropolitan Life Insurance Building, the *Herald*'s beam (from a lamp thirty-two inches in diameter) could be seen in New Jersey and Connecticut. A steady horizontal beam circling the horizon meant a victory for Hughes. A zigzagging beam was good news for Wilson. A red "flame burning in the tower" would be lit if the Republican gubernatorial candidate won; green if the Democrat. The *Herald* warned its readers that both beams would have the appearance of a slanting line but held out hope that one would be steadier than the other. The *San Francisco Chronicle* followed the Chicago example by shooting off skyrockets from its tower—red for Hughes, blue for Wilson. But because the night weather is chancy in San Francisco, and to guard against a campaign of disinformation from its competitors, the *Chronicle* also prepared to announce the returns in theaters and auditoriums all over the city. The game of one-upmanship was carried to still greater heights by the *St. Paul Dispatch and Pioneer Press,* which hired a celebrity aviator, Laddy Laird, to fly over the city in a monoplane with color-coded lights rigged beneath the fuselage. The signaling of election results was now airborne.

In some cities a newspaper arranged with the electric company to have the lights blink off and on all over town according to a pre-announced code when the winning candidate became known. Factory managers would also blow the whistles at their establishments to complete what was billed as the "toot-and-wink" plan.

At 6:30 P.M., New York time, long before the polls closed on the West Coast, the *New York Tribune* studied the figures from the big eastern and midwestern states. Hughes received more votes in New York than any of the straw polls had predicted. He also carried Illinois and Indiana. Gambling that it was a nationwide trend, the editors of the *Tribune* went ahead and signaled the election of Charles Evans Hughes. At 7:31 P.M. the *Herald*'s "strong light flashed out its news [of Hughes' election] far ahead of any similar notification." This item in the next morning's paper apparently disregarded the earlier but presumably weaker light from the hated *Tribune.*

Meanwhile, a crowd estimated at 100,000 people had gathered in Times Square. Two circles of lights blazed from the top of the *Times* flag pole—

white on top while Wilson was ahead, red while Hughes was in front. Shortly before 9 P.M. the red searchlight began swinging around the building and the white lights were extinguished—the sign that Hughes had won.

At 9:15 P.M., the 16,000 arc lights in the streets of Philadelphia flashed off and on twice, based on the *Ledger*'s decision that Hughes had won. Fifteen minutes later, the *New York World,* though supporting Wilson editorially, conceded on the basis of Hughes' sweep of the eastern states that the president's cause was hopeless.

All of this made the decision-makers at the AP extremely nervous. Melville Stone related in his autobiography:

> Early in the evening and long before the polls had closed in the Far West the Democratic papers of the East conceded Hughes' election. Of course it was not our business to announce anybody's election until we knew what the count would disclose. Then began the clamour. Message after message came asking if I was owned by the Democrats, and why on earth I did not accept the admission of the Wilson papers and announce Hughes' election.[18]

Later that night, after Minnesota's twelve electoral votes were awarded tentatively to Hughes, the AP succumbed to the pressure. AP wrote that Hughes had won, unless Wilson scored a landslide victory on the West Coast, which it said was highly unlikely although the tabulation there had not been completed. The United Press continued to insist that the outcome was uncertain.

In St. Louis the *Post-Dispatch* arranged with the electric company to jiggle the master switch in the main power plant when the decision was determined. Lights would blink twice if Hughes won, three times if Wilson were reelected. Young Sidney James remembered being allowed to stay up late on a school night to await the flickering of the lights. Finally, sometime after midnight, the lights all over St. Louis County faltered twice. "Wow, Hughes had won," Sidney recalled, saying he went to bed "tingling with excitement over the drama of it all."[19]

Charles H. Taylor—now General Taylor—sat at his desk in the offices of the *Boston Globe,* not so sure. A searchlight had been mounted on the Custom House Tower. For twenty-five miles around, people watched the tower. One sweep every thirty seconds would mean victory for Wilson; two flashes would mean Hughes had won. All night long the "lofty beacon remained wrapped in persistent darkness," as James Morgan wrote later. Boston's most influential magnates were gathered in the *Globe* building as usual to await the general's judgment. He had analyzed the *Herald* group's straw poll data differently than the others in the combine. Taylor said the figures pointed to a Hughes electoral college victory, "although a shift of 30 electoral votes in some very close states could elect Wilson," which is what the *Globe* preferred editorially. The general was troubled by the absence of figures from California on Tuesday night. So, as one extra edition rolled off the presses after another, the *Globe* stuck to the story that while it looked like Hughes had won, the lack of definite news from the West made it uncertain—the only major circulation morning paper to take that tack. "Race Close, Hughes Leads," said the headline, explaining "No Guessing on the Election by the Globe . . . Nine States With 59 Votes in Doubt."

An article printed later in the *Globe* captured some of the drama:

> The *Globe* office seethed with anxious men. They accused us of refusing to concede a manifest victory, of holding back the truth because of our political complexion. . . . We saw only two columns of figures. We flashed no signal. . . . We telephoned to special correspondents in the Middle West. Telegrams were sent to the capital of every doubtful state. Telephone calls were put in for Minneapolis and San Francisco. Daylight came without any thought of sleep. All through the day the *Globe* was receiving the latest estimates and figures. The same men who kept the tables for the morning paper did so for the evening editions. The time was too vital, the test too severe to warrant any thought of rest.[20]

In New York, the *Herald* had the peculiar problem on Wednesday morning of rejoicing in the news of Hughes' election while defending the reputation of its straw poll, which had predicted that Wilson would win. This the *Herald* did without missing a beat by claiming, in an editorial labeled "What the Herald's Poll Did for Mr. Hughes," that it had been responsible for his victory! When the first installment of the poll was released October 8, Republicans complained, the editorial said, that this would lead to "a sudden outburst of Wilson sentiment." But what also happened, the *Herald* suggested, was that the poll "waked the [Hughes campaigners] from their dreams of certain and easy victory. It showed them the weak spots. It was responsible for the life that was put into the Republican campaign in the last three weeks, turning the tide from defeat to victory. So it is that wherever there is Republican rejoicing today there should be thankfulness for the Herald's poll."

In Boston, the *Globe* told its readers the next day: "Watch Custom House Tower Again Tonight. Three Flashes Will Mean Contest Still in Doubt." At intervals all through the night, the light flashed three times. The outcome would depend on California, the Boston paper said on Thursday, explaining in an editorial that "The *Globe* Does Not Guess."

> A great nation is standing stock still with fascinated eyes fixed on a row of cold figures—figures big with destiny. Whence comes this about? It comes from west of the Mississippi. Westward the course of decision takes its way . . . the decision has leaped from Hell Gate to Golden Gate.
> We found ourselves submissively awaiting the judgment of the Yon Yonsons and the Ole Olesens of the great North West. It is their innings. . . . We stand at one of civilization's crossroads. In the dead of night there is a sound as of the trampling of many feet. Democracy is marching on.[21]

That evening the headline said, "Wilson Is In Lead," followed by: "Again tonight the *Globe* searchlight will flash from the tower."

The last mountain-slope precincts from Humboldt County, California, were not tallied until Thursday. Some of the correspondents in the West Coast bureaus of the UP had come to work on 7 A.M. on election day and were still at the helm, dressed in the same clothing, unwashed and unrested, on Thursday evening.

Morris DeHaven Tracy, the UP stringer from Eureka, the Humboldt County seat, had been summoned to San Francisco to help with the election report. All Thursday afternoon Tracy kept a telephone line open to his boyhood friend back home, the county clerk, who was trying to verify the figures from Eureka.

At 7 P.M. the clerk shouted into the phone, "I got it. I just found an error in the counting. About 1,800 votes in the wrong column. Wilson carries the county by about 3,600 votes!"

The San Francisco bureau chief studied the numbers for a few minutes, then broke into the trunk wire with: "Flash! Wilson Carries California."[22]

Indeed the president won the state by 3,896 votes and was reelected with 277 electoral votes to 254 for Hughes. Wilson's edge in the national popular vote was calculated at just under 600,000.

UP beat the AP by ten minutes with the decision from California.

"Wilson Wins—Took California—Majority of 13 in the Electoral College," reported the *Herald*, which took the news with remarkable aplomb. This it did—how else, of course, but by applauding its straw poll! "The *Herald* wins nationwide commendation for the accuracy of its election forecast," the story declared nonchalantly. "Anyway, Hats Off to The *Herald* Poll," trumpeted an editorial on Saturday. "Again will political managers, politicians and the people doff their hats and agree: 'If you see it in the *Herald* it's true.'"

On the morning after election night, the *Chronicle* in San Francisco said, "It Looks Like Hughes." On the second day, the headline read, "Hughes Probably Elected." The third day it was, "Hughes Leading in New Mexico, Vital State." And on the climactic fourth day, the headline said simply, "Woodrow Wilson Reelected President."

Besides the lingering effects of partisanship, the campaign of 1916 demonstrated the intense competitiveness of horse-race journalism, the great national influence of the New York dailies, the flaws of straw polling, and the limitations of forecasting of any kind in a close election. The straw polls of 1916 severely underestimated Wilson's strength and created an atmosphere in which the projection of a Hughes triumph was instantly credible. According to Claude Robinson's study, the *Herald* combine missed the winning plurality in California by 31 percent, in Illinois by 17 percent, in Michigan by 24 percent, in Kentucky by 26 percent, in Wisconsin by 17 percent, in New York by 8 percent, in New Jersey by 7 percent.[23]

The election of 1916 gave an unexpected lift to the career of a young correspondent for the *New York Evening Post* named David Lawrence. Only recently graduated from Princeton University, Lawrence distinguished himself by predicting Wilson's electoral vote margin almost on the head. He capitalized on that feat and the perception that he enjoyed the president's confidence to become the first of a new, elevated class of journalists—the nationally syndicated Washington columnists. James Gordon Bennett and the other letter-writing correspondents of the previous century were professional ancestors of the syndicated columnists, but with far less exposure. Lawrence left the *Post* to sign on as the first stellar attraction of a feature syndicate—Consolidated Press Association—formed in 1919. Consolidated and other news feature syndicates contracted with the best-known political reporters to sell their columns of analysis and opinion to newspapers around the country. Their nationwide exposure gave unprecedented prominence and influence to the so-called "pundits" of political journalism.

The impact of national columnists struck both of the principal strains of political journalism. A hybrid product of factual reporting and opinionated interpretation, syndicated columns represented yet another alternative to the straight, plodding, predictable literature of election campaign debate. Equally important, the columnist stepped forward as the only continuing counterforce to horse-race political reporting. Here were journalists who were telling the people not the arithmetical sums of their opinions but what they *ought to be thinking* about the issues of the day. While the opinion polls were measuring and reporting as objective reality the collective opinion of the electorate, the columnists were employing their insight and expertise to shape public opinion. In a real sense, the columnists and the pollsters were antagonists. To this day, one of the most persistent sources of criticism of public opinion polls is the fraternal order of syndicated columnists.

A new hierarchical system in the Washington press rubbed off on all reporting of national politics. Political reporters always relied on their symbiotic relationship with news sources. Mark Hanna talked to reporters with the implicit understanding that they would sense what would be off-the-record without being told. A political reporter for the *New York Sun* once estimated that he and his colleagues printed about 1 percent of what they knew. "Otherwise," he said, "something like a revolution might occur in American politics."[24]

The new columnists competed for newspaper outlets all over the country, and for influence in the Washington Establishment. They occupied an elite position. The best political reporters jockeyed for access to sources, for the prestige and respect of their colleagues on the political beat, and for the approval of their editors. As reporters disentangled from their patronage obligations and/or the partisan demands of their editors, they competed more vigorously to climb higher in the pecking order. Political activity being by its nature disorderly and confusing, the pack looked to the inner circle of journalists for interpretations of orthodoxy, for an acceptable understanding of the meaning of what was going on around them. Within the fraternity a few journalists acquired reputations for industry, sagacity, insight, access to power. The modern journalist David Broder expressed this phenomenon this way: "Every day, the national political reporters are competing with each other. Within the club we know which reporters are doing well and which ones aren't. And nothing so influences those collective opinions as each individual's skill or lack of skill to gauge the course of the campaign—knowing who is up and who is down."[25]

Grounded in the Progressive and other protest movements of this period, investigative reporters (labeled muckrakers by Teddy Roosevelt) were, like the columnists, another outgrowth of the new individualism in American journalism. David Graham Phillips, who wrote sensational exposés for Hearst's magazine *Cosmopolitan,* is described by Thomas C. Leonard in his history of political reporting as a different kind of political reporter, "a celebrity and a scoffer" who "snarled at the political process."[26] Phillips and the other muckrakers closed their minds to politics as a process of negotiation, shady bargaining, and compromise. They saw a horror chamber of "interests" conniving in a shadowy world against the public good.

The antipolitician fervor of the muckrakers had the no doubt unintended effect of further spurring the decline of news about campaign discourse. The muckraker could not help but build on the people's distrust of politicians. Syndicated columnists, meanwhile, offered a more compactly reasoned substitute for windy speeches and editorials. They filled some of the void left by the deaths of the great personal editors of the nineteenth century. Then people talked about "what Bennett said today" or "what Greeley said today." Greeley answered William Cullen Bryant in print, "You lie, villain! willfully, wickedley, basely lie!" Greeley had no qualms about denouncing Bennett as a "low-mouthed, blatant, witless, brutal scoundrel." When a politician whom Bryant had criticized threatened to pull his nose, Bryant responded by stalking ostentatiously three times around the bully at their next meeting in public, daring him to try. That was, said one of their contemporaries, "the golden age of our craft, when every editor wore his conscience on his arm, and carried his dueling weapon in his hand, walked always in the light where the whole world could see him, and was prepared to defend his published opinions with his life if need be."[27]

In their quest for rising circulation, editors valued columnists who were provocative. A former newspaperman penned this complaint in 1910: "More circulation can be got only by keeping the public stirred up. . . . Blow the trumpet, and make ringing announcements every day. If nothing new is to be had, refurbish something so old that people have forgotten it, and spread it over lots of space. Who will know the difference? What one person did, others were forced to do or be outdistanced in the competition. It all had its effect. A craving for excitement was first aroused in the public, and then satisfied by the same hand that had aroused it."[28]

The author of those words marveled at "the progressive acceleration of the pace of our twentieth-century life generally."

> Where we walked in the old times, we run in these; where we ambled then, we gallop now. It is the age of electric power, high explosives, articulated steel frames, the long-distance telephone, the taxicab, and the card-index.
>
> What is the effect of all this on the modernized newspaper? It must be first on the ground at every activity, foreseen or unforeseeable, as a matter of course. Its reporter must get off his "story" in advance of all his rivals. Never mind strict accuracy of detail—effect is the main thing; he is writing

not for expert accountants, or professional statisticians, or analytical philosophers, but for the public; and what the public wants is not dry particulars, but color, vitality, heat.[29]

The "dry particulars" of democracy may have been just what Jefferson and
Madison had in mind, but the journalists of 1910 were driven by a need to
"spread over lots of space" stories that were saturated with color, vitality,
heat. For political journalists that meant stories in which "strict accuracy to
detail" was less important. It meant not stories about the dry particulars of
partisan debate. It meant more horse-race reporting.

While these changes were occurring in political journalism, the technical
means of delivering campaign speeches to mass audiences were being made
easier. At last, voters could attend a mass meeting and expect to hear what
was said. The presidential campaign of 1916 is believed to have been the
first in which a candidate's remarks from the rear of a train platform or in
a meeting hall or an outdoor park were amplified electronically. The Bell
Telephone Company conducted the first open-air public address demonstration on Staten Island in June of that year.

The cynical style of some journalists alarmed others. The AP's Melville
Stone was worried about where the entertaining news of election campaigns
as spectacles would lead. Here is an excerpt from a speech Stone delivered
to journalism students at Columbia University on January 12, 1914:

> We are a peculiar people. Drawn from all quarters of the globe, with
> many millions having no just conception of the mission ordained for this
> Republic, with racial prejudices which are natural and inevitable, we as a
> people are facing problems of tremendous import. It is imperative that
> somebody somehow shall do some thinking. And I cannot help believing
> that there is a great body of the people who would like to do this thinking
> if they only had a chance.
>
> I suppose it is true that, as a rule, we are superficial. The late Price
> Collier wrote a book in which, in speaking of another people, he said:
> "They are great nibblers, intellectually." And this seems to be true of us.
> T. P. O'Connor once said, when I asked him what he thought of the citizens
> of this country, that they seemed to him to be "the finest half-educated
> race on earth."
>
> One of the reasons for our deplorable superficiality may be traced to
> the wonderful development of inter-communication in recent years. It is
> only little more than half a century since our range of vision was limited
> to our immediate neighborhood. Now by the extension of the telegraph,
> the cable, and the wireless transmission the remotest corners of the world

are brought close to us and we are as familiar with the activities of mankind everywhere. Every man, indeed, is akin to Goldsmith's teacher.

> . . . And still the wonder grew
> that one small head could carry
> all he knew.

In such circumstances it is impossible that we should dip very deep into the Pierian spring.

Are we doing all we can to better such a condition, which I am sure you must admit is an unfortunate one? The newspaper has practically driven out of existence in this country the review [journal of ideas]; even the magazines are devoted, as a rule, to fiction of the most inconsequential character; even in the newspaper, in large measure, editorial opinion has disappeared. Where then, I ask you, shall you turn for a serious, thoughtful consideration of any public question? May I suggest that I believe there is a great longing on the part of many people for real information, and that I believe it would prove profitable to attempt to minister to this desire. The vast multitude who assemble every year at the various Chautauqua meetings give some evidence of this. . . . It follows from what I have said that I think it is as reporters and not as advisers or as entertainers that we rise to our highest stature.[30]

Eleven

You're on the Air

The first election returns transmitted over the air waves by "wireless telegraphy" were beamed to steamers on the Great Lakes in 1906. Thomas E. Clark, an electric-appliance store owner in Detroit, offered the election night reports as an added bonus for clients who subscribed to his off-shore Morse Code weather service.[1] Not long after that, on Christmas Eve of the same year, the sound of the human voice was first carried through the air by radio, uncoded and without wires.

Newspaper publishers had become concerned, belatedly, about their dependence on the two wired network monopolies—the telegraph and the telephone. So newspaper companies began making plans to get in on the development of the new communications system. For them, radio telegraphy meant a cheaper alternative to telegraph and telephone. Journalists could visualize Marconi's invention as a vehicle for the movement of news over long distances into newspaper offices. A wire service without wires.

Few either in or out of newspaper offices seem to have thought very seriously just then about the potential of radio *broadcasting* to a mass audience. Radio would be for point-to-point messages: from a transmitter on shore to ships at sea; from a newsgatherer to the editors and the printing presses. Whether the messages were coded or straight from the voice box didn't matter much.

Ten years later, in 1916, New York newspapers improvised a special presidential election-night radio service, mainly for ships at sea. The erroneous news of Hughes' election was relayed by the *New York Herald* to wireless operators on ships and to a few hundred amateur receiving stations on the mainland. A direct phone line from the offices of the *Herald* carried the information to the radio station transmitter in the ship news office at the Battery in New York, from whence the signal was sent through the airwaves out over the Atlantic Ocean.

After World War I, any mechanically minded person with a crystal and a head set could hook up a receiver and listen intermittently to music by using a bedspring as an aerial. Westinghouse, which was in the business of producing radio receivers, built a shack on the roof of its plant in East

Pittsburgh to house the first federally licensed experimental radio station. A transmitter operating with all the power of a 100-watt light bulb was ready just a few days before the election of 1920. An antenna was strung from a steel pole to one of the powerhouse smokestacks. At 8 o'clock on November 2—election night—the station that later became KDKA went on the air. Leo Rosenberg of Westinghouse's publicity office began reading returns that had been phoned to the shack from the newsroom of the *Pittsburgh Post*. During lulls between his reports, Rosenberg played records on a hand-cranked phonograph. Periodically, he asked his listeners to send him a postcard reporting their location. At midnight, he stopped reading. Westinghouse executives invited a number of prominent community leaders to join them for the evening at the Edgewood Club, where a receiver and loudspeaker system had been installed to hear the broadcast. Otherwise, the audience probably numbered between 500 and 1,000 crystal set owners. The corporate officials saw the evening's demonstration as a merchandising gimmick to sell more radio sets. The Pittsburgh papers reported news of the broadcast, but otherwise the first commercial radio station election-night service passed without notice.[2]

Meanwhile, the *Detroit News* had set up its special "radiophone" service— call letters 8MK—among the stacks of clippings in a corner of its morgue. On election night, an office boy rushed with the latest figures from the newsroom to the makeshift studio. If no one was available, the lad was instructed to switch on the voltmeter and read the numbers into the microphone himself.

In the streets outside, people crowded closer to see the slide projections from the *News'* magic lantern and hear the results announced by a man using a megaphone. Upstairs, 8MK was "hissing and whirring its message into space," but only about fifty technologically blessed amateur wireless operators within a radius of twenty or thirty miles could pick up the sound of the *News* radiophone.[3]

The significance of the new technology for election-night journalism was demonstrated by a simple incident that happened in central Illinois a short time later. The Atlass family was in the wholesale poultry business in the little town of Lincoln, Illinois. After his father started a bank in Chicago, Les Atlass applied for a federal license to operate an amateur radio station in Lincoln. He wanted the station to talk with his father about chicken prices and other financial information. Radio was cheaper than the telephone. In April of 1923 the voters of Lincoln elected a new mayor. George Newcomer, a prominent Logan County politician who lived in the nearby community of Mount Pulaski, wanted to learn the results of the Lincoln election as soon

You're on the Air

as possible without leaving home. Tall buildings with searchlights were in short supply on the Illinois prairie. The ever resourceful Les Atlass arranged to pick up the election figures from the local newspaper, the *Lincoln Courier,* and to broadcast them over his 10-watt transmitter, call letters 9DFC, to Newcomer in Mount Pulaski. The *Courier* ran a story about this, informing its readers in advance that there was no law preventing other people from tuning in too. "The air is not private," the newspaper noted. Hundreds of curious citizens who were lucky enough to own receivers listened in that night. The Atlasses later moved their equipment and their license to Chicago for a station that became WBBM (World's Best Broadcast Music), still one of the CBS network's owned and operated flagship stations.[4]

By 1924, the number of factory-made receivers in use in the United States had increased to over 2,500,000. More than 500 commercial radio stations were on the air. Broadcasting networks were hurried into service to provide the programs so that purchasers of radios would have something to listen to. In many communities newspaper owners used their political muscle to obtain one of the federal licenses for a place on the radio spectrum. By then, most newspaper editors were reconciled to the fact that radio would be the technology through which the score of a game or the outcome of an election could be announced first. It would be done, they realized, much faster than by any of the imaginative audiovisual devices that had occupied so much of their creative energies over the years. The coming of commercial radio took away most of the incentive for newspapers to project election results onto canvas screens draped across the entire side of a building, launch aerial bombs into the night sky, hire circus barkers to blare out the figures in a voice that could be heard in all corners of a vast arena, sweep the horizon with intricate patterns from the beams of powerful searchlights mounted on the tops of skyscrapers, persuade the power company to make lights blink off and on in unison all over town, arrange light bulbs in huge electric signs, or attach colored lights to the fuselage of low-flying airplanes.

By maintaining their control over the newsgathering facilities (the wire services), and by owning some radio stations themselves, newspaper publishers thought they could dictate the future of radio news. They were determined that that future of radio would be only as a bulletin service that would stimulate and not cut into the sale of newspapers.

Communications historians have noted a special irony in the 1920 election. Both of the major parties chose that year to nominate newspaper publishers from small towns in Ohio as their presidential candidates—Warren Harding, the owner of the *Marion Star,* by the Republicans; James M. Cox, owner of the Dayton and Springfield papers, by the Democrats. The selection of two midwestern publishers for the highest elective office in the land—a symbolic acting-out of the historic power of American newspapers in the political system—occurred just as newspapers were to about to lose their ability to report breaking news first. No longer would the American people have to wait for newspapers to tell them who had won an election. No longer would they have to ride a trolley car downtown and stand in a crowd of inebriated strangers shivering in the cold in front of a newspaper office window. No longer would they have to step out into the back yard in the middle of the night and peer into the distant sky first to identify the appropriate searchlight beam and then endeavor to translate the coded patterns of light.

Expenditures for newspaper political advertising dipped in the 1920 campaign, presumably because the race was so one-sided. The Republican Party hired advertising men Albert Lasker and Robert G. Tucker as publicity consultants. Tucker's task was to set up campaign activities that today we call "photo opportunities," but these were for another exciting new entertainment medium: the motion picture theater newsreels.

The Republican candidate in 1924, Calvin Coolidge, was the first to use radio effectively as a campaigning device. The Republicans operated their own radio station, which broadcast from New York City in the last weeks before the election. The Associated Press, owned by its newspaper members, still refused to sell its news to radio stations and networks. At that time, members of the AP were legally obliged to make their news product available for reuse by the AP and no one else. The *Chicago Tribune* defied the AP policy by making plans to share election returns with its own radio station—WGN. Come election night, the *Tribune* and more than two dozen other newspapers also supplied election-night returns to "their" broadcasters through an increasingly successful competitor wire service—the United Press.

Already the newspaper industry was divided between papers that owned radio stations and those that did not. Being more numerous, the latter faction dominated the AP, whose interests were different from those of the other wire services. UP and International News Service (owned by Hearst) were looking for customers and therefore more willing to serve broadcasters.

Editor & Publisher, the industry trade journal, did not miss the significance of what was happening. "Newspaper extras and bulletin boards looked like stage-coaches in the airplane age," *E & P* commented after the election.[5] Newspapers were advised by *E & P* either to "capture and control radio as an auxiliary force" or get ready to do battle with an increasingly formidable competitor. Karl Bickel, the president of UP, suggested to newspaper clients that they think of radio as "an extension of the bulletin board" on election night. If radio listeners understood that the returns were being made possible only through the big-hearted generosity of newspapers and their wire services, newspapers could only benefit from all the publicity and good will, or so Bickel said. AP faced up to competitive realities by agreeing to radio's use of news of transcendent national and international importance, beginning with election returns.[6]

Four years later, Herbert Hoover ran against the Democratic governor of New York, Al Smith. Between them the two national party committees spent more than a million dollars for the purchase of radio time in that campaign. Hoover, who spoke in a flat, bland but soothing voice, delivered a series of carefully prepared radio speeches. His opponent was ill at ease addressing what he thought of as a cold piece of metal suspended on a string. Smith's raspy, tinny East Side New York accent only reminded rural voters of his big-city origins. Nor could he be persuaded to sit still behind the microphone while he was speaking. He could not resist peering around the pie-plate-shaped gadget, which caused his voice to fade in and out over the "raddio," as he called it. Far from being mesmerized by the candidates' speeches, many listeners and sponsors rang up the station to complain when their favorite entertainment programs were preempted by the paid political broadcasts.

All three wire services went to the opposite extreme by making returns available to radio stations free of charge. The *New York World* and the Columbia network (now CBS) organized a cooperative election night broadcast from the city room of the newspaper. Microphones were placed alongside the telegraph and linotype machines to create the newsroom atmosphere.

Not all of the traditional methods of reporting the results were retired, however. More than 100,000 people stood outside the *Times* building watching the new "Motograph news bulletin"—a moving stream of words 5 feet tall in 13,200 electric lights that disappeared around the corner of the building sixty feet above Times Square. The *Boston American* and the *Richmond Times-Dispatch* sent their airplanes aloft. Green lights flashed beneath the wings when Smith was ahead; red lights signified good news for Hoover.

When the campaign was over, a veteran reporter for the *World*, Samuel G. Blythe, wrote in the *Saturday Evening Post* that radio "has slain the political orator. He is out. The day of the spellbinder is over."[7] Blythe was not alone in predicting that candidates henceforth would rise or fall on the tonal quality of their radio delivery. The substance of a speech would be lost, it was prophesied, unless the speaker possessed a good radio voice.

The best of the radio campaigners, unquestionably, appeared in 1932 when Franklin D. Roosevelt defeated Hoover. Told that a space between two of his lower front teeth produced a slight whistling sound over the air, Roosevelt ordered a removable dental plate that he stored in a heart-shaped box in his bedroom and inserted only when he was about to talk on the radio.

His fireside chats connected with troubled Americans in all parts of the nation. Social workers found that destitute families would sometimes give up their furniture and bedding before parting with their radio. Compared to FDR, Hoover's on-air delivery "had all the aural attraction of a bulldozer at work on a stone highway," according to one commentator.[8]

Radio stations, in the meantime, had been linked by long-distance telephone lines into coast-to-coast networks. NBC and then CBS were the first radio networks to form their own news departments in 1933. When phone lines were available on the whistlestop campaigns, radio journalists occasionally reported live from the field. But the job of hooking up amplifiers and switching equipment was technically so forbidding that few live "spots" were broadcast. Much of the time the radio reporters filed twice-daily telegraphic reports from the campaign trail, the same as their newspaper brethren. Their stories were then read over the air from the studio.

On election night in 1932, the Federal Radio Commission strongly prompted stations to either broadcast the latest returns or stay off the air and avoid interfering with their neighbors' signal on the radio dial. Morse code operators received returns from the AP and INS in the New York studios of the radio networks until 2 A.M.. To total the votes, CBS engaged Dr. Salo Finkelstein, described as a "lightning calculator." The figures were posted on a chalk tally board and read over the air by announcers.

Already the sports influence affected how broadcasters reported election night news. One of CBS's announcers was Ted Husing, a star sportscaster. On NBC, the returns were read in his most excitable ringside voice by another great sports announcer—Graham McNamee.

In Los Angeles, the Great Atlantic and Pacific Tea Company grocery stores gave shoppers free election tabulation charts and bought up all the available election night commercial time on the two leading radio stations. That way their customers could keep score while listening to the returns on radio (and munching on A & P snack food).

However different the technology, the spirit of horse-race journalism

proved irresistibly contagious. In Rockford, Illinois, one station—WROK—
even started its own straw poll, sponsored by the Central Illinois Electric
and Gas Company. Survey results were read over the air every night, and listeners were invited to keep their own charts of the running results. Broadcasters were not content merely reporting the returns much faster than the
pencil press could; they, too, entered the race to anticipate what was going
to happen instead of waiting for it to happen.

As economic conditions worsened in the early 1930s, publishers put
aside their differing interests and agreed that radio should be denied the
AP's election night service. INS did likewise. UP proposed to charge the
radio networks half the total cost of its entire election night operations.
The networks refused and began organizing their own news departments.

At the end of 1933, representatives of NBC, CBS, the American Newspaper Publishers Association, and the wire services met at the Biltmore
Hotel in New York to hammer out a strange compromise which came to be
called "the Biltmore Agreement." First of all, the networks agreed not to
engage in nonlocal newsgathering on their own—disarming, in effect, their
own news services. In return, the newspaper executives authorized the crea-
tion of a new entity called the Press-Radio News Bureau. Beginning in
March of 1934, the bureau culled news from AP, UP, and INS for just
enough news bulletins to fill two five-minute radio news segments each day.
The news items could be no more than thirty words in length. Neither of
the daily news programs could be commercially sponsored. Radio commentators were specifically prohibited from talking about news of events less
than twelve hours old. Occasional other bulletins "of transcendent importance" were to be provided the broadcasters, but only "in such a manner
as to stimulate interest in the newspaper report." The agreement bound
only the 86 stations affiliated with CBS and the 84 stations affiliated with
NBC. The more than 400 independent stations were free to sign up with
one of several rival newsgathering agencies.

UP and INS pulled out of the agreement in 1935. The uncontrollable
competition finally led to the dissolution of the Press-Radio News Bureau
in 1938. Most publishers knew it was futile to deny broadcasters access to
election night returns. Due partly to the cross-ownership of some of the
leading radio stations and newspaper companies, the print media persisted,
however, in what seems today like a blindly misguided fantasy that broadcast
news could be restricted to skimpy bulletins.[9]

Twelve

The Trials and Tribulations of George Gallup

As the theory and practice of consumer market research became more sophisticated in the 1920s, planners of voting-behavior news polls knew only enough to be jittery. Newspaper and magazine editors did not have to be statistical wizards to understand that the electorate consisted of disparate groups of voters, that they did not all turn out to vote all the time, and that the sampling of their opinions was tricky business. For a mayoral election in 1923, the editors of the *Chicago Tribune* realized that: (1) the rich and the poor had different voting concerns; (2) though the rich almost always found the time to vote on election day, they were not inclined to mingle in public places as others did, shopping for groceries and performing other menial chores; (3) the affluent, therefore, might not be adequately represented in a poll conducted on a street corner or at some other public place. The *Tribune* dealt with this problem by conducting what may have been the first newspaper telephone poll. Most upper-class families had telephones in their homes. So reporters from the newspaper called up some of Chicago's Gold Coast citizens and inquired about their voting intentions. The results were sprinkled in with the other straws to arrive at a more comprehensive measure of voter sentiment.

The significant question here was not so much whether people who lived in the high-rent district and had telephones were different (which in some respects they obviously were) but whether, as a class, their *voting preferences* were likely to be different. The voting habits of telephone subscribers were on the minds of the editors of the most widely acclaimed of the national polls, the *Literary Digest,* for other reasons. The editors of the *Digest* were flabbergasted by the nationwide attention that their poll received every election season. Going into the 1930s, *LD* had predicted the winner of every presidential election with impressive electoral-vote accuracy. The magazine accomplished this by soliciting the voting intentions of lists of Americans drawn primarily from telephone directories and automobile registration records. Flattered by the publicity generated by the poll, *LD* used it to sell subscriptions to the magazine. Preparing the sample ballots for mailing was made to appear almost as dramatic as the election itself. "The rumble of activity stirs the blood," readers were told, as 2,500 clerks (all "men and women of superior penmanship") addressed more than 20 million sample ballot solicitations that were lugged to the post office in 12,000 mail bags.[1] When Democrats complained in 1924 that "Republican postmasters" were collecting undelivered ballots and voting them en masse for the Republican candidate, LD shrugged off the possibility. Most of the postmasters were Democrat holdovers anyhow, the editors replied, so it couldn't be much of a problem.

Behind the promotional hype, the editors were as aware as anyone of the vulnerability of their system. Upton Sinclair and other social critics pointed out repeatedly what the magazine editors recognized to be true: that the Republican vote was invariably overestimated in any mailed ballot poll. And LD's sample had to be unrepresentative because the only eligible participants were people who could afford telephone service or cars.

Literary Digest conceded that the poll results from some states had to be unbelievable. These the magazine simply disregarded. The poll was actually a highly selective interpretation of straw-poll findings. On October 11 in 1924, for example, the magazine noted that "Democratic returns [from southern states] have been slow to come in, due partly to technicalities in the mailing of the ballots."[2] When it came time for electoral vote predictions, the *Digest* ignored the straw poll in favor of the time-honored wisdom of past experience. Then in 1928 the *Digest* said up front that Hoover could not be expected to carry the two solidly Democratic southern states of Alabama and Arkansas even though the poll indicated (quite erroneously) that he would. The magazine made no attempt to explain away its repeated underestimate of the Democratic vote. In 1928 it forecast 63.2 percent of the popular vote for Hoover. He actually received 58.8 percent, a substantial discrepancy.

Because all the presidential elections in the 1920s were quite one-sided, however, and the results divided less along socioeconomic class lines than would shortly be the case, LD was able to come close to the correct electoral vote totals.

Just before the election of 1932, the magazine nervously informed its readers: "We make no claim to infallibility. We did not coin the phrase 'uncanny accuracy' which has been so freely applied to our polls. We know only too well the limitations of every straw vote, however enormous the sample gathered, however scientific the method."[3]

Again this time the poll badly overestimated the Republican vote for President Hoover, misallocating five of the forty-eight state electoral outcomes. In one of its 1932 poll reports, the *Digest* had to admit that "our ballots have somehow failed to come back in adequate quantity from large bodies of Democratic voters" in Massachusetts and Rhode Island.[4] The poll also showed Hoover carrying New Jersey, but the magazine warned its readers that "silent Democratic voters" would probably deliver all three states to Roosevelt. *LD* projected a national popular vote of 59.85 percent for Roosevelt, remarkably close to his actual 59.14 percent. It is now apparent that the *Digest* was saved in 1932 by the fact that the anti-Hoover protest stretched across all income levels—including people with telephones and motor cars.

Basking in the national notoriety, *LD* came to believe that the dangers could be buried by mailing out more and more ballot solicitations and reaching still more new potential subscribers. In 1928, 19 million ballots were put in the mails, of which 2,767,263 were returned. James Farley, the Democratic national chairman, had nothing but praise for the "fairly and honestly conducted poll."

Others were disturbed though by the "profound impression" the *Literary Digest* poll had made on the conduct of the election. Those were the words of Walter Lippmann, editor of the liberal *New York World*. Lippmann questioned the social usefulness of a device which he said "caters to mere curiosity, makes debate a pretense and argument futile." "Is it in the best interest of popular government," he asked, "that the people should have an infallible device by which the result of an electoral campaign is known before the issues have been seriously discovered?"[5]

Other news organizations grew increasingly envious of *Literary Digest*'s quadrennial fame. Several of them made plans to start their own national polls. A thirty-year-old statistician named Archibald Crossley had quit his job as director of research for *LD* in 1926 to begin a national poll for the Hearst newspapers. In 1936 another young man, Elmo Roper, developed a presidential election survey for *Fortune* magazine.[6]

The third of the newcomers—the one who would have the greatest impact on political journalism—was a former farm boy from Iowa: George Horace Gallup. His father, an eccentric agrarian philosopher who was obsessed with the study of theoretical logic, made a living by speculating in farmland. The family lived in an eight-sided farm house, his father's logical scheme to deny the terrible prairie windstorms a square target. Knowing that the senior Gallup hated Theodore Roosevelt, the others in the household twitted him by calling young George "Ted," a nickname he carried into adulthood. Ted Gallup also inherited the fanatic distrust of big-city "machine" politicians that was prevalent in the Corn Belt. He believed in pure country-style democracy unfettered by ward heelers and ghost pay-rollers.[7]

As a graduate student in psychology at the University of Iowa, Gallup devised a method of gauging the interest of readers in the contents of news-papers and magazines. He found that ads using sexual appeals and exploit-ing the vanity of readers caught their attention. Although this must have struck his father as utterly logical, Ted Gallup went on to conduct surveys for newspapers and other commercial clients while teaching college jour-nalism and advertising. In 1932, at age twenty-two, he moved to New York as research director of the Young & Rubicam advertising agency.[8]

In the meantime he had married the daughter of a weekly newspaper publisher in Iowa who was also something of a rarity in that state—a Demo-cratic Party politician. Gallup's father-in-law, Alex Miller, ran for governor of Iowa but died before the election. In Miller's honor, the party slated his widow, Ola Babcock Miller, for the elective office of Iowa secretary of state in 1932. Much to everyone's surprise, including Ted's, the Roosevelt land-slide proved so strong that the widow Miller and the entire Democratic state ticket were swept into office. Gallup was fascinated by voting patterns. Partly to help Mrs. Miller prepare for her reelection campaign, he mailed questionnaires to a sampling of voters in the 1934 off-year congressional elections. Adapting Colonel Taylor's key-precinct system, Gallup picked a few "barometer districts" and then assembled a mailing list that included the decisive demographic subgroups in proper proportions—what came to be called the quota sampling method.

He showed the 1934 results to a friend, Harold Anderson, who was the president of a syndicate that sold comic strips and other features to news-papers. Anderson thought Gallup's poll could be sold to editors. He in-vested enough of his own money for Gallup to rent a one-room office across the street from the campus of Princeton University. The original name of the enterprise—Editors Research Bureau—was quickly changed to the aca-demically more impressive American Institute of Public Opinion. A mail poll could succeed only if enough people took the trouble to send back their ballots, and Gallup thought the Princeton address would lend legiti-macy to the business.

Anderson set out to sign up users of a weekly public opinion poll to be called "America Speaks!" His task was made easier by Gallup's contacts with newspaper executives who had retained his readership consulting services. Their first client turned out to be an important trend-setter: Eugene Meyer, the publisher of the *Washington Post*. To promote the first installment in October of 1935, the *Post* chartered a blimp that cruised over the nation's

The Trials and Tribulations of George Gallup

capital towing a banner advertising "America Speaks!" Meyer generally supported Republican candidates (and did so in 1936) but he thought "there was a useful opportunity for checking editors, pressure group representatives and politicians in their unsupported statements with respect to public opinion."[9]

Gallup gambled his future by promising his thirty-five subscribing editors that their money would be returned if his 1936 preelection forecasts missed the mark. His preliminary inquiries told him that 59 percent of telephone subscribers and 56 percent of automobile owners would vote against Roosevelt—but only 18 percent of the many people who were on relief would oppose the president.

This revelation inspired Gallup to make an even bolder gamble. In one of his weekly reports barely a month after Governor Alf Landon of Kansas had been nominated by the Republicans, Gallup predicted what the *Literary Digest* poll would show—56 percent of the vote for Landon—and told the world that this time the *Digest* poll would be wrong. He was risking the future of his business on (1) a rival opinion poll over which he had no control; and (2) the outcome of an election that would not occur for another four months.

Wilfred Funk, the editor of the *Digest* was livid. He denounced the audacity of the inexperienced young ad man, in effect accepting the challenge. Even then *Literary Digest* made no effort to change its methods.

Roper, in the pages of *Fortune,* used a quota sample of only 4,500. He made a point of including 10 percent of the most prosperous citizens, 30 percent in the upper-middle range, 40 percent in the lower-middle bracket, and 20 percent of the poor. Roper warned, however, that a lower turnout by the most impoverished Americans could unsettle the equation. Nor did *Fortune* venture to guess the state-by-state electoral vote breakdown.

The third of the upstarts, Crossley, used a new sample every two weeks, combining telephone and personal interviews totaling about 30,000.

Ballots were said by *Literary Digest* to be "pouring back in an ever increasing stream" in early September. Funk panned the efforts of his competitors, making the familiar complaint that he had never heard of anyone who had ever been asked for an opinion by Gallup and the others. The only special precaution taken by *LD* was to mail ballots to one-third of all the registered voters in Chicago. Landon was shown to be the choice of 49 percent of Chicago's voters. In its final forecast, the magazine predicted that Landon would receive 54.89 percent of the popular vote and win 32 states with 370 electoral votes. FDR was given 40.7 percent of the vote—enough to carry but sixteen states.

Calling Elections

Roper's poll for *Fortune* gave Roosevelt 59.4 percent of the national vote. Crossley had a special problem with the Hearst empire, which was rabidly anti-Roosevelt in 1936. His projections were suspected of having been trimmed to pacify his employers. His 55 percent vote prediction for FDR was accompanied by headlines like this in the Hearst press: "Roosevelt in lead, but Crossley Poll finds Landon victory quite possible."

As election day drew near, Ted Gallup was having trouble sleeping. He suffered from severe "palpitations." Many of his now seventy-two newspaper subscribers were editorially opposed to Roosevelt's New Deal. Their editors did not hesitate to remind him that he'd better be right or there would be hell to pay. Finally Gallup's wife insisted that they wait out the last few days in the balmier surroundings of Sarasota, Florida.

The final Gallup Poll predicted that Roosevelt would receive 55.7 percent of the popular vote. The Democrats were said to be securely ahead in thirty-one states; Landon in only three. Fourteen other states were leaning Democratic; three were leaning Republican. Connecticut and Rhode Island were too close to call.

The Gallups bought a radio for their hotel room in Florida. Operating out of a four-room suite in Radio City New York, NBC posted the figures on a board as they came in from the Press-Radio News Bureau and from affiliated stations with access to newspaper returns. Hearing Graham McNamee read the first scattered results from northeastern states, Gallup and his wife split a bottle of champagne and retired for the night—happier and healthier than before.

When all the figures were in, President Roosevelt had received 62.5 percent of the two-party vote. He carried 46 of the 48 states and collected 523 of the 531 electoral votes. *Literary Digest* had placed 32 states in the wrong column. Landon wound up with 37 percent of the popular vote (32 percent in Chicago).

Because the betting odds on the election had anticipated the landslide, many Americans thought they could make a killing by following the *Digest*'s tip and betting on Landon. "It would be hard to estimate the enormous sums of money that were lost by enthusiastic Landonites in the last days of the campaign," complained Senator Kenneth McKellar, Democrat of Tennessee, who did the only thing he could upon receiving the angry complaints of his constituents: He demanded a Senate investigation of the *Literary Digest* poll.[10]

Gallup did not gloat for long. His poll had under-estimated the Democratic landslide, missing four states, plus the two that he had called even. He knew that the error lay in the low return of mailed ballots by low-income voters, and vowed never again to use the mails in a presidential election poll. The *New York Times* and the now-merged *New York Herald-Tribune* (which had printed the Gallup reports) criticized presidential polls in their postelection retrospectives.

Funk reacted differently. Insisting that the mistakes could not have been avoided, he ridiculed the quota sampling methods of his three competitors. "The *Literary Digest* has never been able to determine how many rich men, poor men, G-men, racketeers, and candlestick makers voted in a given election," he told the *New York Times*.[11]

The *Digest* folded within a year. Although the 1936 poll snafu is widely blamed for the demise of *LD*, there were other factors as well. Economic conditions were dreadful, and *Fortune*'s sister weekly, *Time*, had taken readers and advertising away from other national magazines.

With or without the *Literary Digest*, the Gallup Poll had found its niche in newspaper journalism. Only two clients cancelled after the election. Most of the major metropolitan markets were represented in Gallup's list of subscribers by prestigious newspapers, the *Post* in Washington, the *Herald-Tribune* in New York, the *Globe* in Boston, the *News* in Detroit, the *Daily News* in Chicago, the *Bulletin* in Philadelphia.

Newspaper polls were part of the presidential campaign scene and would remain so. "A new and exciting venture in journalism," Gallup called it, "reporting not just what people do but what they think."[12] The popularity of the polls had shown that people were just as interested in the outcome of an election as they were in the winner of an athletic event, he remarked after returning to New Jersey.

Thereafter Gallup referred often to an opinion poll as the equivalent of a nationwide primary election that would diminish the hidden power of pressure groups. One day, he predicted, newspapers would have a public opinion editor on the staff.

The three best-known practitioners of public opinion polls understood the necessity of sampling groups of voters in proportion to their presence in the electorate. If the rich and the poor were expected to vote differently, then it was important to be certain that your sample included the proper numbers of rich and poor. Gallup also entered the commercial market-research field, giving his company a dependable base of year-round financial support. It was their news polls, however, that made household names of Gallup and Roper and Crossley. Moreover, the methods and procedures for conducting those polls—polls to be reported as election campaign news—would be made to conform to the competitive specifications of newspaper and magazine editors—which is to say, the needs of horse-race journalism. Editors had no desire to spend money on what they derisively dismissed as "thumb-sucking" stories about abstract policy issues. Readers were interested in the race, and the polls would tell them about the race.

Gallup tried to apply "scientific" methodology to polling. His 700 part-time interviewers were paid 65 cents an hour to contact assigned numbers of particular types of voters. At first, interviewers set out to fill their quotas wherever they could find the right combinations of male-female, urban-rural, Catholic-Protestant, rich-poor, etc., who would answer their questions. Gallup's supervisors did not care where the interviews took place.

Another feature of the system bothered politicians. The raw figures were adjusted to allow for differences in probable voter turnout. If there was reason to expect, for instance, that people on relief would not bother to vote at the same rate as others in the population, then the responses from that group would be discounted accordingly.

The Gallup Poll underestimated President Roosevelt's reelection margin against Wendell Willkie in 1940 and against Governor Thomas E. Dewey in 1944. The poll understated the president's vote both years in two-thirds of the states. To please his customers, most of whom were opposed editorially to the policies of the New Deal, Gallup put the best possible Republican spin on the news releases that accompanied the poll reports. At the end of October 1944, while professional gamblers were quoting odds heavily favoring FDR, Gallup reported that the election could go either way.[13] The president won handily.

After the election of 1944, the House of Representatives impaneled a "technical committee" to review Gallup's methods. Gallup might have balked on First Amendment grounds, but he chose to cooperate with the committee. The panel, made up mainly of government experts in survey research, faulted the training and supervision of interviewers and the basic sampling process.[14]

Gallup had experimented in 1944 with some "pinpoint sampling"—concentrating on certain "barometer counties" that had a history of crossing party lines to vote for the winning candidate. Some of the experts argued that the quota sampling system should be replaced by a more precise random selection of specific households. The pollsters from Gallup's company listened to the advice but were put off by the formidable logistical task of reaching a predetermined assortment of specific individual voters.

With the presidential election of 1948, this turned into considerably more than a methodological quarrel at a convention of statisticians. Harry S. Truman had succeeded to the presidency upon the death of Roosevelt.

The Trials and Tribulations of George Gallup

Running on his own in 1948, Truman was opposed by Governor Dewey. During the election season, Gallup was supplying four poll reports a week to 126 newspapers with 20 million readers. From the beginning, his polls and those of his competitors agreed that Dewey had a big lead.

Embarking on a whistle-stop train tour across the country, Truman accused the pollsters of conspiring with his Republican foes in a deliberate campaign of misinformation to discourage his supporters from voting. Gallup struck back. He said the president would be singing a different tune if the numbers showed him in front.

Apart from the historic fact of Truman's dramatic come-from-behind victory, the campaign provided the first stark evidence of how news polls influenced journalistic interpretations and the substantive coverage. The modern era of horse-race journalism had arrived.

The influence touched even those newspapers, such as the prestigious *New York Times,* that avoided the publication of polls. In October William H. Lawrence wrote for the *Times* from Cleveland that "the final Ohio political story *will be* written in the figures of Dewey's majority for President in that state" (my emphasis).[15] Truman would wind up carrying Ohio.

Although the *Times* did not publish the Gallup Poll, it did refer to state polls and to "man-in-the-street" surveys to buttress its many outlook stories. Star political reporter James A. Hagerty reported in his national roundup that Dewey "appears certain to win." His story was accompanied by a table listing the probable division of electoral votes state-by-state. Dewey was awarded 333 of those votes to 90 for Truman. On the last Sunday before the election, Hagerty's lead story proclaimed that Dewey "will win . . . based on reports from correspondents of the *New York Times* in each of the 48 states."

"Dewey Holds Commanding Lead in Poll," headlined the *Los Angeles Times* on October 20. The *Times* ran seven Gallup poll stories in thirteen days. Gallup's figures fed their way through the other coverage in cyclical fashion. The Los Angeles paper, for example, ran another story a few days later reporting that "Man-in-Street Sees Victory of Gov. Dewey." Having been told by the Gallup Poll that Dewey would win, readers told reporters that they thought Dewey would win. A week before the election, the *Times* in Los Angeles informed its readers: "Speculation Rife on Dewey Cabinet" and "Guards [meaning the Secret Service] Ready for Task if Dewey Wins."[16] The final Gallup Poll story in Los Angeles started with this lead: "Governor Dewey will win the presidential election with a substantial majority of electoral votes." There was no mention of the size of the sample or when the last poll was conducted.[17]

Other pollsters reported similar results. Roper was so certain of the out-come that he stopped interviewing two months before the election.

Correspondents who traveled with either candidate knew the game was over. Richard L. Strout wrote in the *Christian Science Monitor* on October 14:

> It is now as certain as anything can be in the course of American politics that Gov. Dewey is elected and the nation knows it, and yawns over the final three weeks of the campaign, whose outcome was certain before it began.[18]

Arthur Sears Henning, the seventy-one-year-old chief of the Washington bureau of the *Chicago Tribune,* sat down at his typewriter before 9 o'clock on election day morning and wrote the story that carried the now-famous banner headline: "Dewey Defeats Truman."

Excluding the third- and fourth-party candidates in that election, Henry Wallace and J. Strom Thurmond, here is how the two-party vote compared alongside the three major polls:

	Dewey	Truman
Roper	52.2%	37.1%
Gallup	49.5	44.5
Crossley	49.9	44.8
Actual	45.1	49.5

Syndicated columnists were taken in as well by the polls. Many of them had already delivered columns for release on the day after the election speculating on the effects of Dewey's triumph. Even the august Walter Lippmann had conceded the presidency to Dewey. All that remained to be decided, he intoned in early October, was control of the Senate. On the day after the election, the *St. Petersburg Evening Independent* in Florida printed a black border around the empty space ordinarily devoted to the columns of analysis. "This space is respectfully reserved for our pundits who were so certain of the election results that they predicated their columns for today on Dewey's election," the newspaper said.[19]

History books now picture Harry Truman as a heroic, courageous figure in that campaign. That wasn't the story line, however, until *after* the election. "Reporters were working on the assumption that Truman would lose," the political scientist Thomas E. Patterson reminds us. "They constructed highly selective images, called up to account for winning or losing. Truman-the-likely-loser was perceived and reported differently by journalists than Truman-the-surprise-winner. His harsh rhetorical style in the first instance was strident and offensive and in the second instance was hard-hitting and appealing." Patterson uses the example as evidence of another important principle of horse-race journalism: reporters assign images to candidates consistent with how well the polls say the candidates are doing.[20]

"The polls colored the thinking of 'the experts' all down the line," the *New York Times* admitted after the election. A correspondent for the *Times* spoke of the vested interest that newspapers had in presenting a consistent story line that did not baffle the reader. One of the experts, James Reston, told his editors that reporters following the candidates were too isolated from voters and "far too impressed by the tidy statistics of the polls."[21]

Radio comedians ridiculed the fallen pollsters. Fred Allen said they were "people who count the grains of sand in your bird cage and then try to tell you how much sand there is on the beach."[22]

Gallup survived the crisis this time by accepting some of the outside advice. A blue-ribbon committee of academics detected some of the obvious problems. Interviews were discontinued too soon. A disproportionate share of those who said they were undecided apparently made up their minds on the final weekend to stick with Truman. Nor did the sample include enough voters on the lower end of the educational scale.

The committee also revived the quota sampling issue. True, the distribution of interviews took note of the diversity in the population, the experts agreed. But the interviewers could range far afield in filling their quotas, creating uncertainty as to the representativeness of the findings.

So, in the aftermath of the debacle of 1948, the Gallup Poll adopted a new probability sampling system. Within the different regions of the country, sampling areas were selected to produce a cross section of the national electorate. The sampling areas were chosen—in areas where interviewers were available—to accurately reflect demographic differences and past voting behavior. The typical interviewer might be a teacher who picked up his clipboard and questionnaires after school. He would be given a map identifying a randomly selected city block or segment of a rural township somewhere in the sampling area. Beginning at 3 o'clock, the interviewer would move from a specific corner or road intersection around the block or down the road, knocking at every other door. Before 6 o'clock, an effort was made to reach the youngest female over age 21 in that household. Attention after 6 o'clock turned to the youngest voting-age male. Typically the political questions would be piggybacked onto a list of commercial product preference questions. Although Gallup's fees might range as high as $500 a week for a large newspaper, it was his far more lucrative commercial market-research business that continued to subsidize the news polls. Reports were mailed from the 160 or so interviewers to Princeton, where they were tabulated. In the final stages of a presidential election campaign, Gallup would increase the sample size from the normal 1,500 to 10,000 or more.

Gallup made one other important policy decision in the wake of the 1948 reassessment. No longer would the Gallup Poll predict the electoral vote breakdown. Not many people realized that the poll underestimated Truman's total vote by less than it had missed Roosevelt's vote in 1936. In 1936 the Democratic margin of victory had been so large that the error did not affect the prediction of the outcome. A smaller error in 1948 caused Gallup to seriously misread the electoral vote projection. He predicted 134 electoral votes for Truman, but the president wound up receiving 304 electoral votes. Gallup and his statisticians knew that their sample was large enough to support the projection of the national popular vote with reasonable mathematical confidence. But the samples were not big enough, usually, to forecast the result in an individual state.

His customers were not pleased by this decision. Editors groused at the possibility, remote as it was, that the candidate who "won" the Gallup Poll could also finish ahead in the popular vote but fail to receive a majority of the electoral votes. Other journalists were suspicious of Gallup's adjustments based on the expected variations in voter turnout. They were convinced, some of them, that the farmer from Iowa had failed to appreciate the ability of big-city machines to bring out Democratic voters.

After the election, the *Saturday Evening Post* commissioned a uniquely talented young man to make sense out of Truman's miracle for the readers of that magazine. His articles announced the debut of a new strain of election campaign analysis that was an extension of—and alternative to—the scientific poll.

Samuel Lubell made it work brilliantly because of his rare combination of skills. He was a master interviewer, adept at steering any conversation with a stranger, who was also blessed with a scholarly mind and a Greeley-like fascination with old election records. Born in Poland, Sam grew up on the Lower East Side of New York. After graduating from Columbia University, he hitchhiked around the United States and tried his hand as a freelance political journalist. He fine-tuned the methods of the pollsters by concentrating his campaign inquiries on specific crucial "streams of voters" and then analyzing the results in the light of past voting returns down to the precinct level. Lubell began his study of an election by identifying groups of voters who might shift from one party to another. He would then visit the places where those people lived and worked. A friendly, garrulous fellow by nature, he chatted with his subjects about the weather, about farm prices,

The Trials and Tribulations of George Gallup

about his interviewee's leaky roof—never straightforwardly about politics. No clipboards or questionnaires were in sight. Only later would the conversation turn to the election. Election returns are "scrolls of the past" that can reveal the present and future as well, he said. "One main difference between my own interviewing of voters and that done by polling organizations lies in this effort to measure the continuity with—and departure from—the past. My techniques, in other words, can best be pictured as sampling not individuals, but streams of voters, moving in continuity with the past and in the context of the communities they live in."

Lubell went on to explain in his book, *Revolt of the Moderates*, published in 1950:

> My talks with voters have impressed me with how much of the vote is determined by things campaigners hardly mention. . . . A prime tool of voting analysis is to plot the contrasts among different groups and how these change from election to election. As often as not Americans vote against rather than for something, and how their ballots polarize bares the underlying tensions and conflicts in our history. . . . This technique of concentrating one's interviews in definable voting areas also corresponds more closely than does random sampling to the actual dynamics of how people decide for whom to vote.[23]

The success of his articles for the *Post* enabled Lubell to branch out into newspaper syndication. He competed for newspaper outlets with the Gallup Poll and other polls. His "The People Speak" interpretive reports appeared in many prominent newspapers on into the 1960s. The *Philadelphia Bulletin, Chicago Daily News, Detroit Free Press,* and *Minneapolis Star* were among his regular users. Some newspapers printed both Gallup and Lubell, using the latter to give a human dimension to the poll numbers. During the 1952 campaign Lubell talked to about 3,500 voters. He went looking not for a cross section of the entire electorate, but for the separate parts of the New Deal coalition that had elected Roosevelt in 1932 and returned Democrats to office in every presidential election since. There, he correctly divined, the election would be decided. Unlike other reporters, Lubell avoided politicians and local political editors. He substituted the techniques of historian and gifted interviewer for Gallup's margins of statistical error.

Gallup lost a few customers after 1948, but not many. Many traditionalists in journalism were faced with a conundrum. They neither understood nor trusted "scientific polls," yet they recognized the necessity of reporting what voters were thinking. The Associated Press ordered its correspondents to do more "grass roots" interviewing. This prompted one skeptical editor to remark that "a grass root usually consists of a local political writer." Member newspapers were asked by the AP to canvass political thinking on the local level and contribute to a nationwide survey of political opinions. Although the AP survey correctly forecast a Republican victory in 1952, the editors were not enthusiastic about entrusting local responsibility to assorted newspapers of multifarious partisan hues. A poll of AP managing editors after the election found 55 percent opposed to the practice.[24]

The *New York Times* had by mid-century established an unprecedented national reputation for thorough, serious, fair-minded journalism. The *Times* was immune from many of the commercial pressures afflicting lesser organs. The *Times* originated all of its editorial matter. It did not publish features syndicated by others. It was not interested in Gallup or Lubell. Nor were its editors of a mind to embark on its own public opinion poll. Turner Catledge, the managing editor, had been schooled in the long-established practices of political reporting. In 1936 he and his friend, Russell Wiggins, then with the *St. Paul Pioneer Press,* later editor of the *Washington Post,* traveled the country by motor car on pleasant junkets that they called "scouting trips." They would sound out a local political reporter and maybe a politician or two.

Catledge reacted to the 1948 disaster by calling for change—in tiny increments. He began by instructing his staff at the beginning of the 1952 campaign to make only those predictions that could be "hung on a qualified source." He made the prescient observation that political leaders were less than totally reliable authorities on voting behavior. Even those who shared their assessments honestly were no longer able to control massive blocs of voters as in the past. The *Times* wanted a brand of horse-race journalism that would strive to anticipate events—including elections. But those forecasts were to be "hung on" knowledgeable sources; and Turner Catledge was not at all sure that the usual coterie of party bosses fit the specifications any longer. "We prefer to subordinate their [political leaders] opinions to those of the voters themselves," Catledge said.

> We should like as much sounding of actual voters as is physically possible. As good sources, the following are suggested for obvious reasons: Filling station attendants, who are virtually automatic poll-takers; hotel desk clerks, hotel lobby cigar stand operators; local newspaper polls, or those conducted by other responsible organizations; club cars on the railroads; taxicab drivers and similar working people who come in contact frequently with the public. Stories can be salted liberally with quotes from these "men in the street," with their names and occupations included.[25]

Thirteen

The Conversion of
the Alsop Brothers

Joe Alsop was in the thumb-sucking business, but he prided himself on being, first and foremost, a good shoe-leather reporter. In the post–World War II years, he and his brother, Stewart Alsop, were coauthors of one of the capital's most influential syndicated columns. Joe made it a point to see in person—not telephone—at least four highly placed news sources every day. He believed that every column needed exclusive factual details underpinning the mushy layers of imperious wisdom.[1]

Born into the Connecticut Yankee aristocracy (they were distant cousins of Franklin Roosevelt), the Alsops had always enjoyed the many benefits of social privilege. Joe used his family's friendships to wangle a job, and eventually the syndicated column, at the *New York Herald-Tribune*. He impressed others as eccentric, foppish, supercilious, "outrageously Anglicized," according to one description.[2]

Successful columnists cultivated the attention of policy-makers in Washington—and vice versa. After Joe shared the column with his brother, some of their best scoops were gathered in at Sunday evening command supper parties in Joe's home on Dumbarton Street in Georgetown. Neither had much interest in the lives of ordinary people. Joe didn't bother even to own a radio.

Before the election of 1952, however, the Alsop brothers arrived at an important understanding. If their column was to thrive in the milieu of Sam Lubell and the Gallup Poll, it would be necessary to learn how to talk to voters as well as secretaries of state.

So, first Stewart and later Joe embarked on field exercises in the mysterious interior of the U.S. They went knocking on doors to feel the pulse of the Midwest. Padding down the grimy streets of South Chicago and the dusty roads of central Indiana, Joe must have been a startling sight in his owlish glasses and Savile Row suit. Neither was blessed with anything resembling Lubell's common touch. Few people would talk to the interplanetary visitors.

Retreating to Washington, they sought out a professional pollster who volunteered to show them how to do it. The man who signed on as their tutor was a rising star in the polling galaxy—Louis Harris. Harris had left his job in the Roper organization to set out on his own. He returned to the hustings with them and demonstrated some of the tricks of the trade. It helped to carry an official-looking clipboard, as, in Joe Alsop's words, "a sign of your bona fides."[3]

Neither of the Alsops would ever be comfortable talking to voters. Joe wrote later that the "doorbell-ringing forays left us more than ever mystified by the strange process that produces majority opinions in democracies like ours." But the important point is that he kept at it. Walter Lippmann, an acknowledged elitist who would never have been caught anywhere near South Chicago, once described the columnist's mission thuswise: If a columnist is doing his job, Lippmann said, the reader will never be surprised when something happens anywhere in the world. Another in the imperial order of columnists—Arthur Krock of the *New York Times*—made a revealing comment after Truman's victory in 1948. "The people," said Krock, "continue to respond to facts and emotions in a way to confound the prophets, including those whose livelihood depends on not being confounded."[4] If they were going to remain the opinion leaders of journalism, Krock, the Alsops, and the others had to aspire also to prophecy. To avoid being confounded by the people, the Alsops knew that it made good sense to seek out individual voters and try to gauge their sentiments.

The conversion of the Alsop brothers symbolized the recognition of the exalted position that the poll-takers had attained in politics and in journalism. In their case, as with many other columnists, this act of acknowledging the existence of the polls did not carry with it an endorsement of all the aggregate measurements of voting intentions routinely performed by Gallup and the others. Early in the campaign of 1960, Joe Alsop wrote a mini-exposé of the Gallup Poll for *The New Yorker*. His article, entitled "Dissection of a Poll," was remarkable for its ignorance of the methodology of probability sampling as practiced by, among others, his now good friend Lou Harris. Alsop could not fathom how the Republican nominee, Richard M. Nixon, could be 3 points ahead on August 17 and 3 points behind two weeks later. The manipulations that went on inside Gallup's counting house struck the columnist as something akin to witchcraft. He accused the pollsters of "cooking" the numbers while endeavoring to screen out likely nonvoters. He also faulted Gallup for what impressed Alsop as the highly speculative allocation of undecided voters into "leaners" for one or the other side. For all the lack of sophistication in his critique for the magazine, the columnist put his finger on two stubborn problems that would

The Conversion of the Alsop Brothers

always plague news polls. Since the objective of a preelection poll was to predict who would come out on top on election day—and not all people of voting age voted or were even registered to vote—it was necessary to weed out the probable nonvoters from the sample. Similarly, if the figures were to be presented to newspaper readers as the score of an athletic contest in progress, the undecideds had to be kept to a minimum. After all, the score of a baseball game is never 4 to 2 at the bottom of the third inning but with two runs undecided. Alsop also considered it vaguely reprehensible that Gallup's interviewers hired out occasionally to rival polling companies.[5]

All three of the syndicated news pollsters were exceedingly gun-shy nonetheless after the carnage of 1948. Appearing together at a conference of marketing executives a few days before the voting in 1952, Gallup refused to be drawn into even a conditional guess as to the probable outcome. Crossley called it a tossup. It could go either way, he said, depending on the size of the vote by traditional Democratic voting groups. Roper hunkered down in an even deeper shelter. He said either candidate could win and could win *by a landslide*.

Editors expected more horse-race definition for their money and less of this wishy-washiness. "We contracted for a service which says something, even if it turns out wrong," one of them complained to Gallup. The multiple "sets of contradictory statistics" were disappointing to another editor, this one a client of Roper's.

Gallup and his fellows in the polling trade need not have been so fretful. His final survey on November 3 listed 13 percent as still undecided, 47 percent for General Dwight D. Eisenhower, the Republican, and 40 percent for Governor Adlai E. Stevenson. the Democrat. The general finished with 54 percent of the popular vote to 46 percent for Stevenson. For the first time ever, Gallup bragged, the Republican presidential vote had actually been *underestimated* by a pollster. The next time around, when Eisenhower won reelection easily with 58 percent of the vote, the Gallup Poll reverted to form, *overestimating* the Republican's share at 59.5 percent.

Election night 1952 witnessed another scene that stands out now as a symbol of change more portentous even than the doorbell-ringing conversion of the Alsop brothers. It happened in what in recent history has been probably the most important nerve center of American journalism: the editors' bullpen in the newsroom of the *New York Times*. The staff of the *Times* organized its vast newsgathering resources in the customary fashion to report the outcome of the election. Following a ritual not much different from that of Colonel Taylor's *Boston Globe* back in the 1880s, the returns were received, tabulated, organized, and swiftly set in type. Reporter Richard Shepard was impressed by the "charm, poise, neat haircuts, preppy rigging, and assurance" of the paper's Washington correspondents who "flooded into 43rd Street, usurping desks and chairs." The key figure on the election night team was the "lean and craggy" veteran political specialist Jim Hagerty. A latter-day General Taylor, Hagerty's "paraphernalia consisted of a prodigious memory of who voted how and also of a fistful of cone-shaped charts that contained the voting history of pivotal districts." Shepard remembered fondly "the efficient hum of pros settling down to write history."[6] Special Western Union circuits connected the newsroom with correspondents across the nation. Between 10:52 P.M. and sunup the next morning, 749,623 papers rolled off the presses with the results of the election. Chartered planes flew copies of the 4:02 A.M. edition to readers in Washington. Among the many calculations made that night, someone recorded that 1,983 company-purchased sandwiches and 2,530 cups of coffee were consumed by *Times* employees during lulls in the work. The main edition contained an impressive 18 columns of tabular material. Edition after edition, the banner headline on the front page progressed from "Eisenhower Takes Strong Lead" to "Eisenhower Men Claim Sweep" to "Eisenhower Wins in Record Vote." The climactic event of the long night occurred shortly before 2 A.M. when Stevenson made a statement conceding defeat. In the bullpen where *Times* editors supervised the coverage, news editor Ted Bernstein turned on a device with an electronic screen that was mounted at the side of his desk. That way Bernstein could see and hear Stevenson's speech as it was being delivered. The editor ordered the presses stopped at once and words added to the front page. This he was able to do without waiting for a telegraphed message from the *Times* correspondent who was with the governor in Springfield. The little box with the little screen was, of course, a television set.[7]

Fourteen

The Story Is
in the Numbers

Election Night on television [is] entertainment about arithmetic.
The story is in the numbers.

Reuven Frank, NBC News

Getting ready for Election Night is not unlike training a horse for
the Kentucky Derby: enormous preparation for an event in which the
stakes are high and which is over very quickly.

Bill Leonard, CBS News

The first election night use of television occurred some time earlier—in
1940. An audience of 3,000 or so spectators wandered through the studios
of NBC's Radio City on that night in New York. Through soundproof windows, the visitors could watch the announcers at work reading the returns
over the radio. Or they could sit in front of one of the several monitors that
showed a motion picture of the Associated Press teletype machine printing the news reports. Occasionally NBC's television announcer, Ray Forrest,
would step in front of the camera and read the vote totals into a microphone.

Another experimental New York TV station, DuMont's W2XWV, was
operating with only 50 watts of power and had video but no audio. Its sound
transmitter was still being built. So DuMont focused its single camera on a
ticker-tape projector, enabling viewers to follow the faintly readable message as the tape flowed across the screen.[1]

World War II put a stop to the commercial development of television.
Four networks were in operation in 1948, however, one of them (DuMont)
owned by a manufacturer of receivers. Many of the major election season
telecasts were sponsored by national magazines as a promotional device.
Often the staffs of magazines like *Collier's, Life,* and *Saturday Evening Post*
played a part in the production of the television program. Cross-country
transmission of TV signals moved through the coaxial cable.

The networks were severely limited in their television coverage of the

Truman-Dewey campaign. Sig Mickelson, one of the pioneers in video news, remembers the coverage as "essentially radio with pictures."[2] The methods of television news were borrowed from radio with the slight influence of cinematic newsreels. Political reporting was seen as a useful way for television franchise holders to impress Congress and the FCC with their concern for the public welfare. The technology was much too formidable at first to treat the campaign as an unfolding narrative.

Election night itself was a different story, though. It was the first big made-for-television news story. In radio studio 22 at CBS, the revered Edward R. Murrow and his war-hardened comrades sat self-consciously on a raised platform. Special reporters had been hired around the country to call in the results on special telephone circuits. Uniformed pages chalked the numbers on a large tally board. Murrow and the others were appalled when the network cut off its live coverage in the early morning hours and treated the staff to a sumptuous breakfast while the outcome was still in doubt.[3] The Mutual Broadcasting Company, from its election night headquarters in the ballroom of the Ritz Carlton Hotel in New York, claimed to be a couple of minutes ahead of the news of Dewey's concession statement at 11:14 the next morning. Ted Gallup, in the meantime, was making the best of his discomfort as an on-camera expert analyst for ABC television.

NBC originated its election night broadcast from studio 8-H. Two stories high, the studio had been ordered by the network founder David Sarnoff in the 1930s. A huge cavity dug out of a midtown skyscraper, it was specially designed for Arturo Toscanini and the NBC symphony. Originally the great room floated on hydraulic springs to shield the music from the vibrations of the Sixth Avenue subway ten floors below.

On this night in 1948 NBC demonstrated its versatility by using eleven cameras in New York City and switching frequently to Washington for live pickups. H. V. Kaltenborn, its authoritarian commentator, pronounced Dewey the likely winner early in the evening. NBC's television signal was displayed on a 15-foot high screen erected in Rockefeller Center by RCA Victor.

When he returned to the air the next day, Ed Murrow said the election had destroyed forever "the mythology that the hopes, the fears, the prejudices, the aspirations of the people who live on this great continent can be measured and pigeonholed."[4]

The next presidential election, in 1952, was memorable for several reasons. It was the first for which the primary elections—the prenomination voting preliminaries coming in sequence—were reported by television much like the innings in a ball game. This week-to-week suspense added enormously to the horse-race nature of the presidential selection process. But it was also the last for which political leaders (led in this case by outgoing President Truman) could disregard the results of the primary tests and ordain their own chosen candidate: Governor Stevenson.

The most profound changes were caused by television itself. Those first television journalists, most of them having come from newspaper or wire-service backgrounds, were tentative and uncertain of what they were supposed to be doing. They were covering the story of the campaign as news, but it (television) had become the centerpiece of the story. The campaign was being conducted *on television*. Spot commercials were now being used to communicate with voters directly in their living rooms. Network crews lugged their ponderous 16mm. film cameras along the campaign trail. "We carried a thousand-pound pencil," said Fred Friendly of CBS. Boxes of lights, shades, lenses, amplifiers, cables, tripods, and the 12-volt storage battery that drove the camera motor weighted the journalists down. Three-minute rolls of black-and-white sound-on-film had to be flown to New York by prop-driven aircraft. A motorcycle courier would rush the cans to the processing lab. Sometimes the film editor would bite off the film with his teeth while the script was being written.[5]

Microwave relays extended the reach of television transmission to more cities. NBC and CBS shared the $80,000 expense of installing a temporary telephone company microwave link to Abilene, Kansas, for Eisenhower's announcement of his candidacy in June of 1952. The candidate scheduled a press conference the next day in Abilene. William S. Paley, the chairman of CBS, thought it would be a good idea for his network to utilize the microwave relay further by carrying the press conference live. When the newspaper reporters heard about this, they objected. They threatened first to boycott the conference. When that failed, the paper-and-pencil press made plans to flood the small theater with teams of Boy Scout messengers who would be kept busy running pieces of their copy to the Western Union telegraphers, disrupting the decorum of the event and probably the candidate's concentration as well. CBS went ahead and set up its cameras. The problem was brought to the attention of General Eisenhower himself, who said let the cameras stay. No Boy Scouts.

For its election night broadcast, NBC rolled out an electronic calculator. The machine, nicknamed "Mike Monrobot," made it possible to total the incoming results more quickly and then guess what the remaining votes would show. Mike was not nearly as advanced or as versatile, however, as the much more elaborate machine made available to CBS.[6]

Only a few weeks before the election, CBS representatives met with publicists from the office-supply company Remington Rand. The two companies worked out what they thought of as a routine promotional deal. Remington would provide at no cost to CBS the typwriters and adding machines needed on election night. In exchange, the cameras would occasionally zoom in close enough to pick up the company's logo on the appliances. Almost in passing, one of Remington's employees mentioned that the firm had recently acquired a subsidiary: the Eckert-Mauchly Computer Corporation. John W. Mauchly, a physicist, and J. Presper Eckert Jr., an engineer, had built the first commercial stored-memory digital-technology electronic computer—a machine that did arithmetic through electronic circuits. It was called UNIVAC—short for Universal Automatic Computer.[7]

How would CBS like to put UNIVAC to work on election night processing, projecting, and, yes, predicting voting returns? It would be a novel gimmick for the network and, if all went well, a windfall of publicity for the company.

A few days later, the top executives of CBS News trooped out to the Remington Rand plant in North Philadelphia to be introduced to UNIVAC. The console, which is on display today in the Smithsonian Institution, resembled a huge organ. Mickelson remembers the system as "a monster, a mass of electronic vacuum tubes interconnected by miles of copper wire and cooled by noisy fans." Its innards were housed in a processor 14 1/2 feet long and 9 feet high. Data entered the machine on reels of magnetic tape, to be stored away in the memory bank at the rate of 7,200 decimal digits per second.

The journalists thought of the gadget as an amusing side show that, Mickelson said, might be a "promotional shot in the arm" for the telecast. Charles Collingwood, an urbane world traveler who was one of "Murrow's Boys" on the news staff, had been assigned the role of election night interlocutor for UNIVAC. Collingwood happened to be late arriving at the factory for the first inspection tour. When he finally did join the others, the Teletype printer that was churning out hard-copy printouts of the messages from the computer began tapping out:

"Collingwood, you are late. Where have you been?" Collingwood and the machine thereby "established instant rapport," according to Mickelson. They got along famously thereafter.

A mathematician from the University of Pennsylvania, Max Woodbury, promised to prepare a program that could predict the outcome of the voting long before all the votes were in. All CBS had to do was supply:

(1) Enough comparative historical information to stock the brain cells of the machine, in advance.

(2) Enough fresh numbers on election night to make some meaningful comparisons.

These data consisted of voting returns from previous elections. If the computer was fed a steady stream of current results it could quickly match those figures with the returns from the same places in previous elections, and project the likely tally when all the rest of the votes had been counted. The machine would be performing two essential tasks—quickly. It would be adding the numbers as they became available, at the rate of 2,000 calculations per second; and it would be using a mathematical formula to compare those numbers with the earlier results. Woodbury and Remington's engineers acknowledged their dependence on an information base of statistical data from the past and on the prompt availability of comparable fresh numbers from easily identifiable places.

The computer scientists at Remington, referred to at the network as "those longhairs in Philly," did not realize the time that would be required to collect voting statistics from all over the country. CBS did the best it could in the brief time available. State-by-state returns were fed into the machine from the 1944 and 1948 elections. More important, the programmers were able to reconstruct the order in which the figures from eight key states had been counted in the previous two elections. Assuming that the new returns would be received from the same places at roughly the same times, it would be possible to project meaningful patterns. The returns from the eight states—New York, Pennsylvania, Massachusetts, Ohio, Illinois, Minnesota, Texas, California—were further subdivided into metropolitan and nonmetro tabulations. Time was too short to consider the construction of a nationwide key-precinct model, which the "longhairs" would have preferred. The phenomenal growth of the suburbs in the postwar years rendered many of the past precinct figures out of date anyway. Woodbury concluded, nevertheless, that there was a reasonable chance UNIVAC would be up to the task on election night.

By the 1950s all three wire services—AP, UP, INS—had devised reasonably efficient vote tabulating networks. Returns flowed from 155,000 polling places into the 3,000 county seats and then on to the regional, state, and national collection points. But the counting could be painfully slow in a paper-ballot county. Even allowing for the different time zones, the voting hours were highly irregular. Polls closed at 4 P.M. in Tennessee, at 9 P.M. in New York. Some ballots would never be included in the wire service count. As many as 300,000 absentee ballots would not be tallied for days.

Students of voting behavior learned the patterns. They knew, for example, that all nine eligible voters in Ellsworth, New Hampshire, would be

waiting at midnight to cast the nation's first ballots on election day. Someone would be there with a walkie-talkie to inform the wire service stringers
who were waiting in a nearby farm house to call the bureaus in Boston with
the information that General Eisenhower had vaulted into a 9-to-0 lead.
Thereafter the availability of returns usually followed a pattern, until
around 10 P.M. when whatever trends had been established usually would
not change.[8]

In any case, Mickelson did not care to gamble the network's journalistic
reputation on an unproven electronic gadget. "We decided to humanize it,
to treat it gently and semihumorously, but at the same time," he said, "give
full attention to the data it would produce."[9]

The journalists were not reassured by their knowledge that Remington
would be employing not one but three UNIVACs. The second would check
the work of the first; the third would be available for backup duty should
either of the other two break down. As the numbers were received at CBS
election headquarters in Manhattan, they were handed to the operators of
special electric typewriters called Unitypers. The figures were converted
into magnetized bits on magnetic tape and then dispatched in triplicate by
Teletype line to the three machines humming away in Philadelphia.

Walter Cronkite occupied the anchor desk in studio 41 on election night
in 1952. Tally boards lined three sides of the room. Wire service Teletype
machines chattered in the center. By 8:30 P.M. EST, the UNIVAC in center ring told its solicitous attendants that Eisenhower looked like a landslide winner. The chances were said to be 100-to-1 that this would happen!
UNIVAC projected 43 states and 438 electoral votes for the Republican
and 5 states and 93 votes for Stevenson.

The professors in Philadelphia could not believe their eyes. They were
dumbfounded. They, like Mickelson and Collingwood, had been reading
the preelection prophecies of the pundits that the election would be close.
Arthur F. Draper, Remington's director of advanced research, looked for
errors or inconsistencies in the work product of the computers, but could
find none. He and Woodbury tinkered with the program, altered some of
the figures, and ran another test. This time it showed 28 states and 317
electoral votes for Ike.

By now it was 9 o'clock and Collingwood was killing time in New York.
"UNIVAC, our fabulous mathematical brain, is down in Philadelphia mull-
ing over the returns that we've sent it so far," he mused over the air. "A few
minutes ago, I asked him what his prediction was, and he sent me back a
very caustic answer. He said that if we continue to be so late in sending him
results, it's going to take him a few minutes to find out just what the pre-

diction is going to be. So he's not ready yet with the predictions, but we're going to go to him in a little while."

In a little while, more adjustments in the hookup between the available totals and the data bank produced a more credible projection: 24 states for each candidate. That was more like it—270 electoral votes for Eisenhower, 261 for Stevenson, a horse race. At 10 P.M. Collingwood reported Ike the probable winner at much tighter 8-to-7 odds.

Not until shortly before 11 P.M. did Ed Murrow report that Eisenhower had definitely won. By this time enough raw figures had been amassed for Mike Monrobot and NBC to arrive at the same conclusion, without benefit of stored memory.

Sam Lubell, over CBS radio, had enough key-precinct information shortly after 8 o'clock to tell the audience that Ike had cracked the Solid South and appeared to be well on his way to victory.

UNIVAC's first projection at 8:30 P.M. estimated Eisenhower's eventual popular vote at 32,915,000. The official canvass counted 33,936,252. The next president wound up with 442 electoral votes, four more than UNIVAC's initial projection.

Later in the night, Collingwood asked Draper what had gone wrong with UNIVAC's "momentary aberration."

Draper responded:

> Well, we had a lot of troubles tonight. Strangely enough, they were all human and not the machine. When UNIVAC made its first prediction, we just didn't believe it. So we asked UNIVAC to forget a lot of the trend information, assuming that it was wrong . . . [but] as more votes came in, the odds came back, and it is now evident that we should have had nerve enough to believe the machine in the first place.

Newspapers naturally considered all this highly amusing. An editorial in the *Washington Post* pontificated: "None of these stupid humans, including his inventors, could believe [UNIVAC] so they started jiggling . . . and ended by throwing the poor thing out of whack entirely, which seems to prove that those old fellows were right after all who said only a hair's line of difference separates true genius from madness."[10]

Collingwood's flippant treatment of his partner's incredible feats helped to blunt the occasional criticism that came later. Some people were disappointed that the customary night-long suspense had apparently been ended with the connivance of a machine. Others noticed that the forecasts were being broadcast nationwide while some voters were still waiting to cast their ballots on the West Coast.

UNIVAC stumbled badly in the mid-term congressional elections two years later. Caught up in the race to be first, the network's over-eager journalists made premature and, as it developed, erroneous projections of landslide Democratic congressional victories based on the computer's fragments of information.

Barring fraudulent manipulation of ballots, an election is always over when the polls close. The decision has been made. All that remains is for the votes to be counted. Then, as always, the reporting of this news depended on the timely availability of the numbers in some sort of predictable, meaningful order. Having computers meant that the mathematical scut work could be done instantly. Problems remained, however—all the more so in off-year elections—and the many pieces of ambiguous information had to be put into some form that could be given meaning. As more jurisdictions changed from paper ballots to machine voting, the order of making the results known to the news media became far less foreseeable.

The shock waves that were set off by UNIVAC's magic had their expected effect. Rival networks engaged in a game of technological leapfrog. For the 1956 election, NBC acquired the services of a computer with an even larger capacity from the IBM corporation. Sixty-two leased wires from AP sped the flow of returns into Radio City. The figures were entered on IBM punched-cards, statistically perused by the computer, and flashed to "Election Central."

NBC also contracted with Teleregister Corporation to dress up the graphic presentation of the numbers. The company developed the first wall-to-wall banks of digital tally boards. Television executives learned that many election night viewers switch to the network that appears to have the most raw figures. That placed a premium on having frenetically active tote boards in sight every few minutes. NBC's spectacular display included a 75-foot wide electronic map of the United States, upon which states were marked off in contrasting colors as the computer awarded them to either Eisenhower or Stevenson. The board game that children had been playing with more than a hundred years before had been adapted to the video age.

In an effort to satisfy UNIVAC's hunger for fresh numbers, CBS posted special collectors of returns in thirty-eight key states with direct wires into the election desk. The third major network—ABC—hired Elecom 125, a computer produced by yet another office-machine company, the Underwood Corporation.

Henceforth the networks would be competing to obtain more returns more quickly than the wire services were providing; to "micro-analyze" selected precinct data; and to call the winners as early as their digital

The Story Is in the Numbers

arsenal—UNIVAC and friends—believed tenable. Reuven Frank, later the president of NBC News, talked about some of the problems of election night coverage:

> The biggest problem was "projecting" results—never, never, never "predicting!" Every election year there is invariably a lot of print and palaver about American journalism over-emphasizing the "horse race" aspects of an election to the detriment of serious treatment of the issues. The public always agrees with the criticism, yet its demand for predictions is insatiable. . . . The same public appetite leads to projecting winners on Election Night programs.[11]

CBS boasted an election night audience more than twice that of its nearest competitor in 1956. The election was a runaway. All of the diverse electronics systems could manage without undue risk to declare President Eisenhower the winner of a second term shortly after 8 P.M. EST.

Trends that started with the coming of radio in the 1920s were carried forward by the merging of television and computer technologies. Newspapers lost their control over the election-night numbers story. Robert Kintner, who was Frank's predecessor at the helm of NBC News, liked to recall one election night when the phone rang at the network news desk. The voice at the other end of the line identified itself as the Associated Press. The AP had a favor to ask: "When you run down the board, could you keep the figures on the screen a little longer? You're going so fast we can't copy them." Kintner, who had been working on a newspaper during the press-radio wars of the 20s and 30s, thought that was funny.[12]

In a blink of the video eye, the print media also lost their edge in telling the stories of politics as spectacle. The colorful, sometimes exciting visual events that happen "on stage" in public view now belonged to television too.

Fifteen

Instincts and Impressions
in the Land of Camelot

The *New York Times* considered one of its necessary missions forecasting the future outcome of the presidential election. How the newspaper went about doing this continued to evolve, however, as the use of preelection polls became more common in other papers. In 1956 three teams of five *Times* reporters each toured the country during the six weeks before the election. Typically they spent three days in a state, interviewing voters along with the customary politicians, local newspaper personnel, and "other informed persons."

"The team operation was not a poll," one of the reporters took pains to point out later, "although some polling was included in the techniques used. The team method had the merit of reportorial checks and balances not available to pollsters." Visits to a particular city would sometimes be as brief as three hours. Team member Gladwin Hill thought it "treacherous to project a 50-person sidewalk sampling into any sort of Gallup-type conclusion about how sentiment is divided."[1]

Some of the surveys turned out "right," others did not. West Virginia, Tennessee, Oklahoma, Texas, and Virginia were all portrayed by the *Times* as likely Stevenson states but were carried by Eisenhower. When it was over, editor Turner Catledge professed satisfaction. "Team members found value," he said, "in not being tied to the arithmetic of polls." "They were free to include their own intangible impressions after days of surveying a state."

The impressions of journalists, tangible and otherwise, were brought to bear, not lightly, in the next election, the election of 1960. John F. Kennedy, the presidential nominee of the Democratic Party, was adored by most political journalists. Young, glamorous, a vibrant personality, Jack Kennedy was enchantingly handsome, irresistibly telegenic, good copy. He cultivated important journalists in Washington, and almost all of the people who covered him loved him.

The dynamics of political journalism cannot be understood without considering the relationship between reporters and their subjects. The reason for this is in Turner Catledge's assumption that the hard data in an opinion poll will be filtered through the admittedly intangible (but presumably fair-minded) impressions of journalists. This is hardly an archaic viewpoint. Marvin Kalb, a former correspondent for both CBS and NBC, said in 1988 that public opinion polls convey only "the illusion of fact." Networks and newspapers find it more comforting, "in the swirl of modern-day uncertainties . . . to rely on a statistic . . . than on their own professional instincts and impressions," Kalb said. More recently, the journal *Press/Politics* published an essay by a former journalist arguing that the tape recorder has had a pernicious effect on journalism. Why? Because in quoting someone's exact words, the reporter is unable to "value them [the words] with his intelligence and qualify them with his morality."[2]

Given the interest of reader/viewers in news of the horse race, should the statistical assessments of voting intentions be tempered by the "professional instincts and impressions" of knowledgeable journalists? An answer to that question must consider whether those instincts and impressions are biased or not. Are political reporters biased? If so, what is that bias and how does it relate to the development of horse-race journalism?

Reporters in any field are necessarily selective in what they report, and they have always understood that most news leaks involve a quid pro quo. An anecdote from 1960 will illustrate how this works. One of the *New York Times* team captains in the 1956 national survey had been William Lawrence, a gruff, hard-driving reporter who made the most of his newspaper's power. After Kennedy won the Democratic nomination in the summer of 1960, the candidate invited the *Times* reporter for a golf game at the Kennedy compound on Cape Cod. After the round, the two men returned to Kennedy's house for a drink, which was interrupted by a phone call from a prominent Democratic official. It was well known that Adlai Stevenson coveted the position of secretary of state in a future Kennedy cabinet, an appointment that many liberals in the party would have applauded. Lawrence heard Kennedy tell the other man that he would never consider naming Stevenson secretary of state. After Kennedy hung up, the reporter told his host that he would have to leave to file his story. They both laughed, knowing that the remark had not been meant for his ears. Nevertheless, "it was a very useful piece of information to have in the back of my head," Lawrence said later, "because after the election Kennedy kept trading me little bits of information against this [knowledge]."

For example, Lawrence called the president-elect one morning and said: "I haven't got a story for Sunday. The election's over, there's no harm in it now. I think I'll write a story saying Adlai won't be Secretary of State."

"Well, that's a speculative story," Kennedy replied. "Why don't you write a story saying that Luther Hodges will be Secretary of Commerce."

"Fine, I'll do that," Lawrence said.

The scenario repeated itself several times, Kennedy leaking other appointments in lieu of the Stevenson story.[3]

Kennedy courted many influential journalists, including Joseph Alsop. Alsop said his friendship with Kennedy began in late 1958, after which he said they would often discuss "practical politics."

After the election, Alsop went abroad. The reason is interesting. "I didn't want to get entangled in all that [competition for news of administration appointments]," he said. "In my business you either *use up your credit* trying to find out who's going to get what job or you go away." (My emphasis).[4]

Q. What does a journalist mean by "using up all your credit?"

A. The "credit" that is established by doing favors for, or otherwise endearing yourself to, a source.

In a journalistic credit/debit system in which reporters are intimately associated with the people they write about (some of whom they like and others they dislike), the very idea of objective impressions and instincts may be naive.

The most common bias of most reporters on the national political beat is not partisan; it is not ideological. They are biased, first and most obviously, in favor of what will produce "a good story." But it's more complicated than that, because most of them entertain another bias that can best be described as "stylistic." On today's scene they are drawn to candidates who embody the stylistic traits identified with Manhattan, the Ivy League, Hollywood. These are traits that were most evident in John and Jacqueline Kennedy, traits which today we call "coolness." Attractive, articulate candidates with laid-back flair, with panache, the stuff of celebrityhood.

This is not entirely a phenomenon of the television age. Here are some examples from the past, beginning with Washington political writer Mary Clemmer Ames: "There is no hint of intellectual grace, no music, no aesthetic culture, no filtering of thought, no finer aspirations." She was talking about President Ulysses S. Grant. Theodore Roosevelt worked hard at his press relations. He would, according to one account, call in the correspondents, "whirl them around a few times until they were dizzy, clap them on the back, assure them they were the best of his friends and order that everybody should have all the news he wanted." Then he would "give to each a large piece of taffy and bid them goodbye with a 'bully for you, boys.'"[5] A reporter who covered the Hoover-Smith race in 1928 said the news was slanted in Smith's favor. Hoover, this observer complained, was "a serious, well-founded information sort of man [who did not] understand either the psychology or the necessities of reporters." Smith, on the other hand, "appealed to the imaginations of the writing folks. His appeal was personal. He had personality, that fellow, and magnetism, and a facility for mixing, and he is a good fighter. . . . There was color about Smith that gave the writers a foundation to work on, and they used their brushes lavishly." Smith understood the reporters' "struggle for the front page," and so did Franklin Roosevelt a few years later. Roosevelt won the hearts of the press corps by supplying them with lots of "news—action—drama! The reportorial affection and admiration for the President is unprecedented," said the *Baltimore Evening Sun*'s Henry Hyde in 1933. "He has definitely captivated a usually cynical battalion of correspondents."[6]

The Roosevelts, Al Smith, and John Kennedy were students of news values, angles, and cycles. They knew how to exploit the competition in the news business to their own advantage. Kennedy came along at the right time to also become the first virtuoso of television campaigning. No public figure ever commanded such devotion by political journalists as John Kennedy. "There was the delightful and delirious love of Kennedy [by reporters] on his plane during the general election campaign," said Theodore H. White, the poet laureate of the Kennedy era (about whom more later). By election day, the correspondents who had covered him felt "they too were marching like soldiers of the Lord to the New Frontier."[7]

Anyone with any political sense could see that Kennedy would attract votes from Catholics who were Republicans and lose votes from non-Catholics who were Democrats. The volatility of this equation led Ted Gallup to hedge his bets. All a poll can do, he said a couple of weeks before the election, is "guess, with a 50–50 chance of being right."[8] Eugene Pulliam Jr., the Indianapolis publisher and like many other publishers an avid Nixon supporter, labeled 1960 "the Year of the Big Hedge."

The *New York Times* tried to untangle the ethno-religious complexities. One day, a story based on "a score of interviews," reported: "City's Catholics Stick to Parties." The next day, a story based on information from politicians was headlined: "Shift to Kennedy by Jews is Noted." A day later, the newspaper cited "most of the usual political criteria," as its foundation for: "Kennedy Appears to Lead in State; Religion a Factor." And finally on the day before the election the *Times* laid out its definitive national survey based on "a nationwide check of informed political opinion." The front-page headline declared: "Kennedy in Lead in Final Survey; 15 States Close." From the states that were not close, the *Times* awarded more than twice as many electoral votes to Kennedy as to Nixon.[9]

Instincts and Impressions in the Land of Camelot

The campaign moved then to the swift pace of jet travel. The candidates chased across the country, trying to touch down in as many different television markets as they could in every twenty-four-hour period. Nixon managed to accomplish his goal of appearing in all fifty states after Labor Day. Correspondents closest to the candidates, in their entourage, spent much of each day trapped in a bus, captives of a debilitating, time-wasting innovation, the motorcade from and back to the airport. The weary men and women accompanying the candidates were least qualified to exercise their instincts and impressions.

The *Los Angeles Times* gave its readers so many conflicting poll stories, including Gallup, Lubell, and Roper, that it felt obliged to compile a "poll of polls" on the final weekend. "So Volatile It Could be a Landslide—Roper," added a brief sidebar at the bottom of the page.[10]

Gallup's final figures showed what the *Herald-Tribune* described as "a dramatic shift" to Kennedy. The Democratic lead was placed at 49 percent to 48 percent for Nixon and an estimated 2 million voters still undecided.

AP had reported Nixon ahead in early October. But in its final national survey, encompassing the judgments of "AP political observers, newspaper analysts and party leaders," the wire service gave Kennedy "a healthy lead," according to the *Herald-Tribune* headline.

Contrary to Roper's quixotic view, not many politicians or journalists thought it would be a landslide election. This would be a close election, the first close election for which newspapers, wire services, and television networks were primed under different competitive conditions to "call" the results as quickly and as definitively as possible. It was a close election, but one in which Gallup and Lubell had both detected an apparent movement toward Kennedy at the very end. It was a close election that most publishers wanted Nixon to win and most reporters wanted Kennedy to win.

Afterwards Catledge would remember election night 1960 as the most nerve-racking night of his life. The job of gathering in the returns and reporting who won remained essentially the same as in the 1880s. The same air of anxiety hung over the newsroom of the *New York Times* that had been present at the *Boston Globe* on election night nearly a century before. This time though, instead of enlisting the "slide-rule boys" from the accounting department downstairs, the figures were punched into data processing cards and fed into one of two IBM electronic tabulators. By rolling in the IBM machines, the *Times* was attempting, Catledge explained dourly, "to satisfy the American lust for predictions."[11]

But it was television that could bring "a continuity of visual excitement" to the dramatic quadrennial epic, one newspaper editor conceded, "a smell of history in motion." Election night now meant "the marathon viewing of TV."[12] At 10:30 P.M. eastern time, 90 percent of all television sets in America—some 83 million—were tuned to election news. The networks fought for audience share, and for bragging rights. Which would call the election first? Robert Kintner delivered a pep talk at NBC that would have made Knute Rockne proud. "Men, you may think this election is a contest between Kennedy and Nixon. It's not," he declared. "It's a race between NBC and CBS."[13]

His network had not fared well in the primary election prognosticating. IBM had overtaken Remington Rand in the development of big mainframe computers. So when NBC began using computers made by its parent corporation, RCA, the way was open for CBS to sign on with IBM. ABC then acquired the services of the newest UNIVAC. IBM's model 7090 could be programmed to analyze demographic voting patterns at the precinct level. It found in the Wisconsin primary, for example, that Kennedy had been successful in the Catholic precincts of Wisconsin's Fox River Valley and did poorly in the Norwegian Lutheran districts in the northwestern corner of the state. Joseph Kennedy, the candidate's father, phoned William S. Paley, the chairman of CBS, to protest that this kind of reporting would promote religious divisiveness and bigotry.

For the election in November, NBC planned to strike back with what it called the "DEW-Line precincts." A takeoff on the Distant Early Warning defense against Soviet air attacks over the North Pole, the system consisted of representative key-precincts that usually were counted promptly. NBC hired people to call in the results from each of the DEW-Line precincts. Colonel Taylor's key-precincts grew out of the same concept long ago in Massachusetts—without the gimmicky label and without the RCA Model 501 computer to do the figuring.

NBC had two popular anchor personalities to showcase on election night. A deck was built over the floor of studio 8-H for the X-shaped desk to accommodate the stern Chet Huntley and the studiously wry David Brinkley. Vote totals were posted on RCA's equipment ballyhooed as "the first digital communications system designed to integrate electronic data processing with remote operations."

Cronkite at CBS sat in front of an equally flashy tally board, IBM's RAMAC 305.

Viewers were inclined to tune in whichever network had the highest raw vote totals on their boards—or so the broadcasters believed. As a consequence, all three networks assembled a running national popular vote com-

Instincts and Impressions in the Land of Camelot

bining the highest individual state figures from three available sources—
AP, UPI (United Press International), or the network's own totals from that
state. Mixing oranges and apples, it was impossible to determine what proportion of the overall vote was actually represented by the figures on the
board.

All three networks expressed the probability ratios of their vote projections in terms of odds. The bigger the spread between the two numbers,
the more certain was the computer. At 7 P.M. EST, ABC reported over the
air that UNIVAC thought the chances were 10-to-1 that Nixon had won.
Wow! A few minutes later, CBS said its computer had projected as many
as 459 electoral votes—a landslide—for Nixon. This information was im-
parted with the same confidence rating of 10-to-1.

Though few votes had actually been counted anywhere but in a few eastern states, that was enough for the *New York Herald-Tribune* to declare Nixon
the apparent winner in its first edition.

Little more than an hour later, the machines did an about-face. More
figures were in. Kennedy was now the apparent winner. CBS reported at
8:14 P.M. that its computer thought Kennedy would finish with 51 percent
of the vote and 297 electoral votes to 49 percent and 240 electoral votes
for his opponent. The odds that this would happen were said to be 11-to-5.
ABC followed a half hour later with essentially the same projection (but
only a 7-to-5 confidence ratio). At 8:23, NBC went public with its first projection: 6.3-to-1 confident that Kennedy would finish with 51.1 percent to
Nixon's 48.9 percent.

The early tally in the eastern states gave Kennedy a sizeable lead. The
New York Times had its electronic tabulator. But it did not have a Colonel
Taylor. The first edition of the paper went to press with an 8-column banner
line across the top of the page:

"Kennedy Elected President."

Perhaps, Catledge wrote in his autobiography, the decision had reflected
"our own prediction as well as the [available] returns" at that early hour.[14]

Depending on the television channel of choice, between 8:14 P.M. and
9:18 P.M. one could learn that Kennedy was projected to win by odds of:
11-to-5, 6.3-to-1, 3-to-1, 7-to-5, 49-to-1, 22-to-1, or 15-to-1. The networks all
projected various electoral vote margins more than enough for the Democratic candidate to be elected. In the next few hours, the predictions spewed
forth with as high as 337.2-to-1 probability odds.

After midnight, as more votes poured in from western states, Kennedy's
raw vote lead began to shrink. The messages from the electronic brains took

on a trembling tone. With the early edition already on the street, Catledge watered down the wording of the next press run to read that Kennedy "seemed almost certain to be elected."

He then took the unprecedented step of ordering the presses stopped for two hours until more returns were in hand and the editors had time to ponder them.

As the status of the race jumped around, the television commentators treated the suspense more lightly. "We have just given our electronic brain its 2 o'clock feeding of warm election returns," said Brinkley on NBC.

Shortly after 3 A.M., Nixon addressed his followers in Los Angeles. AP flashed a bulletin before the statement was made that he would concede defeat, which he didn't. He said merely that he was behind and would lose unless things changed. Toward daybreak, apparently sensing that the Republicans knew something they didn't, the *Times* editors ratcheted up their rhetoric again, stating that Kennedy had been elected. But Catledge suffered another jittery spell as the Democratic lead continued to dwindle. The language in the 7 A.M. "extra" reported only that Kennedy "appeared to have won."

Huntley and Brinkley were due to vacate the studio for the *Today Show* at 7 A.M. Someone ordered them to declare a winner, wrap up the show, and make room for *Today Show* host Dave Garroway. Accordingly, at 7:20 NBC's "concession desk" awarded California to Kennedy and proclaimed him the next president. UPI then did the same.

The only problem with that report was that it was wrong. When all the absentee ballots had been counted eight days later, Nixon, not Kennedy, carried California. The first one-third of the votes counted in California gave Kennedy a 4 percent lead that disappeared when the votes from the southern counties came in.

California would not have been enough for Nixon to win, however. Kennedy scraped through in Illinois, and Nixon's press secretary, Herbert Klein, read the Republican concession statement at 12:45 P.M. EST. The long night was over.

In the end, John Kennedy prevailed with 50.2 percent of the popular vote and 303 electoral votes. Gallup had forecast 51 percent for the winner. Though more cautious with its computer projections, NBC had used its key-precinct system to come closest to a coherent explanation of the status of the vote count all along. Among the three, only NBC had not prematurely declared Nixon the winner.

"The fact is," said the *Columbia Journalism Review*, "that only the narrowest of margins saved newspapers and broadcasters from a massive error—a declaration of the wrong winner in a national election—simply because they could not wait until enough votes were counted."[15]

The managing editor of the *Washington Post,* Alfred Friendly, added his critique: "The worst of TV was having those damned calculating machines. They were whimsical and changing, and came up with odds—in the light of an election that is probably going to be decided by less than 200,000 votes—that certainly didn't warrant such figures as 400-to-1 or 331-to 1, the maximum that the machine could tolerate."

Friendly said he was offended by NBC's "Victory Desk" giving states to one or the other candidate "as if they had the God-given right to make such disposals. I found it not only arrogant but of course wrong."

"Could it have been that some of us [newspaper editors] were panicked by the Idiot Box?" he concluded. "Did we forget our role of chroniclers and tend to become forecasters?"[16]

As Friendly must have realized, the role of the newspaper adapted to the revolutionary influence of the "Idiot Box." Sam Lubell noticed that exposure to national networks had smoothed away many of the regional variations in voting behavior. He had to revise his own methods. Voters no longer moved as predictable parts of ethnic and economic streams. Group identifications were less meaningful. Past behavior was a less dependable yardstick. Attitudes could be altered more precipitously by events and leadership.

Even before Kennedy, Lubell also could see that campaigns were focusing less on issues and more on "image making." One senior citizen told an interviewer from the University of Michigan that she voted against Nixon because she "didn't like the look in his eye—especially the left one."

Beyond what anyone understood at the time, one chronicler of the 1960 election left a profound imprint on political journalism. His name was Theodore H. White—Teddy to his friends. Teddy White grew up in a Russian Jewish family in the Dorchester section of Boston. He went to Harvard and became a correspondent for *Time* magazine. Henry Luce trained his journalists at *Time* to string countless little details together in narrative tales wound around themes of unmistakable simplicity. Good and evil clashed between the covers of the magazine. The human drama was told in weekly installments, carried along by exciting personalities in the news. White reported from China during and after World War II, which happened to be a beat that his boss, publisher Luce, having lived in Asia as a youngster, thought he knew a great deal about. The two men had a disagreement about the Communist takeover of China, which led to White's separation from the omniscient company.

Teddy White thought of himself as "a bespectacled hustler carrying one suitcase and a secondhand typewriter."[17] In 1960, at age forty-five, living off the income from his novels, he hit upon the idea of writing a book about the "real" presidential campaign. He applied the *Time* technique to what was going on behind the scenes, which now meant behind the television screen.

Over the decades journalists depicted politics as battlefield combat. White approached the story as a novelist would, creating mood, suspense, heroic figures, a sense of dramatic adventure. He went into the back rooms to remove the veil from the strategy and the tactics. He treated as literature the thrust and counterthrust of the campaign. Here was something beyond videography: mythology brought to life by the myriad details that only a *Time*man could appreciate. What the characters wore, what they had for breakfast, who said what to whom when nobody was around. Fortunately for White, the candidate whose trust he won turned out to be the central character in the drama—and the next president.

Later, after the horrific assassination of young President Kennedy, White fell into another role. He was chosen by the widow, Jacqueline Kennedy, to tell the story of the Camelot legend as the fallen leader's romantic epitaph.

Teddy White was not a cynic, like most journalists. He was a romanticist, a spinner of heroic legends. His book, *The Making of the President 1960*, established a new genre of political journalism. Aspiring writers across the country awakened as one to the belief that the penetrating reporting of "the inside story" would yield captivating literature. This, they thought, would be the salvation of words on paper.

The Teddy White syndrome influenced print reporters through the balance of the twentieth century. Inspired by his example, journalists scratched and dug for the hidden details that would unmask the play-acting on the public stage. Some of his imitators added more than a pinch of cynicism to the recipe. Few wrote as gracefully as White, but some were better reporters. This desire to take the reader behind the closed doors, helped along no doubt by the increasingly unsubtle news management efforts of campaigners, represented another nail in the coffin of issues-reporting. Polls "gave a new level of sophistication to inside reporting," as E. J. Dionne Jr. of the *Washington Post* has noted. "The inside story overwhelmed the outside story. . . . Looking at the numbers they generate and the statements and advertisements of the candidates, reporters can know *often even before they talk to the insiders* why a candidate is doing what he is doing and what the insiders themselves are thinking." [Dionne's emphasis].[18]

Sixteen

EVA and the Exit Polls

Teddy White and television were both instrumental in fostering a presidential "cult of personality" that lived on after John Kennedy. Campaigners played to television audiences. Voters (and journalists) formed fleeting impressions based on the theatrical quality of the images on television. Political brokers were no longer able to deliver blocs of votes as they could in the past. Party organizations deteriorated as control over the nomination of candidates passed from their hands into those of the voters. This led to the propagation of presidential primaries in almost all the states. The primary test in a state became what Lubell described as "a stage across which the candidates play to the whole nation."[1]

Some of the reasons for the weakening of the parties had nothing to do with the media: the civil service system of public employment; universal educational opportunities; government welfare programs instead of the precinct captain's holiday basket of food; the organizational energy of single-issue movements. But the most important influence was television. The new presidential selection system was made for television. Viewers were treated to a prime-time weekly serial that left the candidates hanging on the edges of cliffs in several different states. Tune in next Tuesday to watch more presidential hopefuls fall by the wayside as the road show moves across the country. An elimination tournament with conflict, drama, suspense, ticking away to the fast pace of the mounting numbers on the tote boards.

Without a central party structure to oversee the competition, the separate state primaries were refereed pickup fashion by the talent scouts and scorekeepers in the media. Someone had to sort out the "serious" candidates and the "spoilers," didn't they?[2]

Preelection polls reported as news took on new significance because the success or failure of a contender was measured not only by the outcome of the voting but also against the standard of achievement established by the journalistic sages. If the candidate won, but not by as much as expected, the victory would be flawed. As the spotlight shifted from state to state and region to region, the illusion of momentum became important. This week's winner had better take advantage of the boost going into next week, or else lose that all-important momentum. In a field with several candidates, the winner could finish first and be applauded as the winner, but with much less than a majority of a small number of votes.

For a time in the early 1960s, most national news organizations did not risk preprimary polls. An intrastate poll is an especially tricky undertaking before a primary election. Screening likely voters is much more difficult than in a general election. Ordinarily only those voters who care to be publicly identified as Democrats or Republicans even think about voting in a party primary; and the proportion of those who actually turn out for a primary can be quite low. The sample for a poll within a state must be considerably larger than the number of interviews from that state included in a national poll.

Early in the selection season, "horse-race polls" favor familiar names in the news. This makes it hard for little-known candidates to demonstrate the popularity that is needed for them to raise money, be able to afford to do the things that will attract media attention so they can become better known, do better in the polls, and (what else?) raise more money. Most of the state polls in the preprimary news were conducted by media within the state or selectively leaked by the candidates themselves.

After NBC's ratings sweep in 1960, the other networks spent heavily for automated equipment that would make them competitive on election night. The broadcasters considered the wire services hopelessly lethargic. AP and UPI still used a trunk wire system of communication attuned to morning and afternoon newspaper deadlines, much too plodding for election night television. So the news departments drew up their own expensive plans to gather returns from the source—the precinct polling places—the better to rush to judgment before all the figures were in. In the past this had been done by projecting the first available returns, on the sometimes valid assumption that they would be representative of the precincts reporting later from the same jurisdiction. Sometimes perhaps, but not always. Statisticians did not like to bank on luck.

CBS hired Theodore White and Louis Harris as consultants. Their objective was simply put, White said. It was to destroy their [election night] adversary, NBC.[3] For the midterm congressional and gubernatorial elections of 1962, including Nixon's comeback try for the statehouse in California, Harris constructed a series of key-precinct models. He called his system the Vote Profile Analysis (VPA).

In each of the eight states with the most newsworthy contests, eighty key precincts were selected as a demographic and partisan composite of the entire state. The network's IBM RAMAC 1410 compared the key precinct

EVA and the Exit Polls

results with the vote profile in the computer's brain, checked the findings against the totals being tallied, and printed out trend analyses. These Harris double-checked against his own poll predictions before calling the race. CBS ran consistently ahead of the others with accurate "calls" all night long.

Working for ABC, Lubell used the same principle to designate key precincts in New York and Philadelphia that produced citywide projections within 1 percent of the citywide vote. Both men were using a computer-enhanced version of Colonel Taylor's Boston Plan.

Bloodied in battle, and in a state of combat readiness, the network forces girded for the presidential campaign of 1964. They were well-armed and well-financed. White was fascinated by the "year-long cannibalistic, desperate and, at times, dangerous rivalry" of the networks. Morale reached such a feverish pitch, Lubell noted, that "the computers themselves were like bystanders."[4]

Vice President Lyndon Johnson had succeeded to the presidency upon the death of Kennedy and was now standing for election. The conservative and moderate wings of the Republican Party fought bitterly for the nomination in New Hampshire, Oregon, and California primaries.

At each week's primary installment, the networks were obliged to hire poll watchers to report the precinct results. It was estimated later that each network spent in the neighborhood of $1.5 million collecting presidential primary returns in California alone.[5]

Governor Nelson Rockefeller of New York, appealing to moderate Republicans, made his last stand against conservative Senator Barry Goldwater of Arizona in the California primary in June. Conceding the superiority of television vote-tabulating systems, the *New York Times* contracted to copy the CBS returns; and the *New York Herald-Tribune* did the same at NBC.

Lubell, who lacked the movie-star panache desired by television, was working for the RKO general radio group on election night. He and both CBS and NBC were experimenting with an innovative device. They were interviewing voters just after they had actually voted—what today we call exit polls.

It occurred to journalists long ago that the best way to find out how people voted might be to ask them. If you could inquire into their voting plans *before* the election, why not do it *after* they had voted? As early as 1940, broadcasters were trying to interview voters after the act, either by telephone or, more rarely, in person. The NBC station in Los Angeles sent college students to ask voters in ten California precincts how they had voted in the 1964 primary. The inquiries were made in a haphazard fashion, however, and no one could figure out a way to feed the data into the network's computer model. NBC apparently gave up the idea of exit polls until many years later.

The origins of CBS's exit interviews are more interesting. On the day of the Maryland primary earlier in 1964, Lou Harris dispatched one of his employees, Ruth Clark, to ring doorbells and question voters about how they had voted. Clark grew weary of trudging to the top floors of apartment buildings in Baltimore. So she hatched a brilliant scheme. She went to the nearby school where the voting was going on and asked the election judges if they minded if she interviewed some voters outside the polling place. They had no objections. Harris liked the idea and added voter interviews in 18 key precincts to his repertoire in California.[6] Again, however, the computer engineers were not up to the task of absorbing the exit poll information into their projections in November.

Lubell had neither the personnel nor the computer expertise to do more than a few interviews in Los Angeles. Two minutes after the polls closed in Los Angeles, he went on the air. "Goldwater has carried Los Angeles County," Lubell said. "This means he has a good chance of winning the state."[7]

Lubell made this startling statement on the basis of the first returns from a few key precincts—and his own exit interviews earlier in the day.

Twenty minutes later, at 7:22 P.M., while voters were still standing in line in the San Francisco Bay area, CBS projected a Goldwater victory with 53 percent of the vote. The polls did not close in northern California until 38 minutes later. VPA issued its projection based on scattered returns, on the numbers from 42 key precincts (among the state's 32,000 precincts), and on voter interviews.

Less trusting of the computers, NBC relied on a double-barreled system. One set of key precincts had been prepared by a mathematician at Princeton, Professor John Tukey. On election night the professor and his associates sat around one conference table in the RCA Computer Center at Cherry Hills, New Jersey. At an adjoining table sat the hulking figure of Richard Scammon, a washtub filled with iced Pepsi Cola bottles at his feet. An experienced election intelligence guru from Washington, Dick Scammon approached the problem from a different direction. He had stocked the computer with "barometer" precincts that had a history of supporting the winning candidate. The two systems would have to agree before NBC would declare a winner. Tukey's system applied mathematical formulas to the results from representative precincts. Scammon's required more human judgment.

When Cronkite called the election for Goldwater, NBC executives up and down the chain of command were watching all three networks on monitors. Robert Kintner, the president of the network, called Bill McAndrew, the president of NBC News, who was in Los Angeles.

"Did you hear that?" Kintner inquired. "Well, what the hell?"

McAndrew called Shad Northshield, a producer who was keeping the mathematician and the political scientist company in New Jersey. "Did you hear that?" McAndrew asked.

Northshield checked with his two experts and reported back that they weren't sure.

"What do you mean, they're not sure?" McAndrew barked back.

Despite increasingly adamant protests from Kintner, relayed at intervals through McAndrew, Northshield would not budge until his two experts said it was all right. This did not happen until 9:50 P.M. in California—well after midnight in the East.[8]

Meanwhile, twelve hours after the counting started, AP and UPI reported Rockefeller leading in a close race.

Eventually CBS had to trim back Goldwater's winning total to 51 percent, a margin of less than 60,000 out of more than 2 million votes. But CBS and NBC had the senator ahead all night long. Their estimates were based not just on the key precincts (and in CBS's case on the exit polls), but on far more actual votes tabulated.

Many morning newspapers, using AP figures, went to press reporting a see-saw race. An AP story around midnight had Rockefeller pulling ahead. The two New York morning papers, the *Times* and the *Herald-Tribune,* enjoying their access to the network numbers, called the win for Goldwater. But in its final edition, the *Los Angeles Times*—3,000 miles nearer the scene of the story and with a three-hour time advantage—headlined:

"Very Close Contest Hangs on Final Vote Tabulations."

Its story was based on the AP's tabulation of only 40 percent of the vote, showing Goldwater 5,600 votes in front. AP did not put the senator ahead to stay until 7:14 A.M. The "snap tallies" from the voting machine counties in the north had been made available faster than the paper ballot counties in southern California. The networks had their precinct stringers, their key-precinct models—and their computers.

It was a humiliating night for the wire services and newspaper editors. They had been brought to their knees by the "Idiot Box." "Election reporting is being re-shaped by a kind of statistical technology that most journalists do not understand," Lubell could not resist remarking.[9]

On the morning after the California primary, the wire services and the television news offices were troubled, for different reasons. Newspaper editors could not allow the vote tabulation gap to continue; network officials had to do something about the runaway spending. So representatives of each of the networks held a peace parley in a hotel room in Los Angeles. Out of that and subsequent meetings with the two wire services came the establishment of a single election night vote-counting cooperative consortium. AP and UPI were in no position right then to quibble over the name of the Network Election System. (It later became the News Election Service.)

The three networks and two wire services each put up one-fifth of NES's $1.4 million budget. Before the November election, the service lined up reporters who were responsible for phoning in returns from some 130,000 of the 172,000 precincts nationwide. At 8:30 P.M. EST on election night in November, 4 million votes had already been counted, compared to 3 million in 1960. By 1:30 A.M., 60 million votes were tabulated, compared to 46 million four years before. The figures were tallied at the temporary NES quarters in a New York hotel and Teletyped to the member newsrooms.

In all but the closest of presidential elections, most people thought the new system would put an end to a social tradition in America: the all-night election vigil. Journalism Professor Penn Kimball remembered waiting out election night in the living room as "an American custom as brimming with nostalgia as waiting for the dinner rolls to rise in the era before the invention of ready-mix."

"Progress," he said, "is not without its price."[10]

Political junkies once had to await the arrival of the weekly newspaper to learn the results of an election. Then they journeyed downtown to scan the newspaper building bulletin board, or the figures flashed by a magic lantern. Then they trooped out into the backyard to watch the searchlight beams on the distant horizon. Then they sat in the living room waiting for the lights to dim. Then they heard the results over the radio. And now the numbers would be collected swiftly, added by a congenial family of electronic machines, and the digits displayed on the screen at home.

Politicians fixed their minds on one of the prices of this progress. They knew that the more cost-effective processing of the results would free the networks to concentrate their attention and their resources on ever more inventive methods of *finding out first.*

Hearings were held and bills introduced in Congress to prohibit news organizations from projecting election outcomes until the voting period had ended. It would be made illegal for the networks to predict a presidential election victory, based on results in the East, as long as the polls were open in the West.

A committee of governors from five states met with network news executives in September to talk further about the problem. The journalists reminded the governors that any effort to restrict their reporting of news would violate the First Amendment. Frank Stanton, the president of CBS, proposed a uniform voting period everywhere in the country. The secretary of state of California suggested that voting in the West begin on Monday evening and end at 4 P.M. on Tuesday (7 P.M. EST). A uniform voting hours bill passed the House twice in the 1980s but was never put to a vote in the Senate. Fred Friendly, the head of CBS News, made some semantic concessions in 1965. His network promised not to "declare" winners prematurely but insisted on the right to use terms like "the indicated winner" or "the probable winner" whenever it felt like it.[11]

Bringing additional sample precincts into its Vote Profile Analysis (VPA), CBS harnessed a tandem team of two IBM computers—a 1440 and a 7010/ 1301 system. CBS promised to do more than tell the score of the November election. It would use its electronic wizardry to provide "the anatomy of a victory," breaking down the demographic parts of the voting only minutes after the figures were received.

NBC brought back Tukey's and Scammon's "tag precincts," which were now labeled the Electronic Vote Analysis (EVA) system. EVA was designed to measure deviations in the key precincts and in county-wide returns as they were delivered by NES.

On another front, NBC jumped ahead in the Visuals Race. RCA developed for the network an on-air display system it called DIVCON—for Digital to Video Converter. By punching a few keys, a technician could direct the computer to convert its digital information into a form that could be shown on the television screen. The home screen became the visible endline of the computer's work. Reuven Frank said he "fantasized that future election nights would require only one good reporter and a DIVCON. Then someone else could do election night and I could go to the movies, or read a book."[12]

The third network, ABC, was determined to catch up with the others. A research and development team consisting of mathematicians and computer specialists from the Corporation for Economic Industrial Research (CEIR) constructed a mathematical model of the national electorate. A polling company executive, Oliver Quayle, then programmed the Burroughs Corporation twin-B 5500 model computer to process and make sense of the returns from 1,300 key precincts across the country. ABC estimated later that it spent $1.8 million on election night news.

With only 2 percent of the precincts in and long before the polls closed on the West Coast, NBC guessed at 6:48 P.M. (EST) that Johnson would receive between 60 and 70 percent of the vote. At 7:49 P.M. ABC reported that President Johnson appeared headed for a landslide victory. CBS "indicated" that Johnson had won at 8:37 P.M. and made an unequivocal landslide prediction at 9:04 P.M. Social scientists who asked westerners whether they had been discouraged from voting by the television projections found a "slight but still important" effect.

The crucial statistics for the networks revealed the Trendex estimate that NBC had captured 52 percent of the audience share to 33 percent for CBS and 15 percent for ABC. NBC used 22 correspondents outside the studio, 58 editors and news writers, and 60 live cameras from 14 remote locations.

CBS had removed Cronkite from the anchor's chair during the summer conventions because of low ratings. He came back for the election night broadcast, however, and the network found solace in kind words from the *New York Times* TV critic, Jack Gould: "In clarity of presentation [CBS] led all the way, and in speed it was way up front for at least an hour and a half."

NBC did its best to hide the main reason for its lack of clarity. EVA had fallen ill. "Not a single 'take' of analytical material came out of the computer," as *Broadcasting* magazine explained later. "DIVCON was struck dumb."[13] Due to the computer breakdown, NBC had to rely on actual returns and a few key precincts, but the contest was so one-sided that EVA's disability didn't matter.

Bill Leonard, who was in charge of CBS's coverage, worried briefly that viewers would be confused by computer declarations while the actual vote postings were showing the loser in front. His post-election mail included this postcard: "You bastards! Election night used to be fun. You spoiled it with your goddamned gimmicks."[14]

On the day after the 1964 election, ABC officials began examining videotapes of everyone's coverage. For the next election, in the off-year 1966 races, ABC introduced its own acronym—RSVP, for Research Selected Vote Profile. Another pollster, John Kraft, fed RSVP. Bill Lawrence was assigned to interpret the machine's findings. Lawrence had quit the *New York Times* and joined ABC in 1961 because the newspaper would not send him on President Kennedy's first trip to Europe. Some *Times* editors believed Lawrence had gotten too close to the Kennedys.

CBS, and later ABC, turned their attention to NBC's visuals lead. In 1966 CBS came up with its own "victorygraph" and "issuesgraph." Before long donkeys and elephants were dancing across the scoreboards, "whizbang protechnics" that reminded *Newsweek* magazine of a video game arcade.

The *New York Times* paid $25,000 for the CBS Vote Profile Analysis. NBC invited a dozen other newspapers, among them the *Herald-Tribune,* the

EVA and the Exit Polls

Washington Post, and the *Boston Globe,* to look on from a room next to the studio while EVA was expected to perform. In future election years this would become standard practice: newspaper reporters covering the vote-counting from a television building and having access to the computer projections in exchange for the goodwill and publicity generated in the print media.

Within the ranks of television journalism, the mechanization of election night news did not occur without some considerable grumbling. Robert MacNeil, who was then a correspondent for NBC, said in his book *The People Machine* that television journalists showed "some anxiety about being gobbled up by the computers. Increasingly, the work of the commentators and political pundits is being pre-empted by machinery. Election coverage is in danger of becoming de-humanized in its fascination with the new technology."[15]

Tension grew between the technologists, who preferred the hard information base contained in numbers churned out by the computers, and the commentators. David Brinkley at NBC and Eric Sevareid at CBS were among those who thought, according to MacNeil, that numbers "cannot generate the intuitive insights of a well-stocked human mind."

"I never could understand the passion to know how people voted before the returns were in," said Sevareid. "Why can't we wait a couple of hours? I can wait. We've gone through a couple of hundred years in this country waiting. It's not a strain on me."

The torrent of raw information needed, MacNeil thought, "to be filtered through a journalistic screen." Many journalists enter the field to help improve the human condition. In television during this period the newspaper distinction between straight news reporting and opinion was not drawn so finely. Some TV correspondents were at liberty to blend facts and interpretations. Wouldn't it be better, MacNeil suggested, if the networks "turned on their big machines the night *before* an election to explain all the issues and give millions of disinterested voters a last-minute cram course?"

CBS remodeled studio 41 for the color telecast in 1968. Cameras glided across the floor hidden in green plexiglas bubbles. Walter Cronkite sat behind a large circular desk. The technology little resembled Colonel Taylor's setup at the *Boston Globe.* Miles of cable under the floor connected Cronkite with the myriad of information sources. Only one of the 180 telephones installed in the studio this night made a ringing noise. Flashing lights signaled incoming calls on all the others. There were 75 Teletype machines and a like number of computer terminals in the studio. A shelf full of short, videotaped "packages" were "in the can" and ready to be aired.

The equipment used by reporters in the field had modernized the coverage of the campaign on television. Cameras were smaller. Videotape could be recorded, played back, and edited electronically. Television signals could be bounced off communications satellites orbiting the earth.

CBS and NBC both spent about $3 million on their election night coverage in 1968, ABC about $2.2 million. In a year of civil unrest over the war in Vietnam, the election promised to be close. Richard Nixon rose from the political graveyard to become the Republican nominee. Vice President Hubert H. Humphrey, who had been beaten by Kennedy in 1960, won the Democratic nomination.

Early in October, Gallup forecast Nixon in front by 12 points. Harris said 5 points.[16] Pulsating social turbulence caused journalists to be extra careful about what CBS was now calling their election night "estimates." Changes in residential patterns were making the key-precinct method of voting analysis less reliable. Families relocated more often over longer distances. Fair housing laws, the flight to the suburbs, the disintegration of ethnic enclaves in the central cities all contributed to neighborhoods that were less identifiable. Living near church and neighborhood shops was less important now. Better highways enabled wage-earners to commute to jobs in distant counties. Precinct lines had never been constant. They were drawn and redrawn by self-serving politicians, not by demographers. As a consequence, there were fewer of what psephologists considered "pure" precincts and more polyglot voting districts.

Key-precinct trends were still reasonably sound reflectors of the overall vote. But the networks wanted to be able to generalize about the voting behavior of demographic groups. As residential concentrations became less predictable, CBS in particular wanted to be able to pick apart and describe individual voting decisions with more certainty.

So in the summer of 1967 the network dropped Lou Harris as a consultant. Like many others in the highly competitive survey research business, Harris had both partisan political and news-poll clients. After working for the Kennedy campaign in 1960, he started his own syndicated newspaper poll in competition with Gallup. Then and later, Harris was a controversial figure in the polling fraternity, mainly because of his more interpretive, Lubell-like interviewing methods.

CBS hired a former U.S. Census Bureau statistician, Warren Mitofsky, to form a permanent in-house election survey unit. Mitofsky sold CBS on the idea that precincts "were fine for geographic categorization, such as urban or rural, but were misleading for presenting personal characteristics."[17]

Mitofsky had been given two missions: The first was to use probability methods to conduct election-day exit surveys that yielded predictably representative samples of the entire electorate. That way it would be possible to report how blacks, women, suburbanites, Catholics, etc., had voted. His second and more ambitious venture was to enter CBS in the booming field of preelection polling. Newspapers and newsmagazines that had once used poll data only to backstop analytical stories were publishing polls as news in and of themselves. The networks were in the position of picking up old news—what the newspapers told them the Gallup Poll or some other published polls were predicting. CBS wanted to undertake its own polls, another significant milestone in the course of horse-race journalism.

Unlike Harris, Scammon and the many instinctual journalists who were becoming involved in election surveys, Mitofsky thought the only way to deal with the chaos of election-night time pressures on television was with quality control of the data managed by an automatic mathematical solution rather than human judgment about the data.

As often as television journalists cited the value of exit polls to the academic understanding of voting behavior, their first priority continued to be winning the race to call the election ahead of the opposition.

After testing election-day telephone interviews in some local contests, Mitofsky concluded that the problems of finding cooperative voters at home were too formidable. Exit polls could be made feasible only when linked with the theory of probability sampling—using a few voters randomly selected to represent all voters—and only with confidential questionnaires collected outside the polling place. For November CBS made plans to question voters at the polling place exits in a few representative precincts in twenty states.

A breakdown in the News Election Service's computer processing of raw figures delayed the delivery of returns from California and Illinois. Because Governor George Wallace of Alabama was also running as a third-party candidate for president, the tabulators had to consider the possibility that no one would finish with a majority of electoral votes. The House of Representatives would then select the president. Shortly after midnight, William Lawrence told ABC listeners that "this race will either go to Humphrey or the House of Representatives."[18]

ABC, renting its computers from International Telephone and Telegraph Company, made the first calls for Nixon victories in Ohio and California the next morning (at 7:32 A.M. EST) and finally in Illinois at 8:19 A.M. Richard Nixon had been elected.

In the studio at CBS, the workers in the room stood and applauded when Cronkite left the premises at 11 A.M. He had been on the air, more or less continuously, since 6 o'clock the night before. CBS posted the highest audience share.

The data yielded by CBS exit polls far exceeded what the network had time to use. So some of the costs were recouped by selling the tabular byproduct to newspapers, including the *New York Times*.

Besides the expense (which climbed to about $500 per precinct in the 1980s), exit pollsters had to contend with sampling problems. Interviewers at CBS were instructed to approach departing voters at intervals sufficient to yield a manageable number of samples—usually around 100 in a precinct. The precincts were chosen to represent the regions in a state proportionally. Party strength was also considered in the distribution of sample precincts within each region. Even if the precincts reflected the voting behavior of all the other precincts in the state on that day, the poll could go wrong because of a high refusal rate. Old people, women, blacks, residents of a "bad" neighborhood are more likely to refuse to fill out a questionnaire. Better educated voters tend to be more cooperative. Foul weather alone can cause the refusal rate to exceed 40 percent in some precincts. The CBS system required that interviewers record the sex, race, and approximate age of refusals. Those figures were reported along with the other information so that the data could be adjusted where necessary to correct the imbalances.

The legislatures of Washington and ten other states enacted laws to keep exit pollsters at least 300 feet away from the polling place doors. But the federal courts struck down the statutes on First Amendment grounds. News media were free to approach voters within a reasonable distance of the precinct polling place.

After years of edging tentatively toward the fateful commitment, the editors of the *New York Times* finally decided in the early 1970s to hire a pollster. They entered into a cooperative agreement with *Time* magazine to commission a series of polls in 1972 by the New York City firm of Daniel Yankelovich, Inc. Ruth Clark, who had serendipitously played a part in the "invention" of the modern exit poll while working for Lou Harris, coordinated the projects for Yankelovich.[19]

Gallup reported in late 1971 that Senator George McGovern of South Dakota was favored for the presidency by 6 percent of Democratic voters. Senator Edmund Muskie of Maine held a big lead in the early polls. James M. Perry, a political writer for the *National Observer* newspaper, wrote a book about the 1972 campaign. In it he said, "if the American people are interested in anything about politics, it's about who's going to win. . . . That being all too true, the little band of believers—the reporters and the politicians and the activists really interested in politics—read George Gallup's figures as if they were chiseled in stone. At this early stage of the game they were, in fact, scribbled in sand."[20]

Looking ahead to the New Hampshire primary, Perry said his instincts told him that McGovern was the only candidate "doing very much" in that state. But he was "swayed by the siren sound of Dr. Gallup's poll and, no doubt, by what my own colleagues were saying and writing."

Shortly before the voting in New Hampshire, Muskie made the mistake of weeping at an outdoor rally while there were reporters present. He received 46.1 percent of the vote and 15 of the 20 delegates from New Hampshire. But McGovern did better than expected—finishing second with 37.1 percent—and was applauded for his moral victory. McGovern's Gallup Poll rating slumped to 5 percent, however.

McGovern went on to win in Wisconsin, nevertheless, with the help of Republican crossover votes. Yankelovich's exit polls in the Florida and California primaries highlighted the problem McGovern would face in the fall. He had the support of a small but extremely enthusiastic segment of the electorate—but not nearly enough to be elected.

Peter Hart, retained by the *Washington Post,* found the same thing in his primary exit interviews. Some of the findings were contradictory, however. When Hart asked some "trial heat" questions in California, McGovern received 66 percent against President Nixon's 28 percent. Trial-heat polls invariably exaggerate the popularity of the name in the news most recently.

After McGovern won the Democratic nomination, Yankelovich conducted four successive preelection polls for the two publications in sixteen pivotal states. The last of the four showed Nixon in front, 62 to 23 percent.

The *Washington Post* deployed eight of its reporters in the fall to survey fifty traditionally Democratic precincts in the ten biggest states. In-depth reports stemming from those 443 interviews were prepared by Peter Hart's organization. The Hart poll examined specific groups of traditional Democratic voters that had defected to President Nixon four years before. The reports all pointed to a Nixon landslide, which is what happened.

The two most influential American newspapers had leaped aboard the polling bandwagon for essentially the same reason. Presidential campaigns were contrived to manipulate the images on the television evening news. All else had become incidental. Pack journalism served only to provide the chorus in the back corner of the stage. Their resistance to the campaigners' news management meant that print journalists generally were more determined than ever to downplay news of the campaign discourse. "To follow only what the candidate is saying doesn't tell you anything about how the country is responding," said Haynes Johnson, one of the *Post*'s reporters. Speaking for the *New York Times*, Jack Rosenthal said that polling had clearly become imperative.[21]

By happy coincidence, mass production preelection polling by telephone became feasible just as door-to-door interviewing became impractical. Metropolitan population shifts brought a morbid fear of crime to many local residents. People chain-locked their doors. Many of them wouldn't talk to a pollster even through the screen door. The refusal rate shot upwards, and pollsters worried that the refusers might have voting plans different from those of the cooperating citizens.

The innovation that came along just then to save the day for the polling profession was long-distance direct dialing. Unlike in the 1930s, well over 90 percent of American households now had access to telephones. Although the refusal rate could still be precariously high, telephone polls before an election were faster and cheaper. Mitofsky and his colleagues led the way in developing techniques for dialing residential exchanges randomly, thus reaching unlisted as well as listed phones in demographically definable areas coded by the telephone company. Soon commercial and media surveyers were tapping opinions across the nation from central phone banks.

When the votes were counted in 1972, Nixon beat McGovern with 61 percent of the popular vote to the loser's 37 percent. Harris had predicted 61–39, Gallup 62–38. For all of their scientific methodology, the pollsters had to be impressed with a straw poll carried out in Illinois the old-fashioned way. Eschewing the statistical mumbo-jumbo, the *Chicago Sun-Times* still conducted its statewide presidential election poll by collecting large numbers of straws at convenient locations around Illinois. The straw poll predicted that Nixon would carry the state with 59.8 percent; he actually received 59.3 percent.

Eventually, all three television networks were conducting exit polls to project outcomes—and in the business of arranging preelection polls for their news programs.

In 1975, the *New York Times* entered into a formal partnership with CBS to operate a joint polling operation. The two organizations have different needs. The broadcasters deliver much less information in their time on the air than the national "newspaper of record" can in its columns of space. Despite those differences, and the clashing egos of their managerial consultants, the marriage has survived through the 1990s. The two media share the same polling data but treat the resulting news reports independently and competitively. Charts based on exit polls—what Martin Nolan of the *Boston Globe* has called "a demographic ouija board . . . guesswork from faceless pigeon holes"—have largely replaced the actual vote tables in the *Times*' postelection report.[22]

Later, ABC joined polling forces with the *Washington Post;* NBC with the *Wall Street Journal;* and Cable News Network (CNN) with *USA Today.*

Increasingly, newspaper reporters covered primary election night from the studio of some kindhearted television station—sometimes with regrettable consequences. In 1976, David Broder of the *Washington Post* awaited the outcome of the Wisconsin Democratic voting in the Milwaukee studio of NBC's affiliated station. At 9:27 P.M. EST, with only 2 percent of the raw vote counted, ABC declared Congressman Morris Udall of Arizona the winner over Governor Jimmy Carter of Georgia. NBC made its call for Udall at 10:22, by which time 76 of Scammon's 100 barometer precincts had been heard from. Facing an 11 P.M. first edition deadline, Broder filed a story reporting that Udall had won. CBS held back until more of the paper-ballot rural counties were tabulated. Carter eventually overcame Udall's lead, won the Wisconsin primary, won the Democratic nomination, won the presidency.[23]

Seventeen

A "Good Story" Trumps the Numbers

Journalists, losing politicians, aspiring opinion leaders, and advocates of reform generally had different reasons for being unhappy with polls. They could all share common cause, though, for protesting a practice that pressured voters to commit themselves prematurely on the basis of sketchy, simplistic information and superficial images. Bill Kovach, the curator of the Nieman Foundation at Harvard and a former *New York Times* reporter and editor, expressed this point of view well. He said the smoke-filled rooms of boss politics had been replaced by "a carnival side-show house of mirrors in which a potential voter is hopelessly trapped in a disorienting hall which is reflecting and re-reflecting the same images."[1]

Entering the 1990s, the transmitters of those images had become reconciled for the most part to the prominence of polls in their political coverage. But many of them resented the loss of their freedom to interpret public opinion. Executives in print and electronic media alike were smitten with the newly discovered need to "connect" with their readers and viewers. They wanted stories that "resonated," to use a buzzword of the 90s. The polls produced tables of flat numbers on a page or screen. Can't we bring the numbers to life? Can't we give them a human dimension?

This concern prompted news organizations to augment the dry quantification in the polls with some real faces and real names. This they did by adapting various forms of a familiar advertising research device: the focus group.

Advertisers bring a small group of consumers together and ask them questions about their product preferences. The questioners are able to probe deeper into the opinions of the subjects, who may or may not be representative of a particular population. Individuals in the room exchange thoughts while the scene is being recorded for later study by the experts.

News reporters used similar methods for television. Assorted individuals would be assembled to watch a political event on TV and then be interviewed, on camera, about their reactions. Their remarks had considerably less mathematical meaning than the numbers in a systematic survey. But the "macro" view provided by a poll was being supplemented by the "micro" expressions of presumably typical voters.

For newspapers, focus groups resembled the old-style man-in-the-street feature. Back before polls, when some big story broke, a reporter would be assigned to go out "on the street," usually accompanied by a photographer, and solicit the opinions of passersby. Readers had to trust the newspapers not to collect three dozen opinions and then discard the two dozen that did not conform to the opinions ordered up by the editors.

Just before the 1992 presidential primary in Illinois, reporters David Broder and Dan Balz arranged a focus group for the *Washington Post* in the Chicago suburb of Oak Park. President Bush and the former governor of Arkansas, Bill Clinton, had clinched their parties' nominations. But Clinton's alleged extramarital philandering had been much in the news. The *Post* wanted to test Clinton's and Bush's standing with swing voters.[2]

First, the newspaper hired a market research agency to summon twelve suburban undecided voters, half of whom voted Republican four years before and half of whom voted Democratic. Sitting around a table with the reporters, for two hours the group recalled the images to which they had most recently been exposed in the news media. When asked to voice "the first thing that comes to your mind when I mention the name Bill Clinton," according to the subsequent newspaper story, the air was filled with epithets: Slick. Slimy. Cunning.

"I call him another (Jimmy) Swaggart or (Jim) Bakker, just from looking at him," said an accountant, referring to two disgraced television evangelists.

A school secretary in the group summarized Clinton's style as "Smooth, smile and screw you."

All of this may have been an apt portrayal of Clinton's image problems that would plague him throughout his presidency. However, respondents were repeating impressions freshly supplied by, among others, the *Washington Post*. In the case of the accountant, his reactions were based on what he knew "just by looking at" the candidate.

The story of the focus group did not appear until after the Illinois primary, which Bush and Clinton both won. The story in the paper was buttressed by the data in a *Post*-ABC national poll that "confirmed doubts [about both candidates] forcibly expressed" by the focus group. "The picture drawn by both the group interview and the poll is of an electorate that has little enthusiasm for either of the likely nominees," the *Post* story reported. When asked to cast a secret ballot between Bush and Clinton, the Oak Park group came down on Bush's side, 9 to 2, with one abstainer.

A "Good Story" Trumps the Numbers

Pictures of people in the act of expressing their ideas make for better television, no doubt, than a screen filled with figures, just as the discretionary intervention of a questioning journalist alters the "scientific objectivity" of an opinion survey. Reporting poll stories in 1996, newspapers began inserting selective illustrative quotes from respondents. By sprinkling the print equivalent of sound bites through their stories, reporters humanized the otherwise sterile numbers. Typically the selective quotes were presented to document the reporter's assessment of a development or trend in the campaign.

Statistical purists like Warren Mitofsky criticized this new hybrid form of horse-race journalism.[3] Unless the participants in the focus groups and the random interviews were chosen by the strict rules of probability sampling, a journalist who is so inclined has regained the opportunity to superimpose professional judgment upon the measurement of public opinion. A small step back in the direction of instinctive, impressionistic political reporting.

On into the 1990s the competition for media audiences intensified, much to the detriment of issues-journalism. Broadcasters had to contend with the growth of cable and satellite channels. Print journalists heard predictions that words on paper would soon be extinct. Many of the very people who constituted the prime political news "market" were off surfing the Internet.

Nearing the end of the century, candidates were thoroughly conditioned to the sound-bite imperatives of an entertainment medium ill-suited for the transmission of ideas. When a metropolitan newspaper—the *Chicago Sun-Times*—offered to make available entire pages in 1996 for the candidates' own unfiltered in-depth exposition of issues, the candidates did nothing but dig out some stale press releases. Treatment of issues in depth proved as foreign to video-conditioned candidates as to journalists.[4]

In most presidential campaigns the top story most of the time is still the race. Who will be nominated (the qualifying heats)? And then who will be elected (the main event)? This story is usually prescripted by the opinion polls. Usually, but not always.

Sometimes the horse-race story is influenced by the stylistic biases of the journalists, acting in their role of handicappers. As noted in a previous chapter, the trendsetters in the press corps admire some candidates and dislike others. Ideology plays some part in these judgments, but not a whole lot. Most White House reporters were personally fond of the conservative Ronald Reagan, the first (but surely not the last?) Hollywood president. In the opinions of two veteran correspondents, Robert Donovan and Ray Scherer, "this contributed to the favorable coverage [Reagan] received." All three of the recent Southern Democrats in the Oval Office—Lyndon Johnson of Texas, Jimmy Carter of Georgia, and Bill Clinton of Arkansas— had to contend with an unsympathetic press. In some part this occurred for reasons of regional culture unrelated to public policy. Anthony Lewis, a columnist for the *New York Times,* commented on this "cultural prejudice" in 1980:

> In the interminable process that we now use to elect a President, the press decides what is news and who is news. . . . Take the case of John Anderson [in 1976], a candidate almost wholly created by the press. We found him different, iconoclastic, a figure of interest in what we considered a dull group of Republican primary candidates. David Broder said reporters liked John Anderson for many of the same reasons we liked Eugene McCarthy [a Democratic candidate in 1968]: "He uses language well, and language is our coin of exchange. He says what he thinks, as we like to think we do. He can be caustically critical of other politicians, which is our stock in trade." And Broder added, "We tend to overlook the moral arrogance implicit in many of his judgments because we have more than our share of that quality ourselves."[5]

In the modern era, the snobbish Ivy League provincialism of the Washington press is typified by one of Kennedy's legion of close friends in the media—Ben Bradlee. Then a reporter for *Newsweek* (and later editor of the *Washington Post*), Bradlee wrote a personal letter to Kennedy after covering Lyndon Johnson's presidential campaigning in 1959: "My own response to Johnson is that . . . he could never make it. The image is poor. The accent hurts. Even if we assume that people say they have no prejudice against a southerner, the fact is that in this country the Texan is partly a comic, partly a horse opera figure."[6]

Sometimes, as it happens, the horse-race story is best advanced by momentarily ignoring the numbers in the polls. If interest in a dull campaign can be revived by an infusion of drama that flies in the face of the numerical logic, so be it. If the race is not exciting (for journalists "exciting" usually means close), the numbers can be disregarded—temporarily.

An example of this occurred in the 1988 contest for the Democratic nomination. Governor Michael Dukakis had a sizeable early lead both in committed delegates and in the popularity polls. Indulging their moral arrogance, some of the leading journalists awaited the entry of the candidate they deemed more suitable—which for most of them meant Governor Mario Cuomo of New York. Cuomo did not step forward, however, and Dukakis held his lead over a field of opponents that included the Reverend Jesse Jackson, a prominent African-American leader from Chicago. Jackson's verbal acuity and his combative nature made good news copy. The polls indicated consistently, however, that many white Democrats were exceedingly hostile toward Jackson, who had been a forceful independent presence on the national scene for many years. In the argot of the polling trade, his "negatives" were extremely high. If the polls held any validity at all, they seemed to be saying that Jesse Jackson was not likely to be nominated, and still less likely to be elected.

The pundits were caught unawares, however, when Jackson won the statewide caucus vote of Democrats in Michigan. Because this development was unexpected, it produced just what was badly needed: a fresh angle for the campaign saga. No one appeared to know how many of which Democrats had participated in the Michigan caucuses, or how the outcome might affect other states. But a new lively story-line sprouted overnight. The next week's Democratic primary would be across Lake Michigan in Wisconsin, a state with fewer black voters. A correspondent for the Knight-Ridder newspapers wrote that Jackson had "emerged as the Democratic front-runner." By mid-week, the *Los Angeles Times* reported "rumors of a stop-Jackson effort." Broder and Paul Taylor said in the *Washington Post* that Jackson's caucus votes in Michigan had "prompted shell-shocked party leaders to question [Dukakis's] ability to compete with him." Robert Shogan told *Los Angeles Times* readers that Jackson's win had "reshaped the race, which seems likely to assure that the contest will be marred by confusion and controversy to its bitter end." For the first time, added R. W. Apple Jr. in the *New York Times,* party professionals had begun "actively contemplating the possibility" that Jackson would emerge from the primaries with more delegates than anyone else.[7]

Dukakis won easily in Wisconsin, the confusion and much of the controversy that would have enlivened the news of the preconvention period lifted, and the governor went on to be nominated. The only remaining conflict at the Democratic convention concerned whether Jackson would acquiesce in Dukakis's selection of somebody other than Jackson for a running mate.

A few lonely editors were still opposed in 1988 to the use of preelection polls. One of them was Gene Roberts of the *Philadelphia Inquirer.* After the Democratic convention ended, while other papers were running Bush-Dukakis trial-heat polls (showing Dukakis in front), the *Inquirer* printed a story headlined "Voters React to Dukakis." Based on interviews in eleven states during and immediately following the convention, the story quoted ten voters in Warren, Michigan; South Philadelphia, Pennsylvania; Brookston, Indiana; Mebane, North Carolina; and Grand Forks, North Dakota.

Some of those who were quoted were for Dukakis; others were against him. The readers were told, without any attempt at quantification, that the account suggested "both the problems and the potential" facing the Democratic nominee.

Especially in the early stages of a campaign, a sudden surge of media attention can produce a corresponding upward blip in an individual's popularity in the polls. An unknown can become a household word almost overnight. Being in the news is what matters. This phenomenon, which is attributable both to the powerful reach of television images and to the uniformity of journalistic interpretations, occurred in the 1996 competition for the Republican presidential nomination.

All during 1995 and early 1996, Senator Bob Dole graded far ahead of the other Republican candidates in the opinion polls. He could also be seen to have cornered most of the big Republican state organizations and money sources. But Dole had run for president twice before. Though widely admired by reporters for his self-deprecating wit, he was in a class novelty-wise with William Jennings Bryan. After retired army general Colin Powell, an exciting nonpolitician, decided against entering the race, the national political press corps had to conjure up their own reality. "We had to report a horse race, even if it meant turning an eye to Dole's advantages," said Washington correspondent Christopher Hanson. "Journalists penned up in Washington for four years by tight travel budgets had been given the go-ahead to hit the trail, and were not about to be denied."[8]

Dole won the first test, the Iowa caucuses, but not by as much as the reporters thought he should have. "Race up for grabs," declared NBC's Tim Russert the next morning. Russert and others agreed that the real winners were the second- and third-place finishers, Pat Buchanan and Lamar Alexander. Then the next week Buchanan won the primary in the tiny state of New Hampshire by a single percentage point. Whereupon Gwen Ifell of NBC declared Buchanan unstoppable. Doyle McManus of the *Los Angeles Times* predicted on a television program that Buchanan would enter the national convention in August with more delegates than anyone else.

When Buchanan's campaign fizzled out, and Alexander failed to win a single primary, the media breathed life into a previously unfamiliar figure (who had finished fourth in New Hampshire)—the multimillionaire magazine publisher Malcolm S. (Steve) Forbes Jr. After Forbes won in Arizona, the media proclaimed *him* the new front-runner, although Dole had taken two other states on the same day and had far more committed delegates than anyone else. *Time* put Forbes' picture on the cover and speculated that Dole might be finished. The splash of media attention raised Forbes' poll

A "Good Story" Trumps the Numbers

ratings briefly. Having elevated Forbes and Buchanan to the status of serious candidates once again, reporters did next what came naturally: they began wondering in print and over the air, as well they might, whether a rich man little known outside Manhattan could be elected president on a platform of lowering his own taxes. By the middle of March, the last suspense had been squeezed out of the story. The game was over. Dole had won.

Sometimes, therefore, the horse-race story requires the suspension of the semi-scientific measurements portrayed by opinion polls. Sometimes instincts and impressions can be teased into a better horse-race story. It is important to understand that journalists compete for space and position in the newspaper and for time on the air. They compete for the esteem of their bosses and their colleagues. They compete for their perceived superiority over their rivals. And they compete for the attention of their readers and viewers. In those who work for a supplemental news service or a newspaper group, the competitive juices flow with special force because they are competing for national exposure.

The horse-race story is almost always uppermost, but there are times in a campaign—usually in brief interludes—when the running story of the race can be sustained only by setting aside the figures in the polls.

Eighteen

And Now . . . the Virtual Horse Race

Aha, the mystery of politics has been quantified. The truth is, I think
we have gone absolutely out of our minds about polls.

Jeff Greenfield, CNN, in 1996.

The presidential election of 1996 spread a veritable groaning board of
horse-race polls before the American electorate. There were four daily national tracking polls and countless national and state surveys. In April, the
New York Times reported: "Poll Points to Close Race in Fall," and suggested
that Dole might even be considered the favored candidate.[1] From the summer months on, however, as the voters began to pay closer attention (and
the journalists were getting bored), the pointers shifted around. With rare
exception, news polls echoed a single consistent theme: Bob Dole was fall-
ing hopelessly behind. This message could not help but seep into the overall
news coverage of the campaign, sapping the interest first of journalists and
then of the voters themselves.

By election day, many Americans were so gorged on preelection polls
that they did not bother to stay for the main course. Voting turnout dropped
to its lowest level in seventy-two years. Using a different metaphor, why
bother to have a ball game (or an election) if everybody knows how it will
turn out?

The previous chapters have told how we got from there to here. The
great dramatists in all languages and all civilizations understood the human
fascination with tales of conflict and suspense. After a brief initial period
of leadership by a privileged few, the United States eased into an electoral
system more fitting for an egalitarian people of many different strains. The
method of selecting the chief executive involved the periodic, visible, and
usually suspenseful settlement of electoral conflict.

Until recently, Americans took pride in lining up on one or the other of
two sides. The people expected to be able to follow the action in the arena.
For many years the lack of voting privacy contributed to the interest in the

voting behavior of others. Keeping score then was relatively easy. In any competitive exercise, the spectators want to know who is favored to win and by what odds; what the score is as the contest proceeds; and when it's over, who won. Over the years, the free and independent press responded to these expectations by functioning as scorekeeper. The relationship of press and politician changed with the diversification of communications technology. When the parties had to control newspapers in order to spread their messages, partisan organs were filled with argumentative propaganda. Scorekeeping reports were sometimes distorted and manipulated for partisan purposes.

It has been shown how newly enfranchised Americans resorted to straw polls for the documentary evidence of the popularity of certain presidential candidates; how, in this newly rooted democratic order, the American people used numbers to nourish and grow important causes; how editors broke loose from partisan servitude after mass-consumer markets and better transportation created a need for advertising; how the profusion of elected governments added to the legions of Americans who were dependent on the spoils of public finance; how interest in gambling created a demand for detailed information about the measurement of risk—at the racetrack and in election campaigns; how the people came to enjoy new spectator diversions more exciting, more satisfying than the oldfangled, long-winded political gabfest.

Most journalists are in the commercial business of telling people things they don't already know—and doing it as quickly as possible. We have explained how Colonel Taylor's concept of key precincts developed into the modern exit poll. Indeed, the idea of representative sampling is at the base of all polling. Bolstered by the voluminous data compiled by the U.S. Bureau of the Census, experts have become adept at using random sampling to predict voting behavior both before and immediately after the casting of ballots. Pollsters have, in the words of one practitioner, "taken away the several hundred years monopoly of journalists to assess what the public thinks."[2]

The impetus for the development of straw polls and their progeny—the modern "scientific" polls—came not from journalists but from The People. One of the oddities in the history of political polls as news is that neither journalists nor market survey professionals were ever very enthusiastic about them. Succeeding generations of newspaper editors and television correspondents fought to preserve a place for their election campaign "instincts and impressions."[3] *Literary Digest* and many of the early newspaper sponsors saw polls primarily as circulation-building gimmicks. Polling companies, ultraconservative by nature, resented being put on such a well-publicized spot. "My advice to all would-be election forecasters is to think again," said Henry Durant, the head of the Gallup Poll in Great Britain. "It is the most stupid job. . . . If you get the election right, everyone takes it for granted. If you get it wrong, you are standing alone and utterly ashamed, and there is nothing you can do about it."[4]

In their election night rush to judgment, the networks sometimes botch the exit polls. Other problems threaten the future of election polls. Apart from an unusually high refusal rate in some areas, the most worrisome danger now facing exit pollsters is absentee voting. California, for example, now permits anyone to cast a ballot before election day without explanation. As more people choose to vote absentee, poll tabulators can only hope that their voting decisions are not significantly different from those who vote on election day.

Oregon elected a U.S. senator by mail over a three-week period in 1996. Because the names of those who voted in the first few days were available, the Oregon media had an opportunity to conduct an on-going exit poll while the voting was in progress, but resisted the temptation.

The growth of commercial "telemarketing" (selling things over the telephone) has increased public resistance to opinion polls of all kinds. More people are refusing to answer questions over the phone. Another problem that developed in the 1996 campaign might have been anticipated. Workers for candidates learned how to gain access to a household by posing on the telephone as independent pollsters and then slipping in a pitch for their candidate. This is a telephonic embellishment of the old-style voter canvass that news organizations fear will further erode public willingness to cooperate in preelection polls.

Because the networks persist in refusing to hold back exit-poll news until the presidential voting has finished in all time zones, the most likely congressional response is (or ought to be) a uniform national voting period—perhaps, as proposed by some, beginning on Monday evening.

The central tabulation of votes, once so vexing to journalists, now occurs expeditiously—thanks to machine voting, computer technology, and the media's cost-cutting cooperative agreements. In the last century, Republican editors were reluctant to accept results relayed by Democratic newspapers. Now the running totals are fast becoming irrelevant to broadcasters who compete to interpret their jointly collected exit-poll data before any votes are actually counted.

Preelection tracking polls do more systematically what Sam Lubell attempted forty years ago by trudging across the countryside in search of voters he had interviewed before to see if their sentiments had changed. The *New York Times* reporting teams did it by checking with politicians and local reporters. Who would argue that the old way was better?

In the final stages of a campaign, there is no better way to find out how people expect to vote than to ask them. If the status of the competition is news—and all but the most cloistered academics must concede that—then I would contend that citizens are better served by a scientific measurement than they are with the impressionistic embellishments of journalists. It is painfully obvious, however, as Jeff Greenfield tells us, that the media have gone out of their minds about polls. It is one thing to project voting intentions in the final stages of the campaign when most voters are paying attention; quite another to litter the civic landscape with estimates of ill-formed opinions on complex issues.

Problems are as likely to occur when journalists apply their professional expertise to the meaning of the numbers. Editors were unhappy with their race-handicapping coverage of the early Republican primaries in 1996. In May, *Editor & Publisher* succinctly headlined the results of a survey of news executives: "News Execs Say Campaign Coverage Stinks."[5]

The veteran pollster Daniel Yankelovich faulted the editors themselves and their "30-second sound bites and snappy headlines," which he said distort survey research. Left out of the news reporting, "is essential information about whether the public's opinion is stable or volatile; whether it contradicts other opinions that people also hold; and whether people are aware or unaware of the consequences of their own views and how they would respond to these consequences."[6]

Newspaper people tend to blame the entertainment imperative of television news for the excesses of horse-race journalism. (Mitofsky says what print journalists really resent is having lost their handle on the election story.)[7] A common complaint in the survey reported in *E&P* was that the news emphasized tenuous perceptions of *the meaning* of "the horserace" while ignoring the substantive issues. "The time has come," said the president of the foundation that sponsored the survey, "for print and broadcast management to recognize the way to improve the quality of reporting is to prepare journalists intellectually to cover the issues and not just the horse race. Our study finds journalists simply aren't providing the analysis citizens need on issues such as immigration, the economy, protectionism and trade."

News of who is ahead and what the issues are about need not be mutually exclusive. Why not have both? If editors acknowledge their responsibilities under the First Amendment, why don't they cover the issues and not just the horse race?

However irrational, some of the reasons can be found in the history of horse-race journalism.

First is that perverse element in the culture of journalism which considers most politicians to be unprincipled knaves and political discourse to be deadly dull. The dismissive cynicism that continues to characterize political journalism originated in the progressive era, a reaction to decades of strong parties, the partisan press, and high political interest. One of the previous chapters spells out in some detail the position taken by the newspaper industry in the early 1900s that because political speech is self-serving (besides being unconscionably dull), it ought to be paid for as advertising. (A similar attitude is reflected in the resistance of television executives to the suggestion today that free air-time should be made available to candidates.) Later on in this century, reports of substantive issues became steadily more truncated as more scintillating fascinations abounded. One newspaper, the *Columbia Daily Tribune* in Missouri, actually initiated a policy in 1996 of charging a fee for letters to the editor that endorsed or criticized a political candidate—$25 for 101–250 words, $10 for 100 words or less.[8]

If most campaign issues stories are not very engaging compared to horse-race stories, as journalists sometimes plead, the fault lies in the newsroom rather than in the living rooms of readers and viewers. One of the reasons was the tradition in the news business that generalists are valued over specialists and that depth can be counterproductive to easy understanding. Bernard M. Kilgore, the former president of the *Wall Street Journal,* helps us understand the origins of this with a complaint expressed in 1961: "This business of urging high-level specialization in journalism . . . is a mistake. . . . I don't know how many times I've had to tell people that we are not looking for economists or statisticians or bankers or whatnot. Almost by definition a good reporter is a generalist. He has a talent for seeking out the new, the unexpected, the unusual and perhaps even the complicated."[9]

One of the exceptions to that rule is the political beat. Campaigns are covered by political reporters, not by journalists who have an in-depth knowledge of immigration, economics, and trade—even in those still rare news organizations where such experts are permitted to exist. The best political reporters live in a world of gossip and speculation and strategic intrigue. They are accustomed to deceptive rhetoric, to practiced hypocrisy and the shifty arts of the spin doctor.

As a consequence, their air of skepticism is easily mistaken for cynicism.

Ruth Marcus, a White House reporter for the *Washington Post,* was quoted in 1995 as saying: "The White House press plane . . . is like junior high school. I have never met a group of people who complain more about what they are doing. It's an ethos of disgruntlement—of which cynicism is a part. And in the group ethos, naivete is just the hugest sin of all. Nothing could make you look more stupid than saying, 'I think, gee, they're doing this because they're right.' There's almost a bidding war of cynicism. It's good to be more cynical."

"You really look like a fool if you take issues seriously," added Gail Collins, then a columnist for *Newsday,* later on the editorial board of the *New York Times.* "Anytime you write something that is really, really positive about a politician, unless he's dead—everyone in the community of journalism says, 'God, did you see how they're sucking up to that person?'"[10]

Hear the ghost of James Gordon Bennett cheering offstage!

Journalists can never cede their control over the reporting of the news. Sam Lubell found long ago that the issues moving voters in a campaign were not always those being addressed in the speeches of the candidates. And Lord Bryce noticed over a century ago that the parties often attempted to sidestep the most sensitive issues.

The Democratic Party's position on immigration, the first of the issues mentioned in the study cited by *Editor & Publisher* in 1996, might have been an example. Some liberals, concerned about overpopulation and environmental degradation, favored curbs on immigration. Other liberals were equally committed to cultural diversity and opportunities for disadvantaged foreigners to make a new start in America.

It was and is possible, nevertheless, for a reporter who knows something about the intricacies of population politics to make the issues understandable. The arguments on all sides can be explained as fully and fairly as possible. Any time the advocate who is making the case omits a bit of relevant information, the reporter should take parenthetical note of its absence. To provide context, the historical background of immigration policy should be summarized. The recent immigration experience should be described, in both macro and micro terms. Who are the American people? Who are the new immigrants? Where do they live? What jobs do they hold? What is known—*really known*—about illegal immigration? Is their presence a depressing influence on wages? One source says this, another says that, this is what I the reporter have done my best to find out is true. Who and what are the forces pressuring Congress in both directions on this issue? What are their motives? If the American Restaurant Association and the Roman Catholic hierarchy are lobbying against a tougher policy on deportations,

And Now . . . the Virtual Horse Race

say so. Who would be helped and hurt by changes in policy? If some of the interested groups are contributing to campaigns, include that information. Leave it to the reader or viewer to make of this information what he or she will. The reporter should try to get to the bottom of baffling contradictions. In some instances, the reporter's clearly labeled opinion might be included, particularly if the reader/viewer is let in on any relevant information about where that reporter is "coming from" on the issue.

Preoccupied as they are with political conflict, most reporters are ill-prepared to understand and explain complicated economic questions. "Are Journalists Too Ignorant To Cover Important News Issues Correctly?" asked the editor of the *Detroit News* recently.[11] Immigration, economic policy, foreign trade are complex issues. No journalistic rendition is ever likely to satisfy the real experts in the field, especially those with strong views on one or the other side who prefer indoctrination to education. But reporting that is clear and penetrating can do much to help citizens make sense of the decisions confronting them. What's more, it can be made *interesting*.

The gamesmanship approach to political activity, so engrained in political reporters, rubs off on legislative reporting as well. A bill passed in Congress is viewed first as a victory or setback for the president. What its passage will mean to the readers or viewers is of lesser significance to the sports-directed generalists in the press box who must deal with (and perhaps sometimes understand) the many different substantive issues that grind their way through the legislative mill. Not infrequently the same reporters are responsible for election-campaign and legislative-session coverage. The result is a style of journalism highly unsatisfactory to many thoughtful citizens.

Lacking the semblance of a horse race, or what they considered worthy issues, the media declared the 1996 campaign over long before the election. "The headlines are very negative and make it sound boring," said Emily Rooney, the political director of Fox News. "I really feel that the press has written it off, as if there's no chance the race could become interesting or that Dole can win it."[12]

"I know what you're thinking," wrote the *Boston Globe*'s David Shribman in *Fortune* magazine in late October. "You're sick of this campaign. You're sick of these candidates. You're sick of those awful network campaign logos. You're sick of the very number '1996.' Come close and let me whisper a secret. So are all of us bedraggled, bewildered political pros. Sick, sick, sick to death."[13]

In the final count Clinton won reelection by almost the exact popular and electoral vote margins forecast by the leading polls.

The origins of horse-race journalism are buried in the American past and in the human psyche. To deplore the status of the contest as interesting news is to ignore the reality of human nature. How newspapers and magazines try to keep pace with a breaking story like election night has come full circle. Whereas once they used kites and flashing lights, now they spread their offerings on the World Wide Web.

It seems likely that advancing technology will continue to nudge horserace reporting along an uncertain path. New interactive digital technology will broaden the media landscape beyond our present imagination. One day soon those with the necessary circuitry will be able to register their opinions by pushing a button on their information console, the results to be tabulated automatically on some cyberspatial scoreboard. The posting of political numbers will have moved from a church door in colonial Massachusetts to a handprinted bulletin in the newspaper office window, to skyrockets and searchlights flashing over the city horizon, to the chalkboard in a radio studio, and to the computerized graphic toteboard on the television cyberset.

Browsing for information, tomorrow's sophisticated citizen will have a "digital agent" to sieve through what is interesting and important, an algorithmic artificially intelligent personality who is familiar with the boss's tastes (and prejudices).

Few people are giving much thought to how this technology can be used to enhance public understanding of things like immigration policy. It can provide a digital tally board accessible day and night to political horse race fanatics; or it can contribute to civic self-enlightenment. The multimedia systems of the future represent an opportunity to process and display "packages" of information in more compelling and easy-to-understand formats. There will, in all available media, be interested parties offering selected versions of the truth. As always, the responsibility for relating the preachments of politicians and propagandists to the lives of people will rest with fair-minded professional journalists. This they can do not so much by disowning the splotchy legacy of horse-race journalism as by reawakening to the words of the First Amendment.

Notes

Introduction

1. Christopher Hitchens, "Voting in the Passive Voice: What Polling Has Done to American Democracy," *Harper's*, April 1992, p. 51.
2. See *New York Times*, Nov. 6, 1996, "Quick Calls: How America Gets the News," p. 16, for a description of the exit polling process in that presidential election.
3. See E. J. Dionne Jr., "The Illusion of Technique: The Impact of Polls on Reporters and Democracy," *Media Polls in American Politics*, ed. Thomas E. Mann and Garry R. Orren (Washington: The Brookings Institution, 1992), pp. 150–67. Also generally Robert M. Entman, *Democracy Without Citizens: Media and the Decay of American Politics* (New York: Oxford University Press, 1989).
4. Daniel J. Boorstin, *The Image: A Guide to Pseudo-Events in America* (New York: Atheneum, 1987), p. 233.
5. The first Broder quote is from Charles Peters and John Rothchild, *Inside the System* (New York: Praeger, 1973), p. 31; the second is from Broder's *Behind the Front Page* (New York: Simon and Schuster, 1987), p. 272.
6. James Reston, *Deadline: A Memoir* (New York: Random House, 1991), p. 205.

1. The Colonel and the Key Precincts

1. Julian Ralph, *The Making of a Journalist* (New York: Harper & Bros., 1903), p. 147.
2. Edward J. Mitchell, *Memoirs of an Editor: Fifty Years of American Journalism* (New York: Charles Scribner's Sons, 1924), p. 260.
3. Ralph, pp. 147, 149–50.
4. The election night description borrows from Ralph; James Morgan, *Charles H. Taylor: Builder of the Boston Globe* (privately published, 1923); Louis M. Lyons, *Newspaper Story: One Hundred Years of the Boston Globe*, (Cambridge, Mass.: Belknap Press, 1971) p. 104; Hartley Davis, "Election Night in a Great Newspaper Office," *Women's Home Companion*, Nov. 1904, p. 3; Allen Churchill, *Park Row* (New York: Rinehart, 1958), p. 13.
5. *Scientific American*, Aug. 30, 1890, published drawings of women operating "electrical counting machines" for the census of that year, p. 132.
6. *Newspaper Maker*, Sept. 3, 1896, p. 6.
7. *Editor & Publisher*, Dec. 27, 1902, p. 2.
8. Morgan, p. 32. The Taylor biographical information is taken from Morgan and Lyons generally.
9. *Boston Globe*, Nov. 1, 1888, p. 1.
10. *Boston Globe*, Nov. 4, 1888, p. 12.

2. Old Hickory . . . and a Passion for Numbers

1. *Virginia Gazette,* Nov. 18, 1786. p. 2.

2. Cortlandt F. Bishop, *Elections in the American Colonies* (New York: Columbia College, 1893), p. 178. See also Robert J. Dinkin, *Voting in Provincial America* (Westport, Conn.: Greenwood, 1977), p. 6.

3. *Virginia Gazette,* Nov. 3, 1738, p. 5.

4. Robert Weir, "The Role of the Newspaper Press in Southern Colonies on the Eve of the Revolution," in *The Press and the American Revolution,* ed. Bernard Bailyn and John B. Hench (Worcester, Mass.: American Antiquarian Society, 1980), p. 114.

5. Patricia C. Cohen, *A Calculating People: The Spread of Numeracy in Early America* (Chicago: University of Chicago Press, 1982), p. 166.

6. Cohen, p. 4.

7. Cohen, p. 3.

8. Cohen, p. 4.

9. Gil Troy, *See How They Ran: The Changing Role of the Presidential Candidate* (New York: The Free Press, 1991), labels this as "the republican code of silence." Edward Pessen in his *Jacksonian America: Society, Personality and Politics* (Homewood, Ill.: Dorsey Press, 1978) describes how difficult it was to find out where Jackson stood on specific issues, pp. 173, 214–15. "Taylor, promise to serve the people" (Gerald L. Baldasty, *The Commercialization of News in the Nineteenth Century* [Madison: University of Wisconsin Press, 1992], p. 45).

10. Tom W. Smith, "The First Straw Poll: A Study of the Origins of Election Polls," *Public Opinion Quarterly* (Spring 1990), pp. 21–36.

11. See generally Samuel Popkin, *The Reasoning Voter* (Chicago: University of Chicago Press, 1991).

12. Smith, p. 26.

13. Smith, p. 27.

14. Smith, p. 29.

15. Smith, p. 27. See also George Gallup and Saul Rae, *The Pulse of Democracy* (New York: Greenwood, 1969), p. 35; and James A. Tankard Jr., "Public Opinion Polling by Newspapers in the Presidential Election of 1824," *Journalism Quarterly,* 1972, pp. 361–65.

16. Smith, p. 28.

17. Smith, p. 30.

18. See Smith, p. 30.

19. *Carolina Observer,* Nov. 3, 1828, p. 3.

20. *Star and North Carolina State Gazette,* Feb. 7, 1828, p. 2.

21. Alexis de Tocqueville, *Democracy in America* (New York: Knopf, 1972), vol. 1, p. 136.

22. *Star and North Carolina State Gazette,* Oct. 13, 1836, p. 3.

23. *Harrisburg Chronicle,* Dec. 20, 1837.

24. James L. Crouthamel, *James Watson Webb: A Biography* (Middletown, Conn.: Wesleyan University Press, 1969). p. 29.

25. *Carolina Observer,* April 3, 1828, p. 3.

26. Frank Angelo, *On Guard: A History of the Detroit Press* (Detroit: The Detroit Free Press, 1981), p. 33.

27. John M. Matheson, "Steam Packet to Magic Lanterns: A History of Election Returns Coverage in Newspapers of Four Illinois Cities, 1836–1928" (Ph.D. diss., Southern Ilinois University, Carbondale, 1967), p. 42.

3. Kicking All Politicians to the Devil

1. Allan Nevins, ed., *The Diary of Philip Hone, 1828–1851* (New York: Dodd, Mead, 1936), p. 712.

2. Beman Brockway, *Fifty Years in Journalism* (Watertown, N.Y.: Daily Times Printing and Publishing House, 1891), p. 414.

3. Thomas H. Baker, *The Memphis Commercial-Appeal: The History of a Southern Newspaper* (Baton Rouge: Louisiana State University Press, 1971), p. 41.

4. Melville E. Stone, *Fifty Years a Journalist* (Garden City, N.Y.: Doubleday, Page, 1921), p. 52.

5. Franklin W. Scott, *Newspapers and Periodicals of Illinois, 1814–1879* (Chicago: R. R. Donnelly, 1910), p. lxxiv.

6. Mark Wahlgren Summers, *The Press Gang: Newspapers and Politics, 1865–1878* (Chapel Hill: University of North Carolina Press, 1994), p. 139.

7. Oliver Carlson, *The Man Who Made News: James Gordon Bennett* (New York: Duell, Sloan & Pearce, 1942), p. 87.

8. J. Herbert Altschull, *From Milton to McLuhan* (New York: Longman, 1990), p. 242.

9. Isaac Pray, *Memoirs of James Gordon Bennett and His Times* (New York: Springer & Townsend, 1885), p. 162.

10. Jean H. Baker, *Affairs of Party: The Political Culture of Northern Democrats in the Mid-Nineteenth Century* (Ithaca: Cornell University Press, 1983), p. 49.

11. Donald Lewis Shaw, "At the Crossroads: Change and Continuity in American Press News, 1820–1860," *Media Voices . . .* ed., Folkerts, p. 146.

4. The Lightning and the Fire

1. Alexander McClure, *Recollections of Half a Century* (Salem, Mass.,: Salem Press, 1902), p. 4. The Massachusetts editor was Charles T. Congdon. See his *Reminiscenses of a Journalist* (Boston: Osgood, 1880), p. 222.

2. *New York Herald*, Nov. 3, 1872, p. 7.

3. *Scientific American*, Nov. 20, 1845.

4. Richard Schwarzlose, *The Nation's Newsbrokers* (Evanston: Northwestern University Press, 1989), vol. 1, p. 125.

5. Schwarzlose, vol. 1, p. 142.

6. Matheson, p. 89.

7. Matheson, p. 102.

8. Carlson, p. 264.

9. Schwarzlose, vol. 1, p. 227.

10. Schwarzlose, vol. 1, p. 164.

11. James W. Carey, *Communication as Culture* (Boston: Unwin Hyman, 1989), p. 211.

12. *Diary of George Templeton Strong*, ed., Allan Nevins and Milton H. Thomas (Seattle: University of Washington Press, 1952), p. 345.

13. Susan Herbst, *Numbered Voices: How Opinion Polling Has Shaped American Politics* (Chicago: University of Chicago Press, 1993), p. 77.

14. Edwin H. Cady, *The Big Game: College Sports and American Life* (Knoxville: University of Tennessee Press, 1978), p. 56.

15. T. H. Breen, "Horses and Gentlemen: The Cultural Significance of Gambling Among the Gentry of Virginia," *William and Mary Quarterly*, April 1977, pp. 239–57.

16. Henry Chavetz, *Play the Devil: A History of Gambling in the United States from 1492 to 1955* (New York: Clarkson N. Potter, 1960), p. 4.

17. For Cleveland, see Arthur H. Shaw, *The Plain Dealer: One Hundred Years in Cleveland* (New York: Knopf, 1942), p. 229; For Chicago, see Pray, *Memoirs of James Gordon Bennett*, p. 124.

18. For Bennett, see, Pray, p. 124; *Journal of Commerce*, Oct. 1, 1834.

19. The Cincinnati controversy is recounted in *Editor & Publisher*, Oct. 22, 1904, and subsequent issues. The Justice Department did not issue its ruling that the lotteries were illegal until after the election.

20. *New York Herald*, Nov. 1, 1876, p. 7.

21. *New York Herald*, Oct, 25, 1908, p. 1.

22. James Bryce, *The American Commonwealth* (London: Macmillan, 1888), vol. 1, pp. 603–4.

5. The Unholy Alliance of the AP and Western Union

1. *Electrical Review*, Nov. 10, 1880, p. 1.

2. Raymond B. Nixon, "Henry Grady, Reporter," *Journalism Quarterly* (Dec. 1935), p. 188.

3. *New York Herald*, Nov. 3, 1856, p. 1.

4. *New York Herald*, Nov. 4, 1868, p. 1. The 1872 quote is from the *Herald* of Nov. 6, p. 1.

5. Edgar L. Gray, "The Career of William Henry Smith, Politician-Journalist" (Ph.D. diss., Ohio State University, Columbus, 1951). See also the Smith papers in the Hayes Presidential Center Library, Fremont, Ohio; and in the William H. Smith Memorial Library, Indiana State Historical Library, Indianapolis.

6. *New York Herald*, Nov. 9, 1876, p. 4.

7. Smith to O. H. Booth letter, Dec. 12, 1876, quoted in Gray, p. 125.

8. Bryce, *The American Commonwealth*, vol. 2, p. 583.

9. *New York Herald*, Nov. 2, 1876, p. 3.

10. Julius Grodinsky, *Jay Gould: His Business Career, 1867–1892* (New York: Arno Press, 1981), p. 462; *New York Herald*, Feb. 21, 1884, p. 4.

11. *Chicago Tribune*, Nov. 1, 1884, p. 3.

12. Matheson, "Steam Packet to Magic Lanterns," p. 113.

13. *New York Herald*, Oct. 20, 1884, p. 3.

14. Matheson, p. 123.

15. For the best account of the anti-Gould demonstrations, see Richard O'Conner, *Gould's Millions* (Garden City, N.Y.: Doubleday, 1962), p. 239 ff.

6. The Journalism of Magic
Lanterns and Heavenly Hieroglyphics

1. *Fayetteville (N.C.) Observer,* Nov. 2, 1896, p. 1.

2. *Harper's Weekly,* Nov. 14. 1896, p. 1122. See also *The Journalist,* Nov. 10, 1900, p. 237.

3. Meyer Berger, *The Story of the New York Times, 1851–1951* (New York: Simon & Schuster, 1951), p. 120.

4. *Chicago Tribune,* Nov. 2, 1896.

5. Berger, p. 121. Ochs' Nov. 3 letter to his wife Effie is reproduced on p. 206 of Richard F. Shepard, *The Paper's Papers: A Reporter's Journey Through the Archives of the New York Times* (New York: Random House, 1996).

6. *New York Herald,* Nov. 4, 1896, p. 1.

7. Berger, p. 121.

8. *Chicago Daily News,* Nov. 3, 1896, p. 1. *Atlanta Constitution,* no advertising, Nov. 1, 1896, p. 1.

9. Nov. 5, 1900, p. 1. Chicago's "Battle of the Colored Bombs" is described in Matheson "Steam Packet to Magic Lanterns."

10. *New York Tribune,* Nov. 1, Nov. 4, 1896. The *New York Times* successfully used four kites to support a camera that photographed a McKinley parade during the 1896 campaign.

11. *Electrical Review,* Nov. 14, 1891, p. 166. See also Carolyn Marvin, *When Old Technologies Were New* (New York: Oxford University Press, 1988), p. 186.

12. *Electrical Review,* Nov. 19, 1892, p. 151.

13. *San Francisco Chronicle,* Nov. 3, 1896, p. 1.

14. *San Francisco Chronicle,* Nov. 4, 1896, p. 9.

7. Pack Journalism and the Modern Campaign

1. Bryce, *The American Commonwealth,* vol. 2, p. 583.

2. Michael E. McGerr, *The Decline of Popular Politics* (New York: Oxford University Press, 1986), p. 122. For the importance of anti-Catholicism in the politics of the 1890s, see Michael F. Holt, *Political Parties and American Political Development* (Baton Rouge: Louisiana State University Press, 1992).

3. Shepard, *The Paper's Papers,* p. 57.

4. *The Fourth Estate,* Oct. 8, 1896, p. 5.

5. Edward G. Riggs, "The Newspaper and Politics," *Bookman,* July 1904, p. 492.

6. Broder, *Behind the Front Page* (New York: Simon & Schuster, 1987), p. 239.

7. Ralph M. Goldman, "Stumping the Country: Rules of the Road, 1896," *Journalism Quarterly* (Summer 1952), pp. 303–6.

8. Stone, *Fifty Years a Journalist,* p. 313.

9. Theodore M. Porter, *The Rise of Statistical Thinking* (Princeton: Princeton University Press, 1986), pp. 4, 8.

10. Richard Jensen, "Polls and Politics: Democracy by the Numbers," *Public Opinion,* Feb.-March 1980, p. 53. See also Charles H. Dennis, *Victor Lawson: His Time and His Work* (Chicago: University of Chicago Press, 1935), p. 172.

11. *New York Times,* Nov. 1, 1896, p. 13. The *New York World* story was Oct. 30, 1896, p. 1; the *San Francisco Chronicle* story, Nov. 3, 1896, p. 3; the *St. Louis Post-Dispatch* story, Nov. 1, 1896, p. 17.

12. *Fayetteville Observer,* Nov. 2, 1896, p. 1.

13. *Fayetteville Observer,* Nov. 4, 1896, p. 2.

14. Robert Batlin, "San Francisco Newspapers' Campaign Coverage: 1896, 1952," *Journalism Quarterly* (1954), pp. 297–303.

15. McGerr, p. 141 ff. J. Rogers Hollingsworth, *The Whirlagig of Politics* (Chicago: University of Chicago Press, 1963), p. 34.

16. McGerr espouses the view that a more independent press represented a victory for the "educational" politics of reform, p. 121.

17. Theodore H. White, *The Making of the President 1960* (New York: Atheneum, 1961), p. 335.

18. *Chicago Journal,* Nov. 3, 1900, p. 1, and Nov. 6, p. 4.

8. Politics as a Sporting Proposition

1. The Tolson excerpt is from the Autumn 1994 issue of the *Wilson Quarterly.*

2. Cady, *The Big Game,* p. 62.

3. The material on Chadwick is from Mac Souders, "Baseball's First Publicist—Henry Chadwick," *Baseball Research Journal* (Nov. 15, 1986), p. 85; John Stevens, "The Rise of the Sports Page," *Gannett Center Journal,* Fall 1987, pp. 1ff.; David Voigt, *America Through Baseball* (Chicago: Nelson-Hall, 1976), p. 93; Melvin L. Adelman, *A Sporting Time: New York City and the Rise of Modern Athletics, 1820–70* (Urbana: University of Illinois Press, 1990), pp. 137ff.

4. See, for example, George Grella, "Baseball and the American Dream," in *Sport Inside Out,* ed. David L. Vanderwerken and Spencer K. Wertz (Fort Worth: Texas Christian University Press, 1985), p. 267; and Roland Garrett, "The Metaphysics of Baseball," in the same work, p. 643. The pastoral retreat theme was developed in Foster Rhea Dulles, *A History of Recreation: America Learns to Play* (New York: Appleton-Century-Crofts, 1965), p. 191. See also G. Edward White, *Creating the National Pastime* (Princeton: Princeton University Press, 1996).

5. Robert Lipsyte, *SportsWorld: An American Dreamland* (New York: Quadrangle, 1976), p. 40.

6. Cady, *The Big Game,* p. 102, from Reston column, *New York Times,* Oct. 11, 1969.

7. Edward White, *The National Pastime,* p. 33. Allen Guttmann, *From Ritual to Record: The Nature of Modern Sports* (New York: Columbia University Press, 1978), p. 100, discusses the "extremes of quantification in baseball." The Greeks, Guttmann points out, produced great athletes and great mathematicians, but "were not obsessed with the need to quantify" (p. 49).

8. James Reston, *Deadline,* p. ix. See p. 59 for his favorable comparison of sports and the "less orderly" and more deceptive realm of public affairs.

9. Richard Lipsky, *How We Play the Game: Why Sports Dominate American Life* (Boston: Beacon Press, 1981). The quoted excerpt is from a condensed version of his

book in Vanderwerken and Wertz, *Sport Inside Out* ("Of Team Players and Sky Hooks: The Infiltration of Sports Language in Politics"), p. 582.

10. Baldasty, *The Commercialization of News*, p. 50; see also pp. 38, 46.

11. Denney, *The Astonished Muse* (Chicago: University of Chicago Press: 1957), p. xxv.

9. Political Speech at Space Rates

1. *The Fourth Estate*, Oct. 8, 1896, p. 5.

2. Thomas H. Baker, *The Memphis Commercial-Appeal*, pp. 175–77.

3. Willard G. Bleyer, *Main Currents in the History of American Journalism* (New York: Houghton Mifflin, 1973), p. 180. First published in 1927.

4. *Newspaperdom*, Aug. 6, 1903, p. 14.

5. *Editor & Publisher*, July 18, 1908. p. 8. *The Nation*, July 9, 1908, p. 26.

6. *Newspaperdom*, Aug. 6, 1903, p. 14.

7. *The Journalist*, Nov. 10, 1900, p. 237. "Doesn't care a rap who won" is on p. 243.

8. Bryce, *The American Commonwealth*, vol. 2, pp. 586, 589–90, 594.

9. *Editor & Publisher*, Oct. 22, 1904, p. 4. *Newspaperdom*, July 13, 1916, p. 18.

10. *Newspaperdom*, June 1895, p. 394. The 1908 editorial is from the issue of Jan. 9, 1908, p. 6.

11. Jean Baker, *Affairs of Party*, p. 280.

10. The Literary Digest and the Pundits: Straws in the Wind

1. *Chicago Record-Herald*, Oct. 25, 1908, p. 3.

2. *New York Herald*, Oct. 18, 1908, second section.

3. *New York Herald*, Nov. 2, 1908, p. 1.

4. *Chicago Record-Herald*, Nov. 1, 1908, p. 1. "Large mercantile concerns," Oct. 22, pp. 1, 7.

5. Troy, *See How They Ran*, p. 129.

6. *New York Herald*, Nov. 3, 1912, p. 1.

7. *Boston Globe*, for Dr. Derolli, Nov. 3, 1912, p. 53; *San Francisco Chronicle* straw polls, Oct. 23, p. 1; Oct. 27, p. 1; Oct. 31, p. 4.

8. Jean M. Converse, *Survey Research in the United States: Roots and Emergence, 1890–1960* (Berkeley: University of California Press, 1987), p. 117.

9. *Fortune*, July 1935, "A New Technique in Journalism," p. 65.

10. Claude E. Robinson, *Straw Votes: A Study of Political Prediction* (New York: Columbia University Press, 1932), p. 67.

11. Robinson, "Bound out ahead in home stretch," p. 81; "Fake straw vote," p. 79.

12. Boorstin, *The Image*, pp. 233–34.

13. Lindsay Rogers, *The Pollsters* (New York: Knopf, 1949), pp. 45, 46, 234.

14. Stone, *Fifty Years a Journalist*, p. 324. Wilson was persuaded to cooperate with the press by the first White House press secretary, Joseph Tumulty.

15. *Literary Digest,* Sept. 16, 1916, p. 659; and Oct. 7, 1916, p. 871. See also Robinson, *Straw Votes,* p. 73; and Gallup and Rae, *The Pulse of Democracy,* p. 39.

16. *Literary Digest,* Oct. 28, 1916, p. 1087; and Nov. 4, 1916, p. 1155.

17. *New York Times,* Nov. 5, 1916, section 3.

18. Stone, *Fifty Years a Journalist,* p. 314.

19. Sidney L. James, "The Power of the Media: How I Watched It Grow and Grow," *Nieman Reports,* Spring 1983, p. 5.

20. Lyons, *Newspaper Story,* p. 200. See also Morgan, *Charles H. Taylor,* p. 125.

21. Lyons, p. 198.

22. The UP anecdote was related many years later in *Editor & Publisher,* Nov. 11, 1986, p. 15.

23. Robinson, *Straw Votes,* p. 67.

24. Riggs, "The Newspaper and Politics," pp. 480, 489.

25. Broder, *Behind the Front Page,* p. 242.

26. Thomas C. Leonard, *The Power of the Press: The Birth of American Political Reporting* (New York: Oxford University Press, 1986), p. 204.

27. Francis E. Leupp, "The Waning Power of the Press," *Atlantic Monthly,* Feb. 1910, pp. 147–50.

28. Leupp, p. 148.

29. Leupp, p. 150.

30. Stone, *Fifty Years a Journalist,* p. 214.

11. You're on the Air

1. Erik Barnouw, *A Tower in Babel: History of Broadcasting in U.S.* (New York: Oxford University Press, 1966), p. 34.

2. Susan J. Douglas, *Inventing American Broadcasting 1899–1922* (Baltimore: The Johns Hopkins University Press, 1987), p. 300. See also James David Barber, *The Pulse of Politics* (New York: Norton, 1980).

3. Barnouw, *A Tower in Babel,* p. 63, quoting *Detroit News,* Sept. 1, 1920. For good, detailed descriptions of the Pittsburgh and Detroit experiences, see Edward Bliss Jr., *Now the News: The Story of Broadcast Journalism* (New York: Columbia University Press, 1991), pp. 7–8; Edward W. Chester, *Radio, Television and American Politics* (New York: Sheed & Ward, 1969); Paul Schubert, *The Electric World: The Rise of Radio* (New York: Macmillan, 1928).

4. William B. Tubbs, "We Broadcast Better Music: WBBM Goes on the Air in Lincoln, Ill." *Illinois State Historical Journal,* Autumn 1996, p. 161.

5. *Editor & Publisher,* Nov. 8, 1924, p. 22.

6. *Editor & Publisher,* Nov. 3, 1928, p. 9.

7. *Saturday Evening Post,* "Political Publicity," Feb. 2, 1929, p. 9.

8. "Social workers found . . . ," *Broadcasting,* Oct. 15, 1936, p. 20; "Hoover . . . bulldozer," in "The Radio and the Election," *The Atlantic,* Sept. 1944, p. 117.

9. The best source for the "radio-press war" of that period is Gwenyth L. Jackaway, *Media at War: Radio's Challenge to the Newspapers, 1924–1939* (Westport, Conn.: Praeger, 1995). The account of that episode in this chapter is based largely on the Jackaway work. See also J. Fred MacDonald, *Don't Touch That Dial* (Chicago: Nelson-Hall, 1979), p. 284.

12. The Trials and Tribulations of George Gallup

1. *Literary Digest,* Sept. 3, 1932, p. 1. "Complaint about postmasters," *Literary Digest,* Nov. 1, 1924, p. 5.

2. *Literary Digest,* Oct. 11, 1924. p. 5.

3. Gallup and Rae, *The Pulse of Democracy,* p. 52. Quote from *Literary Digest,* Nov. 5, 1932, p. 8.

4. *Literary Digest,* Sept. 3, 1932, p. 41.

5. Lippmann in James Boylan, *The World and the Twenties* (New York: Dial, 1973), p. 292.

6. *Public Opinion Quarterly,* Jan. 1937, p. 4.

7. David W. Moore, *The Superpollsters,* (New York: Four Walls, Eight Windows, 1992), pp. 55–56.

8. The Gallup biographical material is from Moore, p. 31–33; James R. Beniger, *The Control Revolution* (Cambridge, Mass.: Harvard University Press, 1986), p. 388; Williston Rich, "The Human Yardstick," *Saturday Evening Post,* Jan. 21, 1939. pp. 8–9, 66; Richard Reeves, "George Gallup's Nation of Numbers," *Esquire,* Dec. 1983, p. 91; Harwood L. Childs, "Rule by Public Opinion," *Atlantic Monthly,* June 1936, p. 25; and an oral history conducted by Paul Sheatsley for the National Opinion Research Center, University of Chicago, March 22, 1978.

9. Eugene Meyer, "A Newspaper Publisher Looks at the Polls," *Public Opinion Quarterly* 1940, p. 239.

10. *Literary Digest,* Nov. 14, 1936, p. 17.

11. Moore, *The Superpollsters,* pp. 54–55.

12. *Editor & Publisher,* Nov. 14, 1936, p. 14. See also Gallup speech, "The Importance of Opinion News," Association for Education in Journalism national convention, University of Iowa, Aug. 31, 1966. In University of Iowa library.

13. The news release was dated Oct. 5, 1944.

14. Moore, *The Superpollsters,* p. 67. Most of the Gallup material in this section is based on Moore's book, by far the best historic treatment of news polls.

15. *New York Times,* Oct. 21, 1948, p. 23.

16. "Dewey commanding lead," *Los Angeles Times,* Oct. 20, 1948, p. 1; "Man-in-street Dewey win," Oct. 24, p. 1; the cabinet and Secret Service stories were Oct. 26, p. 10.

17. *Los Angeles Times,* Nov. 1, 1948, p. 1.

18. Strout pulled out a clipping of this story in his oral history interview with Jerry Hess for the Truman Library, Feb. 5, 1971.

19. For Henning and the *Chicago Tribune,* see Walter Trohan, *Political Animals* (Garden City, N.Y.: Doubleday, 1975). Quote from *St. Petersburg Evening Independent,* in *Editor & Publisher,* Nov. 13, 1948, p. 72.

20. Patterson described this phenomenon in a paper, "News Polls and Their Effects on Voters, Candidates and Reporters," for a conference on polls and presidential selection, Oct. 8, 1987, at the University of Illinois, Urbana-Champaign.

21. Polls colored the thinking. Louis Lyons, "The Press and the Election," *Nieman Reports,* Jan. 1949, pp. 6, 17. Reston's comments, in *Editor & Publisher,* Nov. 6, 1948, p. 5.

22. Michael L. Young, *The Classics of Polling* (Metuchen, N.J.: Scarecrow, 1990), p. 37.

23. Samuel Lubell, *Revolt of the Moderates* (New York: Harper), p. 262.

24. Bruce H. Westley, "On Predicting Elections," *Nieman Reports,* July 1952, p. 7.

25. Catledge's memo was reprinted in *Nieman Reports,* Jan. 1953, p. 15.

13. The Conversion of the Alsop Brothers

1. Alsop's ideas about column writing are spelled out in his and his brother's *The Reporter's Trade* (New York: Reynal, 1958), pp. 6ff.

2. This is from David M. Kennedy's review, Feb. 25, 1996, of Robert W. Merry's book, *Taking on the World* in *New York Times Book Review,* p. 11. The best sources of biographical background on Joe Alsop are Edwin M. Yoder Jr., *Joe Alsop's Cold War* (Chapel Hill: University of North Carolina Press, 1995); Leann Grabavoy Almquist, *Joe Alsop and American Foreign Policy* (Lanham, Md.: University Press of America, 1993); and Joe Alsop's own interview conducted by Elspeth Rostow for the John F. Kennedy Library, June 18 and 26, 1964.

3. *The Reporter's Trade,* p. 38. The Alsops' introduction to polling by Harris is related in Moore, *The Superpollsters,* p. 76.

4. Westley, *Nieman Reports,* July 1952, p. 7.

5. Sept. 24, 1960, pp. 170–74.

6. Shepard, *The Paper's Papers,* p. 205.

7. The Bernstein television story and many of the other details of the *Times*'s election-night scene were related in *Nieman Reports,* Jan. 1953, p. 15.

14. The Story Is in the Numbers

1. The 1940 scene at NBC was described by *Broadcasting,* Nov. 15, p. 20.

2. Sig Mickelson, *From Whistlestop to Sound Bite: Four Decades of Politics and Television* (New York: Praeger, 1989), p. 96.

3. Bliss, *Now the News,* p. 214.

4. Bliss, p. 216.

5. Jeff Kisseloff, *The Box* (New York: Viking, 1995), p. 349ff. See also Bill Leonard, *The Storm in the Eye* (New York: Putnam's, 1987), p. 82.

6. *Broadcasting,* Nov. 10, 1952, p. 27. The Abilene episode is from Mickelson, chap. 4, "The Struggle for Parity with Print," pp. 49ff.

7. For the UNIVAC story in 1952, I am relying chiefly on chapter 10 of Mickelson, pp. 137–41; chap. 14 of Harry Wulforst, *Breakthrough to the Computer Age* (New York: Scribner's, 1982), pp. 161–71; Joel Shurkin, *Engines of the Mind* (New York: Norton, 1984), pp. 252–53; and *Editor & Publisher,* Nov. 1, 1952, p. 46. "Promotional shot in the arm," Mickelson, p. 138.

8. *Editor & Publisher,* Nov. 17, 1956, p. 82.

9. Mickelson, p. 139.

10. Wulforst, p. 170.

11. Reuven Frank, "Election Night on Television," The *New Leader,* Oct. 5, 1992, p. 2.

12. Robert E. Kintner, *Broadcasting and the News* (New York: Harper & Row, 1965), p. 1.

15. Instincts and Impressions in the Land of Camelot

1. Donald D. Janson, "New York Times Election Survey Came Close," *Nieman Reports,* Jan. 1957, pp. 8–10.

2. Marvin Kalb, "How the Media Distorted the Presidential Race," *Editor & Publisher,* Nov. 19, 1988, p. 56. The article in the Spring 1997 issue of *Press/Politics,* by Gabriel Garcia Marquez, is quoted in *Wilson Quarterly,* Summer 1997, p. 130.

3. Lawrence told the story in the oral history interview for the Kennedy Library conducted April 22, 1966, by Ronald J. Grele. See also Lawrence's autobiography, *Six Presidents, Too Many Wars* (New York: Saturday Review Press, 1972), p. 235.

4. See n. 2, chap. 13, above, Alsop's interview for the Kennedy Library.

5. "Mary Clemmer Ames," Summers, *The Press Gang,* p. 173. "Theodore Roosevelt," William E. Curtis Papers, Item A-13, Western Reserve Historical Society Library, Cleveland.

6. "Al Smith style," Blythe, *Saturday Evening Post,* p. 142. See also Thomas L. Stokes, *Chip Off My Shoulder* (Princeton: Princeton University Press, 1980), p. 243. "Franklin Roosevelt," Henry M. Hyde, *Collier's* Oct. 28, 1933, p. 26.

7. Theodore White, *The Making of the President—1960,* p. 339.

8. *Editor & Publisher,* Oct. 22, 1960, p. 12. The Pulliam statement is from *E&P,* Nov. 11, 1960, p. 68.

9. *New York Times,* "City's Catholics," Nov. 2, p. 30; "Shift . . . by Jews," Nov. 3, p. 28; "Religion a Factor," Nov. 6, p. 1; "Final survey," Nov. 7, p. 1.

10. *Los Angeles Times,* Nov. 1–6. "Poll of Polls," Nov. 6.

11. Catledge tells of his anxieties in his autobiography, *My Life and the Times* (New York: Harper & Row, 1971), pp. 212–14.

12. Robert C. Smith, "The Campaign on TV," *Nieman Reports,* Jan. 1961, p. 2. Smith was associate editor of the *Norfolk Virginian-Pilot.*

13. Mary Ann Watson, *The Expanding Vista: Television in the Kennedy Years* (New York: Oxford University Press, 1990), p. 15. See also Frank, *"Election Night,"* p. 163.

14. Catledge, p. 214.

15. Fall 1961, *Columbia Journalism Review,* p. 18.

16. *Editor & Publisher,* Nov. 26, 1960, p. 68.

17. The best book-length biographical study of Theodore White thus far is Joyce Hoffmann's *Theodore H. White and Journalism as Illusion* (Columbia, Mo.: University of Missouri Press, 1995). See also Nora Ephron, *Scribble Scribble* (New York: Knopf, 1978), p. 40ff.

18. See Dionne chapter in Mann and Orren, *Media Polls,* p. 153.

16. EVA and the Exit Polls

1. Sam Lubell, "The New Technology of Election Reporting," *Columbia Journalism Review,* Summer 1964, p. 5.

2. Broder in Charles Peters and Timothy J. Adams, eds., *Inside the System* (New York: Praeger, 1970), p. 12. The best academic analysis of the changing media role is F. Christopher Arterton, "Campaign Organizations Confront the Media-Political Environment," in James David Barber, ed., *Race for the Presidency* (Englewood Cliffs, N.J.: Prentice-Hall, 1978), pp. 3ff.

3. Theodore H. White, *America in Search of Itself* (New York: Harper & Row, 1982), p. 169.

4. "Cannibalistic" from White, *The Making of the President 1964* (New York: Atheneum, 1964), p. 378. "Computers as Bystanders," Lubell, *CJR*, p. 7.

5. Penn T. Kimball, "California: Last of the Long Counts," *Columbia Journalism Review*, Summer 1964, pp. 22–23; Kintner, *Broadcasting and the News*, p. 4; *Broadcasting*, Nov. 2, 1964, p. 30.

6. This anecdote is contained in Warren J. Mitofsky, "A Short History of Exit Polls," in Paul J. Lavrakas and Jack K. Holley, *Polling and Presidential Election Coverage* (Newbury Park: Sage, 1991), chap. 4, p. 88.

7. Lubell, "Computers as Bystanders," pp. 4–8.

8. NBC's California primary experience is recounted in Frank, "Election Night," pp. 217–19.

9. Lubell, "Computers as Bystanders," p. 8.

10. Kimball, "California," p. 23.

11. *Broadcasting*, Sept. 7, 1964, p. 37; Oct. 26, 1964, p. 60.

12. Frank, *Thin Air*, p. 230. Throughout this chapter, most of the basic information about the networks' election night machinery is adapted from various issues of *Broadcasting* magazine just before and after the elections.

13. Frank also tells of EVA's swoon, *Thin Air*, pp. 231–32, more humorously than he might have on election night.

14. Bill Leonard, *In the Storm of the Eye* (New York: Putnam's, 1987), p. 113.

15. Robert MacNeil, *The People Machine* (New York: Harper & Row, 1968), pp. 119ff. Sevareid quote is from Broder, *Behind the Front Page*, p. 297.

16. *Wall Street Journal*, Oct. 28, 1968, p. 1. The network expenditure estimates is from *Broadcasting*, Nov. 11, 1968, p. 30. See also Av Westin, *Newswatch* (New York: Simon & Schuster, 1982), pp. 126, 170.

17. Mitofsky, "A Short History," p. 94. Harris controversial figure, in Moore, *The Superpollsters*, p. 96. For CBS's start in polling, see also Everett Carll Ladd and John Benson, "The Growth of News Polls in American Politics," p. 19, and Kathleen A. Frankovic, "Technology and the Changing Landscape of Media Polls," p. 33, both in Mann and Orren, *Media Polls*.

18. *Broadcasting*, Nov. 11, 1968, p. 30.

19. The details of the 1972 polling experience are mainly as related by Stephen Isaacs, "The Pitfalls of Polling," *Columbia Journalism Review*, May-June 1972, p. 28.

20. James M. Perry, *Us and Them* (New York: Clarkson N. Potter, 1973), p. 49.

21. Isaacs, p. 40.

22. *Nieman Reports*, Spring 1991, p. 18. CBS-NY Times tensions and direct dialing techniques, Moore, p. 270, 277.

23. Broder, *Behind the Front Page*, pp. 249–51.

17. A "Good Story" Trumps the Numbers

1. *Nieman Reports,* Autumn, 1990, p. 19.

2. *Washington Post,* National Weekly Edition, March 20–27, 1992.

3. See Richard Morin polling column, *Washington Post,* National Weekly Edition, Dec. 18–24, 1995.

4. *Editor & Publisher,* Oct. 12, 1996, p. 10.

5. Michael P. Beaubien and John S. Wyeth, eds., *Views on the News* (New York: New York University Press, 1994), p. 49.

6. The Bradlee quotation is cited by Seymour Hersh in his *The Dark Side of Camelot* (Boston: Little, Brown, 1997), p. 377, from a letter in the files of the Kennedy library.

7. "Front runner," *Philadelphia Inquirer,* March 27, 1988, p. 7-A; "Stop-Jackson rumors," *Los Angeles Times,* April 1, column page; "Confusion and controversy, March 28, p. 1; "Formidable contender," *Washington Post,* March 28, p. 1; "Contemplating possibility," *New York Times,* March 28, p. 1.

8. Christopher Hanson, "Lost in Never-Never Land," *Columbia Journalism Review,* May-June 1996, p. 41.

18. And Now . . . the Virtual Horse Race

1. "Close Race in Fall," *New York Times,* April 7, 1996. The numbers in polls do sometimes shift dramatically, usually in response to noncampaign events in the news. During the last seven months of the 1976 presidential campaign, the Gallup Poll swung by 31 points; in 1988 by 23 points; in 1992 by 21 points.

2. Wolfgang Donsback, in J. David Kennamer, ed., *Public Opinion, the Press and Public Policy* (Westport, Conn.: Praeger, 1992), p. 131.

3. An interesting example of this occurred in the 1996 Senate race in North Carolina. Newspapers there responded to a plea that the voters and not the candidates ought to decide what the issues should be. They did this by conducting a poll of what North Carolinians thought the issues should be. But, as so often happens, journalists from outside the state disagreed with the expression of priorities. The media from New York, Washington, and Boston then denounced the state press for "pandering to readers." See *Columbia Journalism Review,* January-February 1997, p. 13.

4. Andrew Kohut, "Rating the Polls," *Public Opinion Quarterly* 1986, vol. 50, p. 9.

5. *Editor & Publisher,* May 11, 1996, p. 10.

6. *Washington Post* national weekly edition, Sept. 16–22, 1996, p. 37.

7. Mitofsky expounded his "sour grapes theory" at a conference on polls and politics at Northwestern University, Evanston, Illinois, Jan. 11, 1989.

8. *Missouri Press News,* October 1996, p. 18.

9. *Columbia Journalism Review,* Fall 1961, p. 57.

10. Marcus and Collins quotes are from Paul Starobin, "A Generation of Vipers: Journalists and the New Cynicism," *Columbia Journalism Review,* March-April 1995, p. 49.

11. *Editor & Publisher,* April 19, 1997, p. 11.

12. *Washington Post* national weekly edition, Oct. 21–27, 1996, p. 6.

13. *Fortune* magazine, Oct. 28, 1996, p. 42.

Index

Index

Index

Index